Fostoria
Useful and Ornamental

THE CRYSTAL FOR AMERICA

IDENTIFICATION
& VALUE GUIDE

Milbra Long & Emily Seate

COLLECTOR BOOKS
A Division of Schroeder Publishing Co., Inc.

The current values in this book should be used only as a guide. They are not intended to set prices, which vary from one section of the country to another. Auction prices as well as dealer prices vary greatly and are affected by condition as well as demand. Neither the authors nor the publisher assumes responsibility for any losses that might be incurred as a result of consulting this guide.

Shown on the front cover: 5093 Vase, 4020 Decanter, 2440 Lafayette Bon Bon, 4099 Candy and Cover, 5092 Cigarette Holder/Ashtray.
On the back cover: Sea Shell Bookend, Mermaid and Bowl, Vertical and Horizontal Fish, Seahorse Bookend.

Cover design by Michelle Dowling and Beth Summers
Book design by Terri Hunter
Color photography by Charles R. Lynch

Searching For A Publisher?

We are always looking for knowledgeable people considered to be experts within their fields. If you feel that there is a real need for a book on your collectible subject and have a large comprehensive collection, contact Collector Books.

COLLECTOR BOOKS
P.O. Box 3009
Paducah, Kentucky 42002-3009

www.collectorbooks.com

Milbra Long and Emily Seate
P.O. Box 784
Cleburne, TX 76033-0784
e-mail: longseat@flash.net
www.fostoria1.com

Copyright © 2000 by Milbra Long and Emily Seate

CONTENTS

ACKNOWLEDGMENTS

We are grateful to the Lancaster Colony Corporation, Inc., of Columbus, Ohio, for permission to use the materials and logo of the Fostoria Glass Company, Inc.

Deepest thanks go to the following people who so generously loaned their glass to us for photographing, or had the piece photographed to the publisher's specifications: Larry Baker and Don Barber, Carol and Larry Bartholf, Kevin Coughlin and Irma Griffin, Jim and Sherry Davis, Tom and Aleeta Herr, Mike and Gina Lodes, and Terry and Carl Naas. Anne Shatrau of DGShopper Online made sure we had the wonderful "shoes" ad featured in the introduction.

It would be difficult to express adequately our appreciation to Billy Schroeder and Lisa Stroup, and to Collector Books' founder, Bill Schroeder. The Crystal for America series stands as testament to the excellence of Collector Books with its superb staff. We could not have had a better publisher to bring to the reader this history of the patterns made by the Fostoria Glass Company as authentically and beautifully as is possible with today's technology.

DEDICATION

This book and all the other books of the Crystal for America series are dedicated to the employees of the Fostoria Glass Company, Inc. whose skilled hands created fine Fostoria crystal.

"Every man's work is always a portrait of himself."
– Samuel Butler

In the nearly 100 years of the Fostoria Glass Company, the glass it offered to the American people over and over again reflected the climate of the times. In its earliest days, hand-painted oil lamps and vases, and heavy, pressed crystal were the norm. After World War I, the feeling of affluence brought on by the peace that followed that terrible time encouraged design and artistry, and eventually, an explosion of color in the glass industry. In *Fostoria Tableware: 1924 – 1943*, we documented the most prolific and extraordinary time in the history of the company. This volume continues to document the depth and abundance of glass produced during the 1924 – 1943 period with the inclusion of some items before 1924 and after 1943.

Presenting the named or numbered pressed pattern lines, the etchings, cuttings, and decorations offered by Fostoria seems, in retrospect, to have been simple compared to the difficulties encountered in the design of this volume. Here we encounter numbered pieces, some on one catalog page, some on another, seldom laid out in order as the named or numbered lines had been. Sometimes, for example, a bowl would be listed with Bowls, sometimes with Appetizers, sometimes with Salad Sets, and on and on. The Contents page kept changing as we understood how one category needed to be combined with another, or a new category created. Providing alphabetical listings worked in some cases, but Bowls, for example, had to be listed numerically. We have cross-referenced pieces both from one section to another, and to previous volumes in the series as much as was humanly possible.

We took the opportunity this volume afforded to list all the Candlesticks, Candelabra, Lustres, and Candle Lamps whether or not we were able to picture them either in photographs or via catalogs. We were fortunate enough to have a 1909 and a 1924 Candlestick catalog, a 1901 Catalog, and a 1910 Lamp and Vase catalog, which we have shared on these pages. Also, we have included some pieces from Milbra's private collection which illustrate the incredible clarity and beauty of Fostoria's early ware. Except for the pieces loaned us from private collections, all the glass in these four volumes is, or has been, in our inventory.

The "New Little Book about Glassware" appears in many of the advertisements from the late 1920s and had long intrigued us. We recently obtained a copy, and are pleased to be able to include it. From 1928, it illustrates the height of ideas for what to do to make one's home beautiful with glassware, even to providing helpful hints for creating a window filled with colorful glass and calling it a "window-garden." The booklet illustrates a time in our history, long before the kind of technology we have today: A time when life was slower, and priorities were different.

Please note the explosion of Barware and Refreshment Sets in 1934, after Prohibition was repealed. Boudoir Accessories featured a variety of items for milady's dressing table, including bon bons and match boxes. The array of ash trays and cigarette holders reflected the proliferation of smoking on the movie screen, at bridge parties, as

House and Garden, April 1944

1951 ad.

smoking for both men and women became socially acceptable. Most of those Smoking Accessories were no longer being made after World War II. Vases comprise the largest single section in the book. We have tried to list them all, again, whether or not we were able to show you what the vase looked like.

Instead of indexing just this volume, the Master Index includes all four books in the Crystal for America series.

The advertisement shown is from the April 1944 issue of *House and Garden* magazine, and illustrates once again, how involved Fostoria was in civic and social affairs. As mentioned in *Fostoria Tableware: 1924 – 1943*, the company is reported to have made bomb sites during World War II. To find an advertisement which shows a woman at the glory hole, blow pipe in hand, says so much about the adaptability, and the social responsibility of this long-lived company.

In 1998, the authors attended an exhibit on Modernism at the Kimbell Art Museum in Fort Worth, Texas, which featured The Norwest Collection. We were both impressed with what a formidable concept modernism was, so much so that only a global war could halt its momentum. From all indications, modernism in its many forms and periods began as a protest against what was perceived as nineteenth century ordinariness. From the time of the 1900 Exposition Universelle in Paris, and to some extent, before that, new designs, new innovations, new materials, were the rule, rather than the exception. The authors would like to believe that the square base, the creations in Ebony and Crystal, and some of the elaborate decorations offered by the Fostoria Glass Company were a direct outgrowth of this tremendous thrust toward the modern.

So much may be learned from a company's advertising. When we found the advertisement for sterling silver on crystal from the 1950s, we felt we had found an answer to a question that has been troubling many collectors. Namely, did Fostoria continue to put silver on crystal as offered during the marvelous Silver Deposit years? It would appear that is not so, but that blanks were bought by other companies and decorated.

Finally, this volume is named to honor the early catalogs of the Fostoria Glass Company, often called "Useful and Ornamental." The glass produced by this great glasshouse nearly always was practical, with stems feeling balanced in the hand, sturdily tempered during the slow cool-down in the lehr. Certainly Fostoria glass was useful, but its elegance both in clarity of manufacture and design, made it desirable ornamentation for the table, the bar, the dressing table, the window garden, the lamp table, and the bridge table.

We wish you great success in your collecting, and hope these volumes serve you well.

The authors first noticed this little booklet mentioned in nearly every advertisement from the late 1920s. On page 47 of *Fostoria Tableware: 1924 – 1943*, one can see the cover of the little book peeking out from the top advertisement. Unfortunately, we were unable to obtain a copy before that book was published because, by all rights, it should have been shown there. As we had thought, the little book is delightful, giving one the taste of a bygone era, and illustrating the many and varied ways Fostoria thought of to use their glassware. We present the booklet to you in its entirety although some of the pages are combined with others to save space.

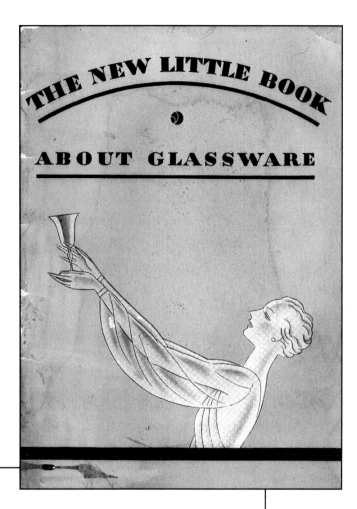

GLASS has a strange power to arrest the eye and intrigue the imagination. It has the remote magic of beauty caught and kept for centuries, mysteriously held enchanted in a crystal prison.

A bracelet from Egypt, a vase from Nineveh or an Assyrian bowl, these glittering treasures of princesses and kings awake fanciful dreams of lives lived long ago!

Such jewel-colored things of glass, now the priceless possessions of the world's great museums, remind us that beauty though fragile is eternal.

Captured bubbles of glass once served as drinking goblets at banquets in Rome. They recall the fact that those Romans of the Imperial Period, artists in living, used more glassware for table service than has been done at any time in history, until glass dinnerware was introduced to American women in the recent years of our colorful twentieth century.

Delight in the color of glass, the brilliance of crystal, its transparency, the play of light flickering through it, the glamorous reflections, is a joy multiplied because it is inherited from countless generations of beauty-lovers.

There has never been a time when glass has been a subject of such great interest and fascination as it is today—to collectors and to decorators and to every woman who takes pleasure in home-making.

And never before has really beautiful glass been so available and so reasonably priced as is Fostoria.

THE NEW LITTLE BOOK ABOUT GLASSWARE

●

Concerning
the colorful magic of glass
and its place in the
modern home

●

Practical and authentic
information conveniently
arranged for reference

Color, Light and Glass

Place a glass bowl or goblet in the sunlight. See how the color of the glass becomes more intense. Again, look at the same piece by candlelight. Notice as the little shadows flicker, how the sparkling lights are multiplied. This real affinity that exists between light and glass affords unending pleasure to the eye. Then—when color and glass are fused, the mystery of the glass, the magic of the color are both increased.

Compare white glass and rock crystal; amber glass and topaz; clear blue and sapphire; green and the emerald; and you see that much of the loveliness of the rarest gems, formed by Nature's chemistry, is found in man's copies.

The keynote of modern decoration is colorfulness. We need color in our lives, for in a subtle way it has an interesting and beneficial effect. And psychologically, gay-colored glass may tone up a weary point of view—the softer shades may rest the jaded nerves.

Housekeeping experts and dietitians agree about color appeal. Meals are more enjoyed, the more beautifully they are served. Glassware offers such a simple means of accomplishing this! Colored glassware, carefully selected and arranged with an eye to art, does make a lovely picture of the dining-room.

The home-maker is wise indeed, who lets glassware help solve her decorating problems, who lets these useful, beautiful things be her daily joy. . . . You need not be a collector or a connoisseur to enjoy the rich amber, clear green, soft orchid, azure, the blue, and dawn, the rose of Fostoria. Prices for Fostoria are so reasonable you can well afford to use it on your table every day!

Crystal *or Clear Glass*

Crystal ware, the white or clear glass, like solid silver, fine linen, real lace, never goes out of fashion. It is ever the most aristocratic glassware, established by tradition and its own magic.

Delicately etched, handsomely cut, crystal tableware is perhaps the most formal sort of glassware. Its icy dazzle, its sparkling brilliance are in keeping with the most elegant table appointments.

Colored glassware is friendly, more appropriate for the informal table-settings and is permanently in the mode; yet for certain occasions many people prefer to have a service of crystal.

The complete Fostoria dinner service is made in crystal, intricately etched, engraved and plain. Fostoria crystal stemware—the goblets, the wine glasses, the sherbets, parfaits, and cocktail glasses as well as the more informal tumblers and iced-tea glasses are made in a great variety of designs and patterns. Some very fragile. Others in the new, more fanciful manner. Also the coin-gold-banded ware that is always correct.

Genuine Fostoria is also made in green, azure, dawn, amber, orchid and a very lovely iridescent ware. The finish of this is absolutely permanent and its delicate colors appeal to those who wish something at once formal and friendly, colorful in a conservative way.

GLASSMAKING is a very, very old art. Its beginnings are veiled in the dim mists of unrecorded days, long before the Christian era. Perhaps in Syria, perhaps in Egypt—it was discovered that chemicals added to sand would work an astonishing transformation and give a permanent transparent material.

Roman glass blowers made many marvelous colors of glass, but it was at Venice in the Sixteenth Century that this art reached the peak of its development. Mastercraftsmen from the island of Murano went out over Europe; to Bohemia, to Ireland, and finally to America. Here in our own country artists like Stiegel and Wistar produced glassware that has cast its spell over many collectors of antiques.

Once the master workers made their wares for the wealthy few. But today science and art and modern business methods make it possible for the average home to possess, for instance, a glass dinner service that a Roman matron with dozens of slaves at her command might well have envied!

Today American glass is designed in a variety of lovely shapes and exquisite colors. The experience of the ages is at the disposal of the people who make, from the special snow-white sand* mined in the mountains of West Virginia, the finest modern American glass—Fostoria.

* Equal in purity even to the sand from the famous fields of Fontainebleau in France.

The Complete Dinner Service of Glassware *

Fostoria has an astonishing power to give gaiety, color, sparkle to the simplest meal. No longer is it surprising to have the soup course, the salad, or dessert, the after-dinner coffee appear in Fostoria dishes. Today the vogue is distinctly for glass for table settings.

At first a complete dinner service of glass sounded like a fairy tale or a glittering dream from Arabian Nights.

But Fostoria is absolutely practicable for serving hot as well as cold foods. Fostoria platters and dinner plates, cups and saucers, vegetable dishes, soup plates, cereal dishes are as serviceable as the stemware, the flower bowls, the candlesticks and compôtes.

Before glass dinnerware was introduced to American women by Fostoria in 1925, tests of many months had proved it perfectly satisfactory for serving all kinds of hot food and drinks.

Fostoria dishes never "craze" (that is because glass is all one material and not glazed). They are so hard it is most difficult to chip them.

The plates stack perfectly, a point much appreciated by the housekeeper whose shelf space is limited.

Many accessory pieces—sauce boats, hors-d'oeuvres trays—have two or three uses.

The complete dinner service of Fostoria is made in amber, green, azure, dawn, crystal and orchid.

For breakfasts, informal luncheons, family dinners, Fostoria suggests the plain ware in the Pioneer (round) or Fairfax (eight sided) design in your favorite color or colors. Fostoria stemware comes to match these patterns. Colors may match or harmonize, as you prefer.

For more formal entertaining, Fostoria suggests colored ware with the delicate tracery of an etched pattern. There are several of these patterns: as in silver, there is one that will especially appeal to you and will look best with your other table appointments. . . . The etched patterns naturally cost more than the plain ware, but you will find Fostoria prices are everywhere most reasonable.

A delightful idea is to have a breakfast service of plain Fostoria in one color, say amber, and an etched dinner service in another shade, perhaps azure. This gives an opportunity for many pleasant changes in the looks of your table and a chance to express your own taste artistically.

Either plain or etched glassware is considered perfectly correct for serving either formal or informal meals. The choice is a matter of personal preference.

* A list of pieces in the dinnerware service is given on page 34. Illustrated on page 14.

The Subject of Stemware *

For many years, Fostoria stemware has been famous for its pure crystal quality, which you may easily test by the clear, resounding tone of the glass. . . . The gracefulness of the designs, created to match the new dinnerware, will please you.

Whether you use stemware to complete a dinner service of Fostoria, or to lend color and sparkle to other table appointments, you will take much pleasure in these fragile magic bubbles. Made in crystal and Fostoria colors.

Crystal twisted stems with colored bowls are charming. Optic effects, spiral and loop, are lovely when the light shines through them.

Footed tumblers find increasing favor, they are so well proportioned, so pleasant to use.

Goblets, as always, are preferred for most formal use.

Fostoria makes all types of wine glasses, cocktail glasses, parfaits, sherbets, champagne glasses in a variety of stemmed and footed shapes. Both fragile and heavy. Plain, etched, engraved and decorated in enamel, gold and silver.

* Several types of glasses are shown on page 16.

SHERBET GLASS (Twisted Stem)

TUMBLER (Etched)

FOOTED TUMBLER (Needle Etched)

FOOTED TUMBLER

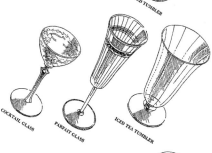

COCKTAIL GLASS

PARFAIT GLASS

ICED TEA TUMBLER

OYSTER COCKTAIL GLASS

COCKTAIL GLASS

CEREAL BOWL

FRUIT SAUCER

FLOWER BOWL

SUGAR BOWL AND CREAM PITCHER

COMPOTE

AFTER DINNER COFFEE CUP

DINNER PLATE

CANDLESTICKS

BOUILLON CUP

PLATTER

CUP AND SAUCER

VEGETABLE DISH

THE HARMONY OF

Glass and Flowers

Fostoria is the friend of sunshine and color. A glass vase or jar or bowl makes possible the perfect arrangement of flowers. From morning till night, as light mysteriously changes, the magic of this fine glass crystallizes each moment's mood. In the sun's full glory, in the soft glamor of candlelight, Fostoria and flowers make an exquisite picture.

The transparency of glass, filled with water, shows flowers to the utmost advantage. For the slender green stems of flowers are a great part of their grace! Seen through crystal or colored glass, simple flowers take on new interest. You can work out amazingly artistic effects—yellow flowers in a blue bowl; splashy red flowers in a green glass jar; the subtler combination of blue and pink flowers in an azure-colored vase; gay zinnias in an amber tumbler —you will be astonished and extremely pleased with the new arrangements your fancy will dictate.

Fostoria makes jolly little flower bowls; the big flip-glasses that are so smart now and so satisfactory; several types of centerpieces with flower blocks (these have candlesticks to match); footed tumblers of course; Oriental jars; and decorative formal vases.

Lovely simple shapes. Clear glass. Optic effects Engravings, etchings, the new brocade patterns. In green, amber, orchid, crystal, azure, dawn and iridescent ware. All sizes—and some pieces are priced very little, though sold in the finest shops.

You will find the right Fostoria "vase" for every room in your home. . . . And when you send flowers to an invalid or a shut-in friend, send with them a Fostoria vase. It will make your gift infinitely precious and your remembrance lasting.

Glassware
for
Bathroom and Bedroom

Once on a time perfume bottles and tear bottles and little glass jars were treasures for princesses. They were cunningly wrought and precious as jewels.

Today powder jars and perfume bottles, jewel boxes and trays of glittering glass can belong to every woman who loves to have pretty things on her dressing table. Fostoria makes all these: Vanity sets (candlesticks with a combination perfume bottle and powder jar), little clocks; water-bottle-and-glass sets, too. Delightful, they are, in glass!

Colored glass is up to date and modern for use in the bathroom. Use a Fostoria jar in a shape you like for bath salts, another for bath powder, in a color that matches your towels, and presto, you have added a bright note and a touch of elegance.

Attractive and practical are the set of glass bottles, matching or in graded sizes, to hold the liquids and lotions that are sometimes a troublesome part of the bathroom equipment. These may fit into the medicine cabinet or be kept on the bathroom shelves, as you like. They may simply be labeled with the name of the contents or decorated in enamel. . . . They are smart, convenient and exceedingly tidy.

And don't forget a vase for flowers in the guest-room. Perhaps a Fostoria box for cigarettes, and an ash tray.

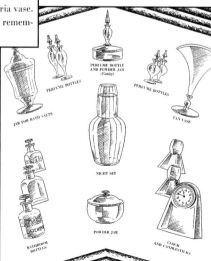

Fostoria
for the Formal Dinner

Candlelight, color and the sparkling magic of glass! A setting that assures the success of your dinner, for as guests sit down at a charming table they are in festive mood.

Here is a simple recipe for setting a table that is modern, and colorful, yet that has the elegance necessary for a rather formal dinner.

A pale yellow damask cloth, with matching napkins (white or pale green if you prefer).
A Fostoria centerpiece, cool green with emerald lights—in this, daffodils.
Fostoria candlesticks, these green with pale yellow candles.
Place plates of Fostoria, green with the new decoration.
Dinner goblets, green, too, etched in the same pattern as the plates. Other stemware as you wish.
Salt and pepper shakers, green Fostoria, etched with another arrangement of the same delicate tracery.
The silver necessary for the courses to be served.

Glass plates are effective for hors-d'ouvres. There are also handsome Fostoria hors-d'ouvres trays. You will want glasses for fruit or oyster cocktails. Cream soup bowls or bouillon cups of Fostoria. There are vegetable dishes and platters, salad plates, dessert dishes, finger-bowls, after-dinner coffee cups, compôtes and bonbon dishes for nuts and candies. Cigarette boxes and ash trays, too!

If your dinner service is green, you may like to have salad plates that are amber, and a dessert service and coffee cups of the new azure shade. Finger-bowls are always lovely in engraved crystal.

Whether your formal dinner is an occasion like Christmas, or Thanksgiving; entertaining for a debutante or an honored guest, it is correct to use Fostoria, and an etched pattern is especially appropriate.

Your artistic sense will suggest many delightful arrangements. Rich red roses with the orchid glass. Blue and orange flowers with amber. Yellow flowers with blue and mixed colors with crystal.

Real Fostoria is made in crystal, amber, green, the subtle orchid, also dawn and azure, and with an iridescent finish that is permanent. Clear glass and a number of interesting etchings. . . . And this finest modern American glass is moderately priced.

For a Bright and Cheerful Breakfast

Here is a table, cheerful and modern, with a colorful simplicity that makes breakfast the most delightful meal of the day. For informal meals, plain Fostoria in one, two or three colors, combined as you like, is a happy choice.

A peasant linen cloth, with a gay border or colored stripes. Orange or blue or green predominating.
A Fostoria bowl—amber, blue or green, with a few hyacinths, narcissus or tulips, in your favorite spring shade, arranged simply.
Fostoria footed tumblers, amber.
Breakfast plates, bread and butter plates, also amber.
Cereal bowls, amber or blue or green.
Coffee cups, amber.
An amber platter. An amber nappy.
Sugar bowl and cream pitcher. Salt and pepper shakers. In amber, blue or green.
Orange juice glasses or grapefruit dishes, in crystal or amber.
Finger-bowls, amber or crystal.
The silver needed for breakfast.

For a Rather Special Luncheon

Nothing makes a table look so lovely as the combination of Fostoria, flowers, light and color. It is easy to arrange this charming table for a festive luncheon or a gay announcement party.

Italian or Spanish embroidered linen runners, with matching napkins.
Pansies, cheerfully smiling in an orchid Fostoria bowl.
High Fostoria Compotes, orchid or iridescent for nuts and bonbons.
Cream soup bowls, place plates, bread and butter plates, orchid etched.
Open salt dishes, and pepper shakers, crystal with green foot.
Orchid tumblers, crystal footed.
Cups and saucers, orchid or crystal, etched.
Dessert plates, iridescent.
The necessary silver.

Do You Entertain at Supper?

There is no pleasanter, more hospitable way to entertain friends than at a simple informal supper. How fresh and colorful this table will be!

A crisp white linen tea cloth, hemstitched, with napkins to match.
Blossoms, apple, peach or cherry, in an azure blue vase.
Candles, pale peach or primrose color in blue Fostoria candlesticks.
Fostoria fruit cocktail glasses, blue with crystal stem, on crystal plate.
Azure goblets with crystal twisted stems.
Place plates, etched crystal or dawn (the new rose).
Bread and butter plates, azure. Salad plates, iridescent.
Salt and pepper shakers, crystal, blue footed.
Service dishes, dawn or azure.
Dessert dishes, azure.
Demi-tasse cups, dawn.
The silver needed for the meal.

The Care of Glassware

You need not fear to use your loveliest glass nor worry about breaking it, if you exercise a little care in using it and in washing it.

When choice glass is to be washed, it is a good plan to lay a folded turkish towel in the dishpan, so that if a cherished piece slips, it falls on a soft substance.

Wash goblets, stemware and tumblers first, rinsing in cold water any that have held milk.

If two glasses or glass dishes stick together, put cold water in the inner one and hold the outer one in warm water and they will separate at once.

Use a soft brush for washing cut glass, and after wiping, place each piece on a soft, dry towel to absorb any moisture which cannot be reached in wiping.

It is dangerous to pour scalding water on glasses that have just held ice water, of course. But if you put a spoon in an iced tea glass that has cracked ice in it, it is safe to pour in the hot tea.

Water pitchers should be washed after each meal. Vinegar cruets are effectively and easily cleaned with diluted ammonia.

Never put gold-decorated glass into scalding water or wash it with strong soap. (Soap will eat off pure gold.)

Fostoria dinnerware is absolutely practicable for serving all kinds of hot or cold food. Treat it as carefully as you would china. That is—let the dishes come to room temperature before you place either piping-hot or ice-cold food on them.

Fostoria will never craze, and it is very hard to chip.

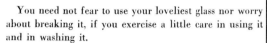

Fostoria is probably sold in your favorite shop. If not, write us for a list of places near you where you can find it. Ask for Fostoria by name. You are then certain to get the finest modern American glassware.

Fostoria Makes

amber, green, orchid, dawn, azure, blue, ebony and crystal glass. *This is plain, etched and decorated.*

Mother of Pearl and Spanish Lustre Iridescent Glass. This finish is absolutely permanent.

Needle-etched glassware, geometric patterns. *Some of these are: Richmond, Sherman, Spartan.*

Plate-etched glassware—here are designs to suit every taste and to harmonize with every type of table appointments—quiet elegance; smart simplicity; fanciful charm; decorative splendor. *Among the popular designs are: Vesper, Vernon, Royal.*

Decorated glassware. Band and encrusted decorations of coin gold. Highest quality. Also colored enamel decorations.

The new brocade ware—developed in the Grape design and the Paradise pattern and the Oak Leaf pattern. Exceptionally effective for flower vases, bowls, jars, boxes. candlesticks and large decorative pieces.

The new dinnerware services in the Pioneer design in amber, green, blue, crystal, and in the Fairfax design in amber, dawn, azure, orchid, crystal, green. Plain or etched patterns. *Pioneer etchings are: Royal, Seville, Vesper, Beverly; and Fairfax etchings are: Vernon, Versailles, June.*

Look for the Fostoria Label

This little brown-and-white label guarantees genuine Fostoria. Every piece of glassware leaves the factory carrying this label.

Fostoria sets the glassware fashions. Fostoria introduced glass dinnerware. The Fostoria artists and chemists and craftsmen are continually working to make newer and lovelier glassware.

One of the most wonderful things about Fostoria is that it does not have to be very expensive to be very beautiful.

For example, you can buy a dozen footed tumblers, in your favorite color for about $6.00.

There are many delightful bowls, jars, candlesticks for as little as fifty cents to a dollar apiece.

A dozen cereal dishes will cost about $6.00.

An eight-place bridge set could be purchased for about $15.00, and larger sets in proportion. Six-place dinner set $30.00 and up.

All Fostoria patterns are open stock—just as with china and silver. You do not have to buy a complete service. You may start a set with plates, cups and saucers and glasses, and add to it platters, vegetable dishes, bowls, or make replacements whenever you wish.

A Complete Dinner Service of Fostoria Includes

12 dinner plates
12 breakfast plates (salad plate size)
12 bread and butter plates
12 soup plates or 12 bouillon cups
12 fruit saucers
12 cereal dishes
12 cups and saucers
12 finger bowls

• • •

12 goblets
12 wine glasses
12 cocktail glasses

• • •

1 10½-inch platter
1 15-inch platter
1 oval open vegetable dish, 9-inch
2 oval vegetable dishes, 10½-inch
1 sugar bowl
1 cream pitcher
1 celery tray
4 sets salt and pepper shakers
1 sauce boat (this may be used for whipped cream or mayonnaise)
1 pickle dish

For Breakfast Sets of Fostoria

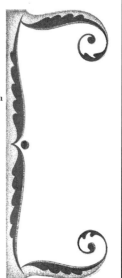

Plates—8-inch size
Bread and butter plates—6-inch size
Cereal dishes or fruit dishes
Platter—for bacon and eggs
Sugar bowl and cream pitcher
Footed water tumblers

FOR LUNCHEON SETS OF FOSTORIA

Bouillon cups or cream soup cups with plates
Plates—9-inch size
Salad plates—7-inch size
Bread and butter plates—6-inch size
Tall ice cream glasses
Footed tumblers
Vegetable dish   Platter

FOR TEA SERVICES OF FOSTORIA

Plates—9-inch size
Bread and butter plates—6-inch size
Salad plates—7 or 8-inch size
Cups and saucers
Iced-tea glasses and pitcher
Hors-d'oeuvres tray
Sandwich plate   Lemon dish
Sugar bowl and cream pitcher

Consider the Gift of Fostoria and think of these things

Footed tumblers
Cocktail glasses
Goblets
Iced-tea glasses
Teacups
A pair of compôtes for candies and nuts
A cake plate

A sandwich tray
Salad plates and a salad bowl
Bread and butter plates
Salt and pepper shakers
A platter
Finger-bowls
Four low candlesticks and a flower bowl

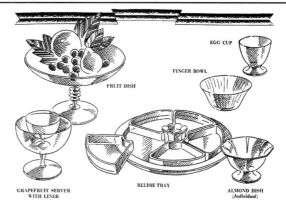

FRUIT DISH

EGG CUP

FINGER BOWL

GRAPEFRUIT SERVER WITH LINER

RELISH TRAY

ALMOND DISH (Individual)

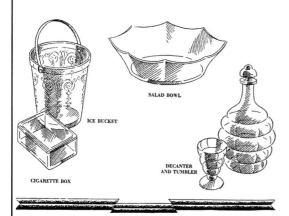

ICE BUCKET

SALAD BOWL

CIGARETTE BOX

DECANTER AND TUMBLER

Rose bowls
Vases, perhaps with flowers in them!
A candy jar
A candy box
Cigarette boxes
Ash trays

A complete dinner service

A refreshment set, a luncheon service or a breakfast service

(Your dealer will include in these the pieces you prefer, with matching stemware)

Ask for Fostoria by name and look for the label.

APPETIZER, BUFFET, and RELISH

Most all tableware patterns contain pieces that would qualify for this category. Some patterns have as many as five different relish dishes. Those are shown with the individual patterns.

The 2528 Appetizer Set which used either the 2056 American inserts or the 2391 inserts is not shown. The only other pieces with number 2391 were the large and small cigarette boxes causing us to speculate that the bottom to the cigarette box might have been used as the appetizer dish. This set would be an interesting find with 2391 inserts in the three strong colors! We have seen the set with the 2056 inserts.

Fostoria made the egg plate in crystal and in milk glass (see Randolph, p. 207, *Fostoria Tableware: 1944 – 1986*). Center handled lunch trays were listed as 11" and 12" at different times. Lunch trays were offered with pressed, etched, and cut patterns and are shown with those patterns. Only the two lunch trays which did not belong to another pressed pattern are listed here.

Oftentimes a note would accompany a piece which said that it was not shown in the catalog. We are listing all the pieces even though there may not be a picture. Turntables were listed in 1935 to fit the 13", 14", and 18" plates. No picture was shown.

2528 Appetizer Set: 2528 Appetizer Tray and six 2391 Appetizer Dishes, two each of Regal Blue, Burgundy and Empire Green, or six 2056 Appetizer Dishes in Crystal, 1935; $400.00

2038 Banana Split, 1915-1928; $15.00

2517 Bon Bon (see Decorator Pattern and Small Bowls, Mints, and Nuts)
Crystal, 1933-1943; $15.00
Regal Blue, 1933-1940; $20.00
Burgundy, 1933-1940; $20.00
Empire Green, 1933-1939; $20.00
Ruby, 1933-1940; $20.00
Lavender, Teal Green, Ruby, 1964-1970; $20.00

2661 Buffet Set: 3-piece, 5-part server and sauce dish with or without cover, 1952-1960; $65.00

2662 Buffet Set: 3-piece, 5-part server (continued to be made through 1961), sauce dish with or without cover, 1952-1958; $54.00

2663 Buffet Set: 4-part server and cover, 1952-1958; $60.00

2375 Canape Set (See Fairfax)

2492 Canape Set (See Bar and Refreshment)

2276 Cheese and Cracker Set: Covered Cheese and 11" Plate
Crystal, 1925-1927; $55.00
Amber, 1925-1927; $58.00
Green, 1926-1927; $65.00
Ebony, 1925; $58.00

2368 Cheese and Cracker
Crystal, 1929-1942; $57.00
Rose, 1928-1934; $68.00
Azure, 1928-1934; $68.00
Green, 1927-1933; $65.00
Amber, 1927-1933; $62.00
Blue, 1927; $75.00
Orchid, 1927-1928; $68.00
Topaz, 1929-1933; $65.00

2511 Cheese and Cracker with or without center Board
Crystal, 1933-1937: $34.00
Regal Blue, 1933-1937; $65.00
Burgundy, 1933-1937; $65.00
Empire Green, 1933-1934; $65.00
Amber, 1934; $65.00
Topaz, 1934; $65.00

2535 Cheese and Cracker with Board, 1935-1940; $34.00

2528 Cocktail Tray 11¾" x 10¾" (see Bar and Refreshment), 1935-1939; $200.00

2000 Condiment Tray
Rose, 1928-1932; $27.00
Azure, 1928-1932; $27.00
Green, 1927-1932; $27.00
Amber, 1927-1932; $27.00
Blue, 1926-1927; $32.00

2675 Egg Plate, 1955-1958; $60.00 (see also Milk Glass)

4147 Jam Set, 3 pieces: 4147 Oblong Tray, Two Jam Pots and Covers (Cover could be notched for Marmalade spoon), Crystal, 1940-1943; $47.00

2517 Lemon
Crystal, 1933-1943; $15.00
Regal Blue, 1933-1940; $20.00
Burgundy, 1933-1940; $20.00
Empire Green, 1933-1939; $20.00
Ruby, 1933-1939; $20.00

2287 Lunch Tray, Center Handled
Crystal, 1925-1932; $28.00
Amber, 1925-1932; $35.00
Canary, 1925-1926; $58.00
Green, 1925-1932; $38.00
Rose, 1928-1932; $42.00
Azure, 1928-1932; $45.00
Ebony, 1926-1927; $30.00
Blue, 1925-1927; $55.00

Seafood Cocktails in Ruby and Empire Green, 2663 Buffet Set, Fish Canape, Seafood Cocktail in Silver Mist

Azure 2000 Condiment Tray, 2375 Canape Set

Orchid, 1927-1928; $48.00
Amber, SO, 1927-1929; $40.00
Green, SO, 1927-1930; $42.00
Orchid, SO, 1927-1928; $48.00
2342 Lunch Tray, Octagon Center Handled
Crystal, 1927-1932; $28.00
Amber, 1927-1932; $35.00
Green, 1927-1932; $38.00
Rose, 1928-1932; $42.00
Azure, 1928-1932; $45.00
Orchid, 1927-1928; $48.00
Blue, 1927; $55.00
2318 Relish Set (see The New Little Book about Glassware, p. 13): 7 pieces, 13" Tray, Crimped Tumbler, five partitions
Crystal, 1929; $75.00
Green, 1926-1929; $95.00
2462 Relish, 5-part
Crystal, 1933-1938; $55.00
Green, 1933-1938; $65.00
Amber, 1933-1934; $74.00
Rose, 1933-1938; $65.00
Topaz/Gold Tint, 1933-1938; $65.00
2462 Relish, 5-part, Metal Handle
Crystal, 1933-1936; $55.00
Amber, 1933-1934; $74.00
Green, 1933-1936; $65.00
Rose, 1933-1936; $65.00
Topaz, 1933-1936; $65.00
2514 Relish, 5-part Square, 1935-1938; $38.00
2664 Relish, 4-part Server, 1952-1965; $40.00
2497 Seafood Cocktail
Crystal, 1934-1943; $20.00
Regal Blue, 1934-1938; $35.00
Burgundy, 1934-1937; $35.00
Empire Green, 1934-1940; $32.00
Silver Mist, 1934-1943; $22.00
Ruby, 1935-1940; $35.00
2330 Sherbet and Plate (one piece) (see Plates)
Amber, 1925-1926; $18.00
Green, 1925-1926; $18.00
2705 Snack Set, 3 piece: two snack bowls on satin finished wood tray, 1959-1970; $48.00
4152 Snack Bowl; $15.00

2015 Spoon Tray, pre 1924-1929; $50.00
1851 Sugar and Cream, 1923-1928; $40.00
2133 Sugar and Cream, 1923-1928; $32.00
2255 Sugar and Cream
Amber, 1925-1927; $27.00
Blue, 1925-1927; $36.00
Green, 1925-1927; $27.00
2321 Sugar and Cream (see Priscilla)
2321 Sugar and Cream set (see Priscilla): 2321 Sugar (Bullion), 2321 Cream, 2000 Condiment Tray
Rose, 1929-1932; $65.00
Azure, 1929-1932; $65.00
Green, 1929-1932; $65.00
Amber, 1929-1932; $60.00
2497½ Sugar and Cream set
Crystal, 1934-1939; $58.00
Regal Blue, 1934-1936; $95.00
Burgundy, 1934-1936; $95.00
Empire Green, 1934-1936; $95.00
Silver Mist, 1935-1936; $75.00
4020 Sugar and Cream, Footed
Crystal, 1931-1933; $45.00
Amber Base, 1931-1933; $50.00
Green Base, 1931-1933; $50.00
Wisteria Base, 1931-1933; $75.00
Ebony Base, 1930-1932; $65.00
Rose Bowl, 1931-1933; $65.00
Topaz Bowl, 1931-1933; $65.00
2517 Sweetmeat
Crystal, 1933-1943; $15.00
Regal Blue, 1933-1940; $20.00
Burgundy, 1933-1939; $20.00
Empire Green, 1933-1940; $20.00
Ruby, 1933-1939; $20.00
2491 Tea Warmer
Crystal, 1934-1943; $47.00
Amber, 1934-1942; $55.00
Topaz/Gold Tint, 1934-1939; $58.00
2056 Turntable (Wood), 14", 1935; $20.00
2056 Turntable (Wood), 18", 1935; $20.00
2440 Turntable, 13" Wood, 1935; $20.00
2510 Turntable, 15" Wood, 1935; $20.00

Milk Glass Egg Plate, Empire Green 2517 Bon Bon, Ruby Lemon

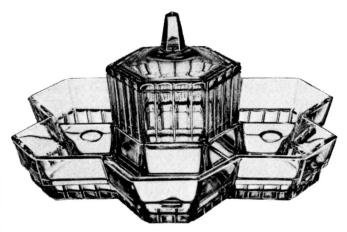

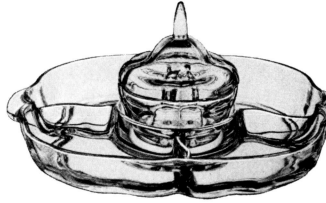

2661
Sauce Dish & Cover
Height 4⅝ in.

2661
3 Pc. Buffet Set
Consisting of:
1/12 Dz. 2661 5 Part Server
1/12 Dz. 2661 Sauce Dish & Cover
Height 6¼ in. Diameter 12¼ in.

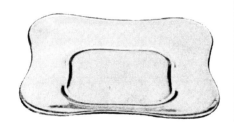

2662
Sauce Dish & Cover
Height 5¼ in.

2662
3 Pc. Buffet Set
Consisting of:
1/12 Dz. 2662 5 Part Server
1/12 Dz. 2662 Sauce Dish & Cover
Height 5¾ in. Diameter 12 in.

2663
3 Pc. Buffet Set
Consisting of:
1/12 Dz. 2663 4-Part Server
1/6   Dz. 2663 Cover
Height 4¼ in. Length 13¼ in.

2665 — 7 in. Plate

2665 — 8 in. Plate

4152 — Snack Bowl
See price list for colors
Height 3⅞ in.

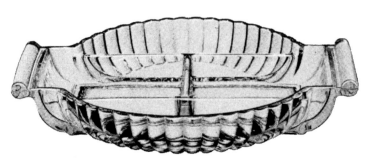

2664
4-Part Server
Length 12½ in. Width 10 in.

2497
Seafood Cocktail
2497½ Sugar
2497½ Cream
Height 3¼ in.

2514—5 Part Square Relish
11½ in. Square

2538—11 in. Nappy
2538—6 in. Nappy
2538—4½ in. Nappy

1831
Mustard and Cover
Height 3⅝ in.

2511—13 in. Cheese and Cracker
Including Board for Center

4087
Marmalade and Cover
Height 5⅛ in.

2491—Tea Warmer
Height 3¼ in.
PATENT NO. 94182

2491—Wax Pot
and Candle included
with Tea Warmer

2535
12 in. Cheese and Cracker with Board

Topaz Tea Warmer

*1934 House
and Garden*

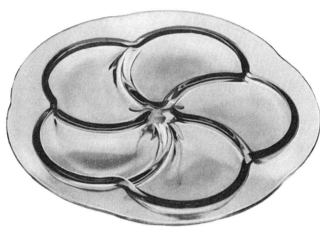

2462—5 Part Relish
Diameter 11 in.
Ro-Gr-Am-Crys-Tz

2276—Cheese and Cover.
2276—11 in. Cracker Plate.
Not made in Blue.

2368—Ftd. Cheese.
2368—11 in. Cracker Plate.

2255—Sugar.

2255—Cream.

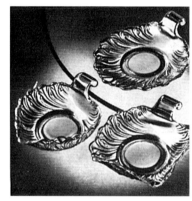

*1934 House
and Garden*

No.1851- Sugar

No.1851 - Cream

No.2133 Sugar.

No.2133 Cream.

4147—7 oz. Jam Pot and Cover
Height including cover 3¾ in.
Top Diameter 3 in.
Capacity 7 oz.

4147—3 Piece Jam Set
Consisting of:
1/6 Doz. 4147 Jam Pot and Cover
1/12 Doz. 4147—7½ in. Oblong Tray

No. 2038 Banana Split
Length 8½ in. including Handle

2705
Snack Set
Consisting of:
1/6 Doz. 2705 Snack Bowl

1/12 Doz. Wood Tray,
Ebony Finish
Height 6½ in.
Width 13¾ in.

2675
Egg Plate
Length 12 in.   Width 9½ in.

2287—11 in. Hld. Lunch Tray.

2342—12 in. Hld. Lunch Tray.

Orchid 2342 Center Handled Tray; Decorated 2287 Center Handled Tray

BAR and REFRESHMENT

An explosion of barware followed the repeal of Prohibition. In 1934 Fostoria offered a new line called Repeal Glassware which included small tumblers and cocktails, decanters, cocktail mixers, and jugs. These were offered in a wide range of colors and are high on the list of popular collectibles. Tumblers in the 4140 – 4142 lines were made in colors. Each dinnerware pattern had its own bar and refreshment pieces, and the reader is asked to refer to a specific pattern for those listings. The 2518 Cordial Bottle and Bitters Bottle were listed in the July 1934 supplement, but were not in the 1935 price list. Thus, they are probably very limited, if ever seen at all. A few of the earlier water bottles were listed through 1927 but none were shown. The 1697 Carafe and Tumbler and several refreshment sets replaced water bottles.

Burgundy 6011 Brandy, Wine, Decanter; 2494 Bitters Bottle with Tube

319 Bar Bottle and Stopper, 1934-1937; $38.00
322 Bar Bottle and Stopper, 1934-1938; $38.00
808 Beer Goblet, 8 oz., 4¾", Plain or Optic; $8.00
810 Beer Goblet, 12 oz., 5⅜" Plain; $9.00
811 Beer Goblet, 14 oz., 5½" Plain; $10.00
1861 Beer Mug, 11 oz., 15 oz., 1933-1934 (see *Fostoria Stemware*, page 176); All Crystal, and Crystal with Amber, Regal Blue, Empire Green Handle; $37.00
2435 Beer Mug, 9 oz., 1933-1934 (see *Fostoria Stemware*, Page 176); All Crystal, Crystal with Amber Regal Blue, Empire Green Handle; $37.00
2464 Beer Mug, 10 oz., 1933-1934; $25.00
2487 Beer Mug, 12 oz.
    Crystal, 1933-1934; $25.00
    Amber, 1933-1934; $32.00
2487 Beer Mug, 14 oz. (see *Fostoria Stemware*, page 177)
    Crystal, 1933-1934; $30.00
    Amber, 1933-1934; $36.00
    Green, 1933-1934; $37.00
    Rose, 1933-1934; $40.00
    Topaz, 1933-1934; $37.00

Wisteria, 1933-1934; $65.00
2493 Beer Mug, 14 oz., Tavern
    Crystal, Amber, Topaz, 1933-1934, $42.00
    Bicentennial Tavern Mug, Crystal, Amber, 1974-1978, $42.00 (see also Miscellaneous Milk Glass and *Fostoria Stemware*, page 177)
2048 Beer Stein, 18 oz., 1933-1934; $30.00
2490 Beer Stein, 16 oz., Crystal with Amber, Green or Regal Blue Handle, 1933-1934; $35.00
4168 Beverage Set, 6 tumblers, 1956-1958; $95.00
4168 Beverage Set, 12 tumblers in 6 colors, 1956-1958; $125.00
2494 Bitters Bottle with Tube
    Crystal, 1934-1942; $67.00
    Amber, 1934-1935; $74.00
    Regal Blue, 1934-1942; $85.00
    Burgundy, 1934-1942; $82.00
    Empire Green, 1934-1942; $79.00
    Ruby, 1935-1937; $88.00
2518 Bitters Bottle and Tube (May not have been made.)
    Crystal, July 1934; $85.00
    Regal Blue, July 1934; $125.00
    Burgundy, July 1934; $110.00
    Empire Green, July 1934; $110.00
    Ruby, July 1934; $125.00
    Mother of Pearl, 1934-1936; $60.00
2492 Canape Set, Fish Canape plate, and 4115 3 oz. or 4115½ 4 oz. footed cocktail, 1934-1942; $22.00

Silver Mist Cordial Tray, Regal Blue 2494 Cordial Bottle, 4024 Cordials

2524 Cocktail Mixer (see *Fostoria Stemware*, page 179)
    Crystal, 1934-1943; $30.00
    Regal Blue, 1934-1939; $48.00
    Burgundy, 1934-1936; $48.00
    Empire Green, 1934-1939; $48.00
4169 Cocktail Mixer, used with 4168 sets, 1956-1958; $35.00
2518 Cocktail Shaker, Metal Top (see *Fostoria Stemware*,
    page 178; Decoration 512, this section)
    Crystal, 1934-1940; $95.00
    Regal Blue, 1934-1940; $125.00
    Burgundy, 1934-1940; $110.00
    Empire Green, 1934-1940; $110.00
    Ruby, 1934-1938; $125.00
2518½ Cocktail Shaker, 7⅜", Gold Top
    Crystal, 1936-1940; $95.00
    Regal Blue, 1934-1940; $110.00
    Burgundy, 1934-1936; $110.00
    Empire Green, 1934-1937; $110.00
    Ruby, 1934-1940; $110.00
2525 Cocktail Shaker, Gold Top
    Crystal, 1934-1937; $75.00
    Regal Blue, 1934-1938; $105.00
    Burgundy, 1934-1938; $95.00
    Empire Green, 1934-1935; $95.00
    Ruby, 1934-1940; $110.00
2525½ Cocktail Shaker, Gold Top (see *Fostoria Stemware*,
    page 179)
    Crystal, 1936-1937; $75.00
    Regal Blue, 1936-1938; $95.00
    Ruby, 1936-1940; $95.00
2528 Cocktail Tray, 1935-1939; $200.00
2429 Cordial Tray, 12" (see Twenty-Four Twenty-Nine)
    Crystal, 1934-1937; $85.00
    Regal Blue, 1934-1937; $125.00
    Burgundy, 1934-1937; $110.00
    Empire Green, 1934-1937; $110.00
    Silver Mist, 1934-1935; $85.00
2429 Cordial Set, 2429 Cordial Tray, 2494 Cordial Bottle,
    six 4024 Cordials
    Crystal, 1934-1936; $300.00
    Regal Blue, 1934-1936; $495.00
    Burgundy, 1934-1936; $475.00
    Empire Green, 1934-1936; $495.00
    Silver Mist, 1934-1935; $335.00
2494 Cordial Bottle
    Crystal, 1934-1942; $75.00
    Amber, 1934-1935; $85.00
    Regal Blue, 1934-1942; $135.00
    Burgundy, 1934-1942; $125.00
    Empire Green, 1934-1940; $135.00
    Ruby, 1935-1940; $147.00
    Silver Mist, 1934-1938; $75.00
    Mother of Pearl, 1934-1936; $80.00
2494 Cordial Set, Cordial Bottle, six 4024 Cordials
    Crystal, 1934-1942; $225.00
    Amber, 1934-1935; $275.00
    Regal Blue, 1934-1942; $370.00
    Burgundy, 1934-1942; $350.00

4024 Regal Blue Sherry, Cordial with Silver Mist Foot, Regal Blue 2494 Decanter, 6011 Footed Whiskey, 6011 Wine, 4024 Rhine Wine, National Cutting, Regal Blue 887 Whiskey

    Empire Green, 1934-1940; $370.00
    Ruby, 1935-1940; $400.00
    Silver Mist, 1934-1938; $250.00

Empire Green 6011 Rhine Wine, 877 Wine, Green 4020 Decanter, Empire Green 877 Cocktail, Bitters Bottle, 6011 Brandy, 877 Cordial, 4024 Cordial

2443 Ice Tub, Green 4101 Jug and Tumblers

2518 Cordial Bottle, Crystal Stopper (May not have been made.)
   Crystal, July 1934; $95.00
   Regal Blue, July 1934; $135.00
   Burgundy, July 1934; $125.00
   Empire Green, July 1934; $125.00
423 Custard, Handled, 1928-1943; $7.00
300 Decanter and Stopper, Pint, Quart, Plain or Optic, Pre 1924-1928; $32.00
1918 Decanter and Stopper, 1934-1939; $42.00
1918 Decanter and Stopper, Handled, 1934; $48.00
1928 Decanter and Stopper, Pinched, 1934; $42.00

Ruby 2494 Decanter, 6012 Wine, Cocktail

2052 Decanter and Stopper, Pinched, 1934; $45.00
2439 Decanter and Stopper
   Crystal, 1930-1932; market
   Amber, 1930-1932; market
   Topaz, 1930-1932; market
   Rose, 1930-1932; market
   Azure, 1930-1932; market
   Green, 1930-1932; market
2439 Decanter Set, 2439 Decanter, six 5098
   2½ oz. Footed Tumblers
   Crystal, 1930-1932; market
   Amber, 1930-1932; market
   Topaz, 1930-1932; market
   Rose, 1930-1932; market
   Azure, 1930-1932; market
   Green, 1930-1932; market
2494 Decanter and Stopper (see *Fostoria Stemware*, page 177)
   Crystal, RO, 1934-1940; $125.00
   Amber, RO, 1934-1935; $148.00
   Regal Blue, 1934-1940; $175.00
   Burgundy, 1934-1940; $175.00
   Empire Green, 1934-1940; $175.00
   Ruby, 1935-1940; $185.00
   Mother of Pearl, 1934-1936; $125.00
2502 Decanter and Stopper
   Crystal, 1934-1937; $125.00
   Regal Blue, 1934-1942; $165.00
   Burgundy, 1934-1937; $165.00
   Empire Green, 1934-1935; $195.00
2502 Decanter Set, Decanter, six 2 oz. Whiskeys
   Crystal, 1934-1937; $225.00
   Regal Blue, 1934-1935; $295.00
   Burgundy, 1934-1937; $285.00
   Empire Green, 1934-1935; $285.00
2510 Decanter (see Sunray)
2518 Decanter and Crystal Stopper (see *Fostoria Stemware*, page 178; Decoration 512, this section)
   Crystal, 1934-1939; $95.00
   Regal Blue, 1934-1937; $135.00
   Burgundy, 1934-1940; $115.00
   Empire Green, 1934-1940; $115.00
   Ruby, 1934-1940; $125.00
2525 Decanter, Crystal Stopper (see *Fostoria Stemware*, page 179)
   Crystal, 1934-1937; $95.00
   Regal Blue, 1934-1938; $125.00
   Burgundy, 1934-1938; $110.00
   Empire Green, 1934-1938; $110.00
4020 Decanter, 1930-1932
   Crystal; $495.00/market
   Green Base; $600.00/market
   Amber Base; $565.00/market
   Ebony Base; $565.00/market
   Rose Bowl; $625.00/market
   Topaz Bowl; $625.00/market
4101 Decanter and Stopper, Quart (see *Fostoria Stemware*, page 180)

Amber, 1928-1934; $85.00
Topaz, 1930-1934; $85.00
Green, 1928-1938; $85.00
Rose, 1928-1938; $95.00
Azure, 1928-1934; $100.00
4101 Decanter Set, Decanter and six Whiskey Tumblers
(see *Fostoria Stemware*, page 180)
Amber, 1928-1934; $150.00
Topaz, 1930-1934; $165.00
Green, 1928-1934; $165.00
Rose, 1928-1934; $165.00
Azure, 1928-1934; $175.00
4132 Decanter and Stopper, 24 oz., 1938-1943; $54.00
Deer Cutting A, B, C, D, and Cutting 779, 780, 781
Decanter and Tumblers
6011 Decanter and Stopper
Crystal, 1934-1939; $95.00
Amber Base, 1934-1939; $105.00
Regal Blue Bowl, 1934-1935; $175.00
Burgundy Bowl, 1934-1939; $150.00
Empire Green Bowl, 1934-1939; $150.00
701 Highball, 10 oz. N.O. or Plain
Crystal, Regal Blue, Burgundy,
Empire Green, Ruby, 1934-1940; $20.00
701 Highball, 12 oz. N.O. or Plain
Crystal, Ruby, 1934-1940; $20.00
4098 Hollow Stem Beer, 12 oz. (also available with Crest
Designs A-F)
Crystal, 1934-1940; $25.00
Amber Base, 1934-1937; $32.00
Burgundy Base, 1934-1938; $32.00
Empire Green Base, 1934-1935; $38.00
Regal Blue Base, 1934-1935; $38.00
863 Hollow Stem Champagne, 1934-1940; $18.00
1554 Hollow Stem Champagne, 1934-1937; $22.00
4132 Ice Bowl, 1938-1943; $28.00
Deer Cutting A, B, C, D, and Cutting 779, 780, 781
4140 Ice Tea Set, 7 piece: Jug and six 12 oz. Tumblers
(see Water Set below for colors and prices)
2443 Ice Tub
Crystal, 1933-1940; $45.00
Rose, 1933-1934; $67.00
Azure, 1933-1934; $67.00
Green, 1933-1934; $58.00
Ebony, 1933-1934; $45.00
Topaz, 1933-1935; $56.00
2464 Ice Jug
Crystal, 1933-1943; $225.00
Amber, 1933-1934; $280.00
Green, 1933-1934; $300.00
Rose, 1933-1934; $300.00
Topaz, 1933-1934; $300.00
2503 Jug, Quart Wine, Colored Handle
Crystal, 1936-1938; $75.00
Regal Blue Handle, 1934-1937; $95.00
Burgundy Handle, 1934-1938; $95.00
Empire Green Handle, 1934-1938; $95.00

2518 Jug, Crystal Handled Wine (see *Fostoria Stemware*,
page 178)
Crystal, 1934-1940; $75.00
Regal Blue, 1935-1937; $95.00
Burgundy, 1935-1940; $95.00
Empire Green, 1935-1940; $95.00
4101 Jug (see *Fostoria Stemware*, page 180)
Amber, 1928-1936; $65.00
Topaz, 1930-1936; $65.00
Green, 1928-1937; $65.00
Rose, 1928-1932; $75.00
Azure, 1928-1936; $75.00
4118 Jug, 60 oz.
Crystal, 1936-1940; $95.00
Regal Blue, 1935-1938; $175.00
Burgundy, 1935-1937; $175.00
Empire Green, 1935-1937; $175.00
Ruby, 1935-1937; $175.00
2283 Luncheon Set, SO (see Plates), Rose, Azure, Green,
Amber (Pieces offered from 1927 to 1929, Set offered 1929)
Cup and Saucer, $12.00
Plate, 6"; $4.00
Plate, 7"; $5.00
Plate, 8"; $5.00
Plate, 9"; $7.00
Plate, 10"; $9.00
Plate, 13"; $15.00
2255 Sugar and Cream (see Appetizer, Buffet, and Relish)
1184 Old Fashioned Cocktail, 3⅜", 1934-1940 (N.O. or
Plain, Crystal, Rose, Azure, Amber, Green Topaz, Wis-
teria); $25.00 to $30.00

Ruby 4118 Jug and Tumbler

Regal Blue 2518 Jug, Ruby 2518 Decanter, Whiskey, Wine, Regal Blue 2524 Cocktail Mixer (Courtesy of Mike and Gina Lodes)

1185 Old Fashioned Cocktail, 8 oz.
    Crystal, Regal Blue, Burgundy, Empire Green, 1934-1940; $32.00
2510 Pilsner, 1934-1936; $45.00
2464 Refreshment Set (see *Fostoria Stemware*, page 177) Jug and six Tumblers
    Crystal, 1933-1943; $295.00
    Rose, 1933-1934; $500.00
    Green, 1933-1934; $500.00
    Amber, 1933-1934; $425.00
    Topaz, 1933-1934; $450.00
4101 Refreshment Set, Jug, six tumblers
    Amber, 1928-1936; $125.00
    Topaz, 1930-1936; $125.00
    Green, 1928-1937; $125.00
    Rose, 1928-1932; $150.00
    Azure, 1928-1936; $150.00
4118 Refreshment Set, 60 oz., Jug, Crystal Handle, six 4118 Tumblers, 12 oz.
    Crystal, 1936-1940; $155.00
    Regal Blue, 1935-1938; $260.00
    Burgundy, 1935-1937; $260.00
    Empire Green, 1935-1937; $260.00
    Ruby, 1935-1937; $265.00
4141 Refreshment Set, 4141 Jug, six 10 oz. or six 12 oz. 4141 Tumblers (see *Fostoria Stemware*, page 182)
    Crystal, 1938-1942; $125.00
    Amber, 1938-1939; $135.00
    Azure, 1938-1942; $165.00
    Regal Blue, 1938-1939; $175.00
4142 Refreshment Set, 4142 Jug, six 10 oz. or six 12 oz. 4142 Tumblers (see *Fostoria Stemware*, page 182)

    Crystal, 1938-1940; $125.00
    Amber, 1938-1939; $135.00
    Azure, 1938-1939; $150.00
    Regal Blue, 1938-1940; $175.00
2706/599 Salad/Punch Bowl, wood base with Ebony finish, 1959-1970; $50.00
2706/615 Punch Cup, 1959-1970; $5.00
2464 Tumbler
    Crystal, 1933-1943; $25.00
    Amber, 1933-1935; $32.00
    Green, 1933-1935; $32.00
    Rose, 1933-1934; $35.00
    Topaz, 1933-1935; $32.00
4118 Tumbler, 12 oz.
    Crystal, 1936-1940; $10.00
    Regal Blue, 1935-1938; $14.00
    Burgundy, 1935-1937; $14.00
    Empire Green, 1935-1937; $14.00
    Ruby, 1935-1937; $15.00
4132 Tumblers (see *Fostoria Stemware*, page 154)
    Deer Cutting A, B, C, D, and Cutting 779, 780, 781, 1938-1943; $12.00
4140 Tumbler, 10 oz., 12 oz.
    Crystal, 1938-1940; $10.00
    Azure, 1938-1939; $14.00
    Amber, 1938-1939; $10.00
    Regal Blue, 1938-1939; $15.00
4140 Water Set, 7 piece: Jug and six 10 oz. or 12 oz. Tumblers
    Crystal, 1938-1940; $125.00
    Azure, 1938-1939; $165.00
    Amber, 1938-1938; $145.00
    Regal Blue, 1938-1939; $175.00
2033 Water Tray, 12", pre 1924-1928; $22.00
2106 Water Tray, 10", 1928; $25.00
887 Whiskey, 1¾ oz. Plain, Regal Blue, Burgundy, Empire Green, Ruby, 1934-1940; $25.00

Amber 2494 Tavern Mug, 2494 Cordial Bottle, Mother of Pearl 2494 Decanter, Crystal Tavern Mug, 879 Mother of Pearl Cordials, 6011 Cordials

887 Whiskey, 1¾ oz., R.O., Crystal, Amber, 1934-1940; $22.00

887 Whiskey, 2½ oz., 2¼", R.O., 1935-1936, N.O., 1936-1940; $25.00

    Crystal, Amber, Rose, Green, Topaz

887 Whiskey Sham, 2⅛", 1936-1940; $20.00

4122 Whiskey Sham, 1½ oz., 3", 1934-1936; $18.00

889 Whiskey Sour, 5 oz. Plain, Crystal, Regal Blue, Burgundy, Empire Green, Ruby, 1934-1940; $25.00

1185 Whiskey Sour, 5 oz., 1934-1940; $20.00

2502 Whiskey, 2 oz.

    Crystal, 1934-1937; $18.00

Regal Blue, 1934-1935; $22.00

Burgundy, 1934-1937; $20.00

Empire Green, 1934-1935; $20.00

2518 Wine, 5 oz., Whiskey, 2 oz., Crystal, Regal Blue, Burgundy, Empire Green, Ruby, 1934-1940; $20.00

2494 Wine Set, Decanter, six 4024 Sherries

    Crystal, 1934-1940; $275.00

    Amber, 1934-1935; $300.00

    Regal Blue, 1934-1940; $425.00

    Burgundy, 1934-1940; $395.00

    Empire Green, 1934-1940; $395.00

    Ruby, 1935-1940; $450.00

RYE

Plate Etching 321

1935 – 1936

319 Bar Bottle and Stopper, 29 oz.; $54.00

322 Bar Bottle and Stopper, 26 oz.; $54.00

1918 Decanter and Stopper, 24 oz.; $54.00

1918 Decanter and Stopper, 24 oz. Handled; $60.00

1928 Pinch Bottle and Stopper, 24 oz.; $54.00

2052 Pinch Bottle and Stopper, 29 oz.; $54.00

DECORATION 512

Gold Bands on Crystal

1935 – 1938

2518 Cocktail Shaker; $95.00

2518 Decanter; $95.00

2518 Whiskey; $20.00

2518 Wine, 5 oz.; $20.00

2435—9 oz. Beer Mug
Height 4¾ in.
Solid Crystal
Crystal Mug with
Am-RB-Emp. Hdles.

1861—11 oz. Beer Mug
Height 4½ in.
Solid Crystal
Crys. Mug with
Am-RB-Emp. Hdles.
1861—15 oz. Beer Mug
Height 5¼ in.
Solid Crystal
Crystal Mug with
Am-RB-Emp. Hdles.

808—8 oz. Beer Goblet
Height 4¾ in.
Crystal, Plain and Optic
810—12 oz. Beer Goblet
Height 5⅝ in.
Crystal, Plain
811—14 oz. Beer Goblet
Height 5½ in.
Crystal, Plain

4098—12 oz. Hollow Stem
Beer—Height 4¾ in.
Solid Crystal
Am-RB-Bur-Emp. Base
with Crystal Bowl

2449—9 oz. Footed
Beer Mug
Height 4¼ in.
Solid Crystal

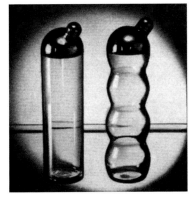

1934 House and Garden

4098—12-oz.
Hollow Stem Beer.
Height 4¾ in.
Crest A

4098—12-oz.
Hollow Stem Beer.
Height 4¾ in.
Crest B

4098—12-oz.
Hollow Stem Beer.
Height 4¾ in.
Crest C

4098—12-oz.
Hollow Stem Beer.
Height 4¾ in.
Crest D

4098—12-oz.
Hollow Stem Beer.
Height 4¾ in.
Crest E

4098—12-oz.
Hollow Stem Beer.
Height 4¾ in.
Crest F

2052—Pinch Decanter and
Stopper—Cap. 29-oz.
Hgt. 9¼ in. Et. 321

1928
Pinch Decanter and Stopper
Cap. 24-oz. Hgt. 8 in. Et. 321

1918—Decanter and Stopper
Cap. 24-oz. Hgt. 10½ in.
Et. 321

1918—Hld. Decanter and
Stopper—Cap. 24-oz.
Hgt.10½ in. Et. 321

319—Bar Bottle and Stopper
Cap. 29-oz. Hgt. 12¾ in.
Et. 321

322—Bar Bottle and Stopper
Cap. 26-oz. Hgt. 12¾ in.
Et. 321

5510—12-oz. Pilsener
Height 8 in.

863—5-oz.
Hollow Stem Champagne
Cut Flute
Height 5⅛ in.

1554
5-oz. Hollow Stem Champagne, Pressed. Height 5 in.

1184—7-oz.
Old Fashioned Cocktail,
Sham. Height 3⅜ in.

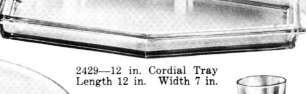

2429—12 in. Cordial Tray
Length 12 in.   Width 7 in.

2511—13 in. Cheese and Cracker

887
1¾-oz. Whiskey, Sham.
Height 2⅛ in.

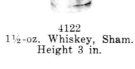

4122
1½-oz. Whiskey, Sham.
Height 3 in.

2502—2-oz. Whiskey
Height 2¼ in.

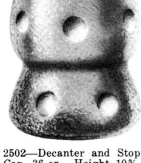

2502—Decanter and Stopper
Cap. 36-oz. Height 10¾ in.

2503—Wine Jug
Cap. 33-oz.   Height 8¼ in.

6011
Decanter and Stopper
Cap. 26-oz. Height 11⅜ in.

2518
5 oz. Wine
Height 3½ in.

4122
1½-oz. Whiskey, Sham.
Height 3 in.

2518—Decanter,
Capacity 30 oz.
Height 9½ in.

2525—Decanter and Stopper
Capacity 28 oz.
Height 10½ in.

6011
Decanter and Stopper
Capacity 26 oz.
Height 11⅜ in.

2518
2 oz. Whiskey
Height 2¼ in.

887
1¾-oz. Whiskey, Sham.
Height 2⅛ in.

887—2½ oz. Whiskey
Height 2¼ in.

4101—2½ oz. Ftd. Whiskey
Height 3 in.

2494—Bitters Bottle
with Tube
Capacity 5¾ oz.
Height 5¾ in.

2494—Decanter and Stopper
Capacity 26 oz.
Height 9¼ in.

2494—Cordial Bottle and
Stopper
Capacity 14 oz.
Height 7½ in.

4101—Decanter and Stopper
Capacity 38 oz.
Height 9¾ in.

1184—7-oz.
Old Fashioned Cocktail,
Sham. Height 3⅜ in.

1184—7 oz.
Old Fashioned Cocktail
Narrow Optic
Height 3⅜ in.

2518—3 oz. Footed Cocktail
Height 3⅜ in.
for use with 2518
Cocktail Shaker

889
5 oz. Whiskey Sour,
Plain
Height 3½ in.

1185
5 oz. Whiskey Sour
Sham
Height 3⅞ in.

1185—8 oz.
Old Fashioned Cocktail
Sham
Height 3½ in.

6012—3 oz. Cocktail
Height 4⅝ in.
for use with 2518
Cocktail Shaker

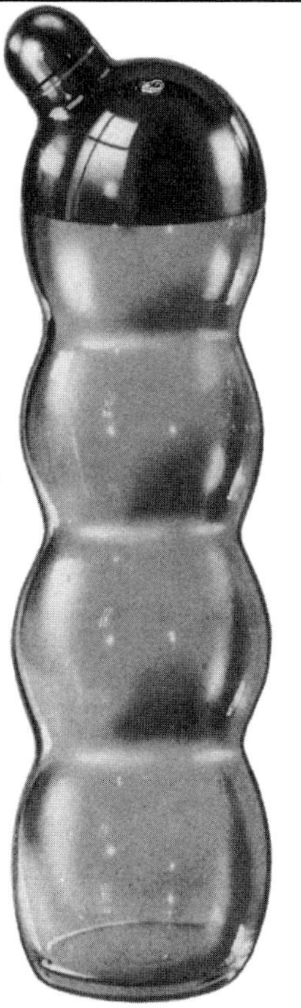

2518—Cocktail Shaker, Metal Top
Capacity 38 oz.   Height 12¾ in.
2518½—Cocktail Shaker, Metal Top
Capacity 28 oz.   Height 7⅜ in.

2524—Cocktail Mixer
Capacity 21 oz.
Height 6½ in.

4115—3 oz. Ftd. Cocktail
Height 3⅛ in.
4115½—4 oz. Ftd. Cocktail
Height 3¾ in.
for use with 2525
Cocktail Shaker

6011—3 oz. Cocktail
Height 4⅝ in.
for use with 2525
Cocktail Shaker

2528—Cocktail Tray
Length 11¾ in.   Width 10¾ in.

2525—Cocktail Shaker, Metal Top
Capacity 42 oz.   Height 12½ in.
2525½—Cocktail Shaker, Metal Top
Capacity 30 oz.   Height 7½ in.

701—Tumbler
See price list for sizes

889—Tumbler
See price list for sizes

4076—9 oz. Tumbler
Height 4¼ in.

2449—12 oz. Footed
Beer Mug
Height 5¼ in.
2449—9 oz. Footed
Beer Mug
Height 4¼ in.

2056
Tom and Jerry Mug
Capacity 5½ oz.
Height 3¼ in.

2056—12 oz. Beer Mug
Height 4½ in.

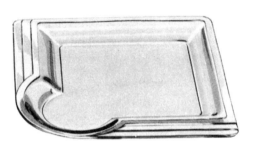

2541—Snack Plate
6¾ in. Square

5510—12-oz. Pilsener
Height 8 in.

4115—3 oz. Footed Cocktail
Height 3⅛ in.
2492—Fish Canape
Length 8½ in.

4098—12 oz. Hollow Stem
Beer—Height 4¾ in.

2518—Jug, Capacity 44 oz.
Height 9 in.

4118—12 oz. Tumbler
Height 5 in.

4118—60 oz. Jug
Height 8½ in.

2518
10 oz. Tumbler
Height 4⅛ in.

2464—11 oz. Tumbler
Height 3¾ in.

4101—Jug
Capacity 80 oz.
Height 9¾ in.

4101— 9 oz. Footed Tumbler
Height 4⅝ in.

2464—Ice Jug
Capacity ½ Gal.
Height 6¾ in.

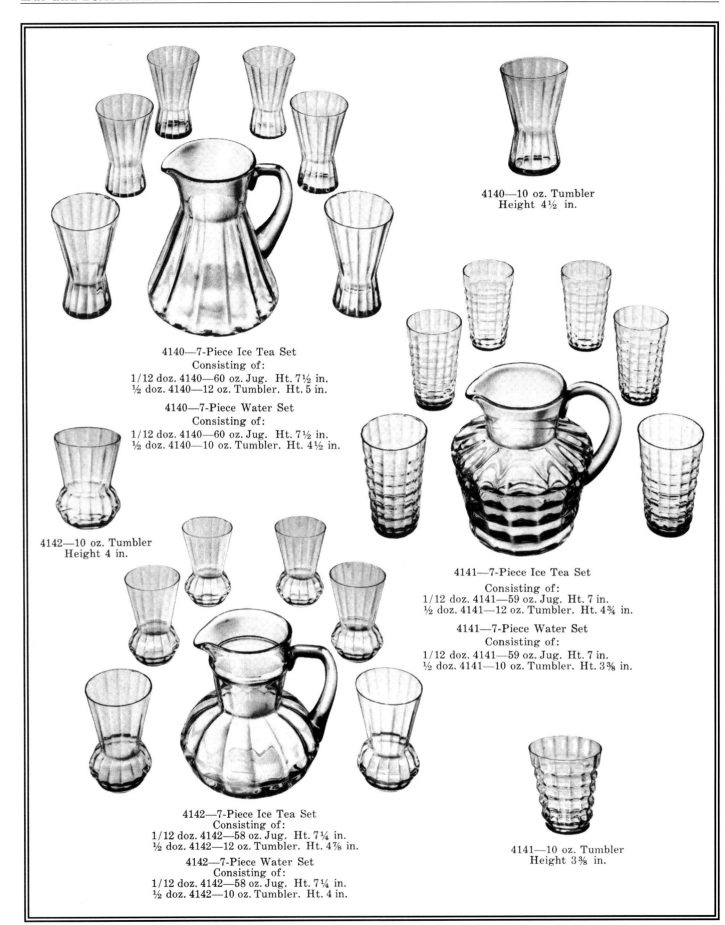

4140—10 oz. Tumbler
Height 4½ in.

4140—7-Piece Ice Tea Set
Consisting of:
1/12 doz. 4140—60 oz. Jug. Ht. 7½ in.
½ doz. 4140—12 oz. Tumbler. Ht. 5 in.

4140—7-Piece Water Set
Consisting of:
1/12 doz. 4140—60 oz. Jug. Ht. 7½ in.
½ doz. 4140—10 oz. Tumbler. Ht. 4½ in.

4142—10 oz. Tumbler
Height 4 in.

4141—7-Piece Ice Tea Set
Consisting of:
1/12 doz. 4141—59 oz. Jug. Ht. 7 in.
½ doz. 4141—12 oz. Tumbler. Ht. 4¾ in.

4141—7-Piece Water Set
Consisting of:
1/12 doz. 4141—59 oz. Jug. Ht. 7 in.
½ doz. 4141—10 oz. Tumbler. Ht. 3⅜ in.

4142—7-Piece Ice Tea Set
Consisting of:
1/12 doz. 4142—58 oz. Jug. Ht. 7¼ in.
½ doz. 4142—12 oz. Tumbler. Ht. 4⅞ in.

4142—7-Piece Water Set
Consisting of:
1/12 doz. 4142—58 oz. Jug. Ht. 7¼ in.
½ doz. 4142—10 oz. Tumbler. Ht. 4 in.

4141—10 oz. Tumbler
Height 3⅜ in.

2510½
2-oz. Whiskey
Height 2¼ in.

2510—18-oz. Oval Decanter
and Stopper
Height 8¼ in.

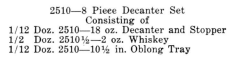

2510—8 Piece Decanter Set
Consisting of
1/12 Doz. 2510—18 oz. Decanter and Stopper
1/2   Doz. 2510½—2 oz. Whiskey
1/12 Doz. 2510—10½ in. Oblong Tray

4132—Decanter and Stopper
DEER CUTTING D Illustrated
Capacity 24 oz. Height 9¾ in.
This Decanter Also Cut in Following Designs.
Deer Designs—Cut No. A-B-C-D. See Catalog Page No. 146-C
Ripple Design—Cut No. 766. See Catalog Page No. 143-B
Beacon Design—Cut No. 767. See Catalog Page No. 144-B
Pussywillow Design—Cut No. 769. See Catalog Page No. 147-C
Athenian Design—Cut No. 770. See Catalog Page No. 147-C
Federal Design—Cut No. 771. See Catalog Page No. 148-C
Tulip Design—Cut No. 772. See Catalog Page No. 148-C

CUTTING A   CUTTING B   CUTTING C   CUTTING D

SOUTH SEAS DESIGN
CUTTING No. 779

SERENADE DESIGN
CUTTING No. 780

DRUM DESIGN
CUTTING No. 781

4020 Decanter and Stopper
Solid Crystal
Gr-Am-Eb Base with Crys Bowl
Crys Base with Ro-Tz Bowl
Priced on page 39

4168
Beverage Set
Consisting of:
½ Doz. 4168 Tumbler
Capacity 10½ oz.

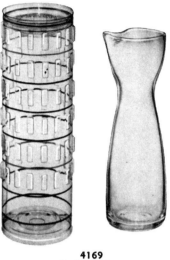

4169
Cocktail Mixer
Height 10¼ in. Capacity 28 oz.

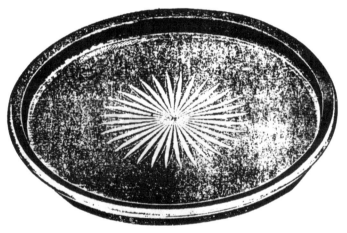

No. 2033 12 in. Round Tray

2443—Ice Tub
Height 4⅜ in.
Width 5¾ in.
Ro-Az-Gr-Eb-Crys-Tz

Azure 2439 Versailles Decanter (courtesy Jim and Sherry Davis)

BELLS

The Fostoria Glass Company made bells for many occasions: for Christmas, for Mother's Day, for Valentine's Day, for weddings, and other special times. They also made bells to coordinate with some major patterns. We've had one in Chintz and one in Heather. No bells were listed until 1977. In that one year bells were added to four main patterns, Sheffield, Richmond, Serenity, and Navarre. A special order bell was made for the Avon Company in the Navarre pattern to be given as a sales award, and is seldom seen in the marketplace. The handle is different from the handle for the Navarre bell. The first Christmas bell, 1977, was a winter scene on the Silver Flutes blank. It is dated 1977 and has the Fostoria "F" mark. A few other bells were marked, but most were not.

In January of 1978 a Mother's Day bell was shown. Made of very thinly blown crystal, this bell has an etched picture of a mother holding a child inside an oval that is framed by scroll-like flowers. Below the oval is etched "Mother's Day 1978." The 1979 Mother's Day bell has the mother and child in oval frame flanked by flowers and vines.The Cameo bell was purchased in the Moundsville, West Virginia, Fostoria Outlet Store. It is not listed in Fostoria price lists.

The bells are about to "ring"

The advent of the wedding bell occurred in 1979. This unusual bell is shaped like the figure of a bride, the handle being the top part of the body and the bell itself serving as the flared skirt of the bride's dress. The soft Silver Mist finish covers the top and about one-third of the bell part like a veil of illusion.

The American pattern (2056) added a bell in July of 1981. Instead of being the expected heavy pressed piece, this bell was blown into a mold resulting in a bell that is very thin, light, and simply exquisite.

Also in 1981 a Ruby bell, "'Twas the Night Before Christmas," with a frosted crystal handle was offered. Although introduced as the first of four limited editions, it became the first and only one made before the production of handmade crystal ceased at the Fostoria factory in 1982. Some pressed bells continued to be made until the factory closed.

In 1986 the Moundsville Chamber of Commerce bought plain Fostoria blanks and had a replica of the old brown label etched on one side. Under the label are the words, "Moundsville, W. Va., Feb. 28, 1986," the date the Fostoria factory was closed. These bells have a gold metal handle. The "Merry Christmas" bell with gold metal handle has not been found in catalogs or price lists, so no date can be determined.

In a group of items made for the Centennial of the Coca Cola Company, Fostoria used a Calendar Girl taken from an 1891 calendar. The bell was Ruby flashed on crystal. This same blank was used for a "Love Birds" bell dated 1987 and was sold through the outlet stores after the factory was closed. A "Peace on Earth" Christmas bell dated 1986 also used the same blank.

American, 1981-1982; $500.00/market
Angel, Silver Mist, 1980-1982; $47.00
Cameo, Crystal; $35.00
Christmas, 1977; $95.00
Christmas, 1978; $95.00
Christmas, 1979; $95.00
Christmas, 1980; $95.00
Christmas, 1981, Ruby with Silver Mist Handle; $125.00
Christmas, 1982; $95.00

Mother's Day Cameo, Mother's Day 1979, 1978, 6020 Spiral Optic (unknown date)

Christmas, 1985, Silent Night, Cobalt Blue, Silver Metal Handle; $25.00

Christmas, 1986, Peace on Earth, Ruby (flashed), Gold Metal Handle; $25.00

Christmas, 1986, Silent Night, Cobalt Blue, Silver Metal Handle; $25.00

Merry Christmas, Gold Metal Handle; $25.00

Coca Cola, 1986, Gold Metal Handle; $75.00

Fostoria Commemorative, February 28, 1986, Gold Metal Handle; $45.00

Kimberly, Gold Metal Handle, 1983; $35.00

Love Bell, 1980-1982; $95.00

Love Bell, 1986; $25.00

Love Birds, 1987, Ruby (flashed), Gold Metal Handle; $25.00

Love Always, Fostoria Outlet Store, 1986, Ruby (flashed), Gold Metal Handle; $35.00

Mother's Day, 1978; $95.00

Mother's Day, 1979; $95.00

Navarre, Crystal, 1976-1982; $95.00

Navarre, Blue, 1976-1982; $125.00

Navarre, Pink, 1976-1982; $110.00

Navarre, Avon, 1980; $135.00

Richmond, 1977-1982; $32.00

Serenity, Crystal, 1977-1982; $65.00

Serenity, Yellow, 1977-1981; $75.00

Serenity , Blue, 1977-1982; $75.00

Sheffield, 1977-1982; $36.00

6020 Twisted Handle, SO; $70.00

Valentine, 1979; $95.00

Wedding Bell, 1979-1982; Crystal and Silver Mist, NO; $95.00

Wilma, Pink, Special Order, 1980-1982; $85.00

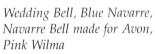

Wedding Bell, Blue Navarre, Navarre Bell made for Avon, Pink Wilma

Commemorative, Merry Christmas (unknown date), Love Always, Peace on Earth, Love Birds

Christmas 1979, 1980, Angel Bell, Christmas 1977, 1978, 1981

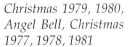

Fostoria
Christmas 1981

Wedding Bell

Navarre Bell
(Crystal or Blue)

Richmond Bell
(Gold Band)
Sheffield Bell
(Platinum Band)

Holiday Bell

American Bell

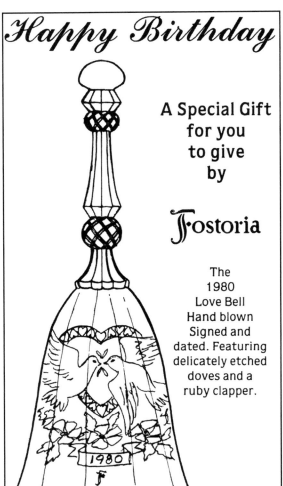

Happy Birthday

A Special Gift
for you
to give
by

Fostoria

The
1980
Love Bell
Hand blown
Signed and
dated. Featuring
delicately etched
doves and a
ruby clapper.

*Kimberly
Bell*

Limited Edition Collectors' Bells
A treat to give, a treasure to keep. Both handsomely gift boxed.

"Silent Night" The 1985 Christmas Bell — graceful snow geese in flight on Cobalt blue with silver handle.

The *"Love Bell"* for Valentine's and Mother's Day 1986. A truly romantic motif etched on Ruby with a gold handle.

The "Love Bell" for Valentine's and Mother's Day 1986. A truly romantic motif etched on Ruby with a gold handle.

"Silent Night" The 1986 Christmas Bell — graceful snow geese in flight on Cobalt blue with silver handle.

Coca Cola Centennial Collection

Coca Cola is celebrating its 100th Anniversary in 1986, and Fostoria helps to commemorate the occasion with a new gift collection featuring art work from Coca Cola's archives.

BOOKENDS

Bookends first appeared in 1939 in the form of a horse and an elephant. Both were made in crystal and Silver Mist through 1943 and the horse remained in production through 1958 in crystal. Both bookends were remade in Ebony in 1980; however, very few turned out as first quality. These were sold through the outlet stores. The owl bookend made in crystal in 1942-1943 was also made in Ebony in 1980 with little success. Eagle bookends introduced in 1940 were made in crystal and Silver Mist with Stars, Carving 14.

The Lyre bookends enjoyed a long run from 1941 to 1958, and along with the horse, are seen more often than the other styles. The seahorse in sparkling crystal is also collected as a figural.

As far as we can determine the Chinese bookends were offered only in Ebony decorated with Gold as shown. The Seashell came in two sizes. It and the Serendipity bookends are seldom seen (see *Fostoria Tableware: 1944 – 1986*). The unusual Plume design in crystal or Ebony is outstanding. All bookends are priced as a pair.

Lyre Bookends, Eagle Bookends

2564 Horse
    Crystal, 1939-1958; $110.00
    Silver Mist, 1939-1943; $125.00

Ebony, Silver Mist, and Crystal Horse Bookends; Ebony and Crystal Owl Bookends

2636 Plume
    Crystal, 1951-1957; $125.00
    Ebony, 1953-1957; $225.00
2626 Chinese, Decoration 522, Ebony with Gold, 1954-1957; $600.00
2825 Small Seashell, Crystal, 1973-1974; $135.00
2825 Large Seashell, Crystal, 1973-1974; $160.00
2856 Serendipity 139, Crystal, 1974; $110.00
2856 Serendipity 140, Crystal, 1974; $110.00
2856 Serendipity 141, Crystal, 1974; $150.00

    Ebony, 1980 Feasibility; $675.00
2580 Elephant
    Crystal, 1939-1943; $195.00
    Silver Mist, 1939-1943; $235.00
    Ebony, 1980 Feasibility; $750.00
2585 Eagle
    Crystal, 1940-1943; $220.00
    Silver Mist, 1940-1943; $250.00
2585 Eagle with Stars Carving, Silver Mist, 1940-1943; $250.00
2601 Lyre, Crystal, 1941-1958; $150.00
2615 Owl
    Crystal, 1942-1943; $450.00
    Ebony, 1980 Feasibility; $700.00
2641 Seahorse, Crystal, 1950-1958; $395.00

Ebony and Crystal Plume Bookends, Ebony Chinese

39

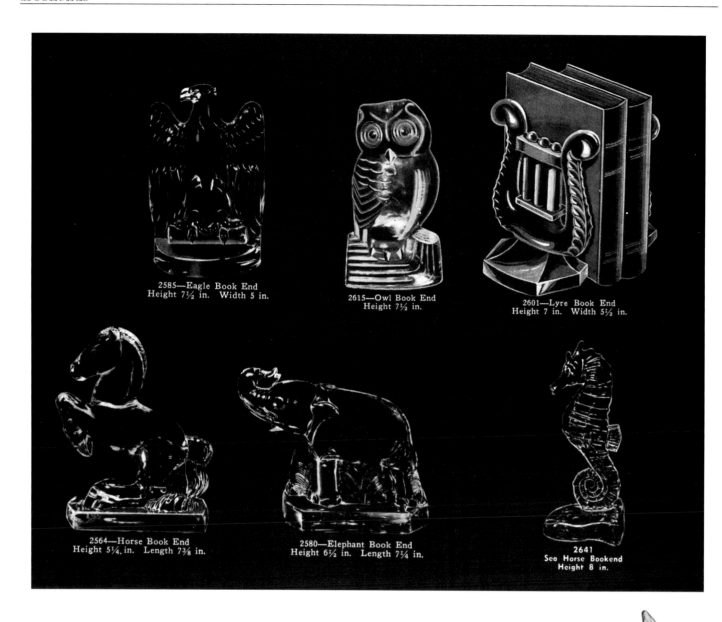

2585—Eagle Book End
Height 7½ in.   Width 5 in.

2615—Owl Book End
Height 7½ in.

2601—Lyre Book End
Height 7 in.   Width 5½ in.

2564—Horse Book End
Height 5¼ in.   Length 7⅜ in.

2580—Elephant Book End
Height 6½ in.   Length 7¼ in.

2641
Sea Horse Bookend
Height 8 in.

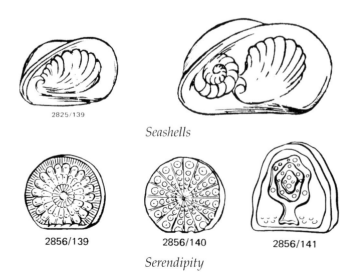

2825/139

Seashells

2856/139   2856/140   2856/141

Serendipity

2639
"Plume"   Book   End
Height   9¼   in.

BOUDOIR ACCESSORIES and JEWELRY

Fostoria had made many items for bedroom and bath in the earlier part of the century. Many of these were made from opal glass and were hand painted. Sets that include large trays, pin trays, hand mirrors, colognes, puff, pomade, match, and cold cream boxes have been found. After 1920 the 2241, 2242, and 2243 colognes were being used for etched patterns until the advent of color in 1924, 1925 when several new designs appeared (see *Fostoria Tableware: 1924 – 1943*, Virginia Etching for catalog picture). A box or tray was created to suit milady's every need. Many of these were delicately or lavishly decorated to reflect trends in style and decor of the time (see *Fostoria Tableware: 1924 – 1943*, Decorations). Another vanity, numbered 2289, was offered from 1925 to 1927 but is seldom seen. After 1930 boudoir offerings waned. However, in 1939 the 2276 Vanity was offered again, in Crystal only. Since this lovely piece seems to top the list of collectible boudoir items we are showing it with some decorations we have not yet identified. It also was used for cuttings and engravings many having only a number. The stopper is cut to form a sharp point at the top and is often found damaged or repaired. Note that the 2276 Covered Cheese and the 2347½ Puff and Cover are very much alike. The cover is the key.

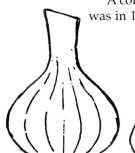

A cologne bottle was offered in the 2743 Crown Pattern in 1962. The last effort to make a cologne or puff was in 1982 for the Navarre line. Jon Saffel, head of the design department at that time, has said in a letter to us: "You show the large carafe and small carafe, of which quite a few were made. I don't know how many were actually etched, however. The puff box and cover were only sampled, and if there were any examples around, there would not be many. The perfume bottle was sampled; I don't recall it ever being etched. The stopper was never made (we didn't even make a mould for it)." See Navarre, *Fostoria Tableware 1943 – 1986*.

The Powder Room and Decorative Accessories group offered in 1958 are unique in design and color. The metal stems on the apple and pear are removable. The Jenny Lind line in milk glass was devoted almost exclusively to boudoir accessories (see Milk Glass).

NA01/790, Table Carafe/Vase; NA01/750, Mini-Carafe/Vase; NA01/842, Perfume Bottle and Stopper; NA01/580, Puff Box and Cover

1478 Lavender Salt and Stopper, Optic, Crystal,
    pre 1924-1927; $75.00
1666 Puff and Cover, Optic, Crystal, pre 1924-1927;
    $65.00
1697 Bedroom Set, 2 pieces: Carafe and 4023 Tumbler
    Crystal, pre 1924-1940; $95.00
    Green, SO, 1929-1940; $110.00
    Amber, SO, 1929-1940; $110.00
    Rose, SO, 1929-1932; $145.00
    Azure, SO, 1929-1940; $125.00
1886 Pin Box and Cover (See Milk Glass)
1886 Pin Tray and Cover (See Milk Glass)
1904 Bon Bon and Cover, Optic, Crystal, pre 1924-1927;
    $75.00
2056 Cologne and Stopper (see American)
2106 Match and Cover, Vogue Pattern
    Crystal, 1924; $68.00
    Amber, 1924; $87.00
    Green, 1924; $87.00
    Canary, 1924; $125.00
2118 Cologne, Crystal, pre 1924-1927; $95.00
2135 Hair Receiver, Optic
    Crystal, 1924; $95.00
    Ebony, 1924; $95.00
2135 Puff and Cover, Optic, Crystal, 1924; $95.00
2136 Pomade and Cover, 2"
    Crystal, 1924; $75.00
    Amber, 1924-1926; $75.00
    Green, 1924-1926; $75.00
    Canary, 1924-1926; $85.00

Canary 2289 Vanity, 2276 Vanity, American Cologne

    Blue, 1925-1926; $85.00
2136 Cold Cream and Cover, 3"
    Crystal, 1924; $75.00
    Amber, 1924-1926; $75.00
    Green, 1924-1926; $78.00
    Canary, 1924-1926; $85.00
    Blue, 1925-1926; $82.00
2136 Bon Bon and Cover, 5"
    Crystal, 1924; $74.00
    Amber, 1924; $85.00

Green, 1924-1926; $85.00
Canary, 1924-1926; $125.00
Blue, 1925-1926; $125.00
2137 Brush Vase, Crystal, pre 1924-1925; $67.00
2183 Puff and Cover (see Colonial Prism)
Amber, 1925-1926; $225.00
Blue, 1925-1926; $250.00
Canary, 1925-1926; $265.00
2241 Cologne (Engraving D, Engraving E, Etching
253, Etching 261)
Crystal, 1924-1926; $85.00
Amber, 1924-1926; $97.00
Green, 1924-1926; $97.00
Canary, 1924-1926; $125.00
Blue, 1925-1926; $125.00
2242 Cologne (Engraving 14, Engraving C, Etching
253, Etching 262), 1924-1926; $95.00
2243 Cologne (Engraving A, Engraving B, Etching
253, Etching 263), 1924-1926; $95.00
2276 Vanity Set
Crystal, 1924-1927, 1939-1943; $95.00
Ebony, 1925-1927; $110.00
Amber, 1924-1927; $125.00
Green, 1924-1927; $125.00
Canary, 1924-1926; $250.00
Blue, 1925-1927; $145.00
Orchid, 1926-1927; $145.00
2276 Vanity, Cut or Engraved, 1924-1928; $110.00 (See Decoration)
2286 Pin Tray, 5"
Ebony, 1925-1926; $25.00
Amber, 1924-1926; $28.00
2286 Comb and Brush Tray, 10½"
Ebony, 1925-1926; $45.00
Amber, 1924-1926; $54.00

2276 Green Royal Covered Cheese, 2137 Brush Vase (Courtesy of Larry Baker and Don Barber), Blue 2347½ Puff and Cover (Courtesy of Aleeta and Tom Herr). The covered cheese is shown with the puff and cover to illustrate their differences.

2289 Vanity Set
Crystal, 1924-1927; $95.00
Ebony, 1925-1927; $115.00
Amber, 1924-1927; $110.00
Green, 1924-1927; $110.00
Canary, 1924-1926; $250.00
Blue, 1925-1927; $145.00
2322 Cologne
Crystal, 1926-1927; $75.00
Ebony, 1926-1927; $85.00
Amber, 1926-1927; $87.00
Green, 1926-1927; $87.00
Blue, 1926-1927; $120.00
2323 Cologne
Crystal, 1926-1927; $64.00
Ebony, 1926-1927; $68.00
Amber, 1926-1927; $74.00
Green, 1926-1927; $74.00
Blue, 1926-1927; $88.00
2338 Puff and Cover
Crystal, 1925-1927; $46.00
Amber, 1925-1927; $52.00
Green, 1925-1927; $52.00
Canary, 1925-1926; $65.00
Blue, 1925-1927; $57.00
2347 Puff and Cover
Crystal, 1926-1927; $55.00
Ebony, 1926-1927; $58.00
Amber, 1925-1927; $58.00
Green, 1925-1927; $58.00
Canary, 1925; $77.00
Blue, 1925-1927; $68.00
2347½ Puff and Cover
Crystal, 1926-1927; $57.00
Ebony, 1926-1927; $65.00
Amber, 1926-1927; $65.00
Green, 1926-1927; $65.00
Canary, 1926; $87.00
Blue, 1926-1927; $75.00
2359½ Puff and Cover

2243 Engraved Cologne, 2276 Green Vanity, unknown Gold decoration, 2323 Decorated Cologne

Crystal, 1926-1927; $35.00
Ebony, 1927; $48.00
Amber, 1926-1927; $48.00
Green, 1926-1927; $48.00
Blue, 1926-1927; $55.00
2519 Cologne and Stopper (see Milk Glass)
2519 Puff and Cover (see Milk Glass)
2561 Bath Bottle
  Crystal, 1939-1943; $97.00
  Silver Mist, 1939-1943; $110.00
  Carved, 1939-1943; $125.00
2561½ Bath Bottle, Wide Mouth
  Crystal, 1939-1943; $97.00
  Silver Mist, 1939-1943; $110.00
  Carved, 1939-1943; $125.00
2562 Bath Bottle
  Crystal, 1939-1942; $95.00
  Silver Mist, 1939-1942; $110.00
  Carved, 1939-1942; $125.00
  Gold Band, 1939-1942; $110.00
2562½ Bath Bottle, Wide Mouth
  Crystal, 1939-1942; $95.00
  Silver Mist, 1939-1942; $110.00
  Carved, 1939-1942; $125.00
2698 Cologne and Cover, Small
  Marine, 1956-1957; $30.00
  Bark, 1956-1957; $25.00
  Pink Clover, 1956-1957; $34.00
  Milk Glass, 1956-1957; $25.00
2698 Cologne and Cover, Large
  Marine, 1956-1957; $35.00
  Bark, 1956-1957; $32.00
  Pink Clover, 1956-1957; $38.00
  Milk Glass, 1956-1957; $28.00
2698 Bath Salts and Cover
  Marine, 1956-1957; $85.00
  Bark, 1956-1957; $67.00
  Pink Clover, 1956-1957; $95.00
  Milk Glass, 1956-1957; $65.00
2698 Puff and Cover, Small
  Marine, 1956-1957; $37.00
  Bark, 1956-1957; $32.00
  Pink Clover, 1956-1957; $45.00
  Milk Glass, 1956-1957; $32.00
2698 Puff and Cover, Large
  Marine, 1956-1957; $54.00
  Bark, 1956-1957; $45.00
  Pink Clover, 1956-1957; $58.00
  Milk Glass, 1956-1957; $45.00
2699 Apple and Cover
  Marine, 1956-1957; $85.00
  Bark, 1956-1957; $65.00
  Pink Clover, 1956-1957; $85.00
  Avocado, 1956-1957; $85.00
2699 Pear
  Marine, 1956-1957; $85.00
  Bark, 1956-1957; $65.00
  Pink Clover, 1956-1957; $85.00

Ebony 2338 Cupid Puff and Cover, Amber 2276 Vanity, unknown cutting, Amber 2338 Puff and Cover

  Amethyst, 1956-1957; $75.00
2699 Melon
  Marine, 1956-1957; $95.00
  Bark, 1956-1957; $70.00
  Pink Clover, 1956-1957; $95.00
  Amethyst, 1956-1957; $85.00
2743/133 Windsor Crown Bottle and Stopper (see Crown)
HO04/292 Mini Box, Hinged Cover, 1984 (see Heritage Giftware); $35.00
JE01/293 Jewelry Box and Cover, Crystal, 1980-1982 (see Heritage Giftware); $20.00
PE05/873 Heart Pendant, 1979-1981; $25.00
PE06; 873 Rose Pendant, 1979-1981; $25.00
PE07/873 Cameo Pendant, 1979-1981; $25.00
RI02/865 Ring Holder, Silver or Gold Trim, Crystal 1978-1981; $20.00
SA05/293 Satin Ribbons (See *Fostoria Tableware 1944 – 1986*, p. 294)

Avocado Apple and Cover, Marine Bath Salts and Cover, Small Cologne, Small Puff and Cover

Pink Clover Apple and Cover, Pear, and Melon, Amethyst Pear

Peach Jenny Lind Puff and Cover; Milk Glass 2519 Cologne and Stopper, Puff and Cover; Jenny Lind Milk Glass Pomade; Aqua 1886 Pin Box and Cover

Samples from the Fostoria archives made sometime after 1950: Jenny Lind Puff, Jewel, and Pin Boxes

Gold 133 Windsor Crown Bottle and Stopper, Satin Ribbons Jewel Box, 2561 Bath Bottle, American Picture Frame

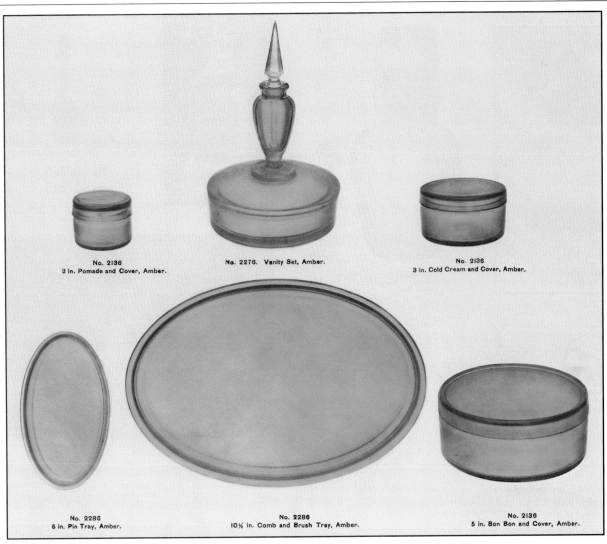

No. 2136
2 in. Pomade and Cover, Amber.

No. 2276. Vanity Set, Amber.

No. 2136
3 in. Cold Cream and Cover, Amber.

No. 2286
5 in. Pin Tray, Amber.

No. 2286
10½ in. Comb and Brush Tray, Amber.

No. 2136
5 in. Bon Bon and Cover, Amber.

No. 2322—Cologne.

No. 2347—Puff and Cover.

No. 2322—Cologne.

No. 2323—Cologne.

No. 2347½—Puff and Cover.

No. 2323—Cologne.

No. 2106—Large Cigarette and Cover.
Not made in Ebony.

No. 2338—Puff and Cover.
Not made in Ebony.

No. 2359½—Puff and Cover.

No. 2289
Vanity Set.

1697—Carafe.
4023—6 oz. Carafe Tumbler.
Spiral Optic.

No. 2241. Cologne,
Drip Stopper.

RI 02/865
RI 03/865

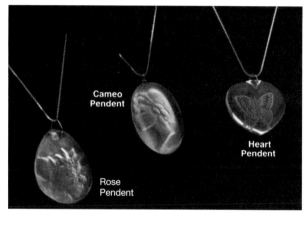

Cameo
Pendent

Rose
Pendent

Heart
Pendent

No. 1904 Bon Bon and Cover
Etched 221

2698
Large Cologne and Cover
Height 6½ in.

2698
Small Cologne and Cover
Height 5¼ in.

2698
Bath Salts and Cover
Height 7¼ in.

N. 1666 Puff and Cover
Etched 221

2698
Small Puff and Cover
Height 2¾ in.

2698
Large Puff and Cover
Height 3½ in.

No. 1478 Lavender Salt and
Stopper, Etched 221

2699
Pear
Height 7⅝ in.

2699
Apple and Cover
Height 5⅞ in.

2699
Melon
Height 8 in.

No. 2276 Vanity Set, Engraved No. 25
Height 7¼ in., Diameter 4½ in.

No. 2276 Vanity Set, Engraved B
Height 7¼ in., Diameter 4½ in.

No. 2276 Vanity Set, Engraved A
Height 7¼ in., Diameter 4½ in.

No. 2276 Vanity Set, Cut 171
Height 7¼ in., Diameter 4½ in.

No. 2276 Vanity Set, Cut Stopper
Height 7¼ in., Diameter 4½ in.

No. 2289 Vanity Set, Engraved C
Height 5¼ in., Diameter 4 in.

2243 Cologne Eng. B.

2243 Cologne Eng. A

2243 Cologne Etch 253

2243 Cologne Etch 263

2242 Cologne Eng. 14

2242 Cologne Eng. C

2242 Cologne Etch 253

2242 Cologne Etch 262

2241 Cologne Eng. D

2241 Cologne Eng. E

2241 Cologne Etch 253

2241 Cologne Etch 261

47

2561—Bath Bottle
Height 5¼ in.
Capacity 6¾ oz.

2561½—Bath Bottle, W.M.
Height 5¼ in.
Capacity 6¾ oz.

2562½—Bath Bottle, W.M.
Height 5 in.
Capacity 6½ oz.

2562—Bath Bottle
Height 5 in.
Capacity 6½ oz.

GOLD BAND DECORATION
2562—Bath Bottle
2562½—Bath Bottle, W.M.

SILVER MIST DECORATION
2562—Bath Bottle
2562½—Bath Bottle, W.M.

SILVER MIST DECORATION
2561—Bath Bottle
2561½—Bath Bottle, W.M.

CARVED DECORATION
2561—Bath Bottle
2561½—Bath Bottle, W.M.

CARVED DECORATION
2562—Bath Bottle
2562½—Bath Bottle, W.M.

BOWLS, CENTERPIECES, and CONSOLE BOWLS

Fostoria made many different bowls for many different occasions. Some of these may fit into more than one category. This is especially true of the large bowls used for salads and fruit, and also for console sets. Every pressed tableware pattern had bowls and those will generally be listed with the pattern. There were numerous blown nappies and footed bowls made prior to 1924 which continued until 1928. We show many of these with patterns in *Fostoria Tableware: 1924 – 1943*.

One interesting fact about the 2297 line in the mid-twenties: The 2297 bowls have three toes on the base while the 2297½ bowls have a round base with collar to fit the Ebony bases. Bowl "A" was made in 10½" Shallow and 10½" and 12" Deep. The 2297½ line was replaced by the 2339 line in 1925. These bowls were suitable for use both as bowls and as console bowls. The 2297½ bowl has a plain collar base (one ring) and 2339 has two rings around the round base. Both were made to fit the 3½" 2314 Ebony base. The 2305 Ebony Base is plain while the 2314 Base has toes.

Console bowls and console sets came into vogue with the advent of the table service made in glass during the 1920s. Since Fostoria pioneered the idea of a complete dinner service in glass, it followed that they would also create accent and decorative pieces to complement each pattern. Some of the dinnerware lines offered two or three styles of console bowls and candlesticks were often available in single, duo, and trindle sizes. A few of the early bowls were referred to as centerpiece bowls.

1925 Fostoria ad

One of the most innovative yet practical sets was the 2546 Quadrangle which used the four-arm candlestick as the centerpiece surrounded by four small bowls for flowers. Also unique is the square bobache used to create the candelabra. A duo candlestick and a candy box made from the four-inch bowl and a cover were the only other pieces in this line. In the late period the Table Charms set is outstanding in color and versatility.

During the Depression years many console sets independent of dinnerware lines were made. Offered in crystal, pastels, and the strong colors of the period, those lovely sets are a real tribute to Fostoria designers, and have transcended time and many fashion trends to remain popular today. Even though bowls and candlesticks were made to match (line numbers are the clue), it is possible to use similar styles together. The 2324 candlestick, for example, was used with many different bowls. Not all the candlesticks are shown in this section, but may be found in the Candlestick section. Prices are for the bowl only unless otherwise noted.

315 Bowls, 4½", 5", 6", 7", 8", 9", Plain or 24-point Cut Star
    bottom, or 24-point Cut Star bottom and cut beaded
    edge, 1939-1942; $10.00-$25.00
315 Berry Set, 9" Bowl, six 4½" Bowls, 1939-1942; $65.00
2267 Bowl, 7" Footed Console
    Crystal, 1923-1926; $26.00
    Amber, 1924-1926; $28.00
    Blue, 1925-1926; $35.00
    Green, 1924-1926; $30.00
    Canary, 1924-1926; $35.00
    Ebony, 1925-1926; $28.00
2267 Bowl, 9" Footed Console
    Crystal, 1923-1926; $28.00
    Amber, 1924-1926; $30.00
    Blue, 1925-1926; $37.00
    Green, 1924-1926; $32.00
    Canary, 1924-1926; $37.00
2267 Bowl, 10" Console, Rolled Edge
    Crystal, 1923-1926; $30.00
    Amber, 1925-1926; $32.00
    Blue, 1925-1926; $40.00
    Green, 1924-1926; $35.00
    Canary, 1924-1926; $40.00

2267 Console Sets included 2269 6" Candles or 2275 7" or 9" Candles
2297 Bowl "D," 7½" Shallow, Regular
    Amber, 1926-1927; $35.00
    Green, 1926-1927; $35.00
    Blue, 1926-1927; $40.00
    Canary, 1926; $45.00

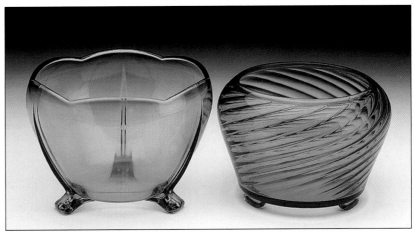

Green 2394 Bowl D, Blue 2297 Bowl D

2297 Bowl "D," 7½" Deep, Plain
    Crystal, 1924-1930; $35.00
    Amber, 1924-1930; $35.00
    Green, 1924-1930; $35.00
    Blue, 1925-1927; $40.00
    Canary, 1924-1926; $45.00
    Orchid, 1927-1928; $40.00
    Rose, 1928-1930; $40.00
2297 Bowl "D," 7½" Deep, SO
    Amber, 1927-1930; $35.00
    Green, 1927-1930; $35.00
    Blue, 1927; $45.00
    Orchid, 1927-1928; $45.00
2297 Bowl "B," 9¾" Shallow Cupped, Plain
    Crystal, 1924-1927; $32.00
    Amber, 1924-1927; $35.00
    Green, 1924-1927; $35.00
    Blue, 1925-1927; $40.00
    Canary, 1924-1926; $45.00
2297 Bowl, 9¾" "C," Rolled Edge
    Amber, 1924-1927; $35.00
    Green, 1924-1927; $35.00
    Blue, 1925-1927; $40.00
    Canary, 1924-1926; $45.00
2297 Bowl, 10½" "B," Deep Cupped, Plain
    Crystal, 1924-1932; $30.00
    Amber, 1924-1932; $34.00
    Green, 1924-1932; $34.00
    Blue, 1925-1927; $40.00
    Canary, 1924-1926; $45.00
    Orchid, 1927-1928; $45.00
    Rose, 1928-1932; $40.00
2297 Bowl, 10½" "B," Deep Cupped, SO
    Amber, 1927-1932; $36.00
    Green, 1927-1932; $36.00
    Blue, 1927; $45.00
    Orchid, 1927-1928; $45.00
2297 Bowl "A," 10½" Shallow Flared, Plain
    Crystal, 1924-1927; $35.00
    Amber, 1924-1927; $40.00
    Green, 1924-1927; $40.00
    Blue, 1925-1927; $47.00
    Canary, 1924-1926; $55.00
    Ebony, 1925-1927; $40.00
    Orchid, 1927; $47.00
2297 Bowl "C," 10½" Deep Rolled Edge
    Crystal, 1924-1932; $30.00
    Amber, 1924-1932; $34.00
    Green, 1924-1932; $34.00
    Blue, 1925-1927; $38.00
    Canary, 1924-1926; $45.00
    Orchid, 1927-1928; $40.00
    Rose, 1928-1932; $38.00
2297 Bowl "C," 10½" Deep, Rolled Edge, SO
    Amber, 1927-1932; $34.00
    Green, 1927-1932; $34.00
    Blue, 1927; $45.00

Blue Vesper 2297 Bowl A, 2324 Candlesticks; Blue Royal 2324 Bowl and 9" Candlesticks

    Ebony, 1927-1928; $32.00
    Orchid, 1927-1928; $42.00
    Rose, 1929-1932; $40.00
2297 Bowl "A," 12" Deep, Flared
    Crystal, 1924-1939; $30.00
    Amber, 1924-1934; $34.00
    Green, 1924-1939; $34.00
    Blue, 1925-1927; $40.00
    Canary, 1924-1926; $50.00
    Ebony, 1925-1937; $30.00
    Orchid, 1927-1928; $40.00
    Rose, 1928-1939; $35.00
    Azure, 1928-1930; $40.00
2297 Bowl "A," 12" Deep, SO
    Crystal, 1927-1932; $30.00
    Amber, 1927-1932; $35.00
    Green, 1927-1932; $35.00
    Blue, 1927; $45.00
    Orchid, 1927-1928; $40.00
    Rose, 1928-1932; $40.00
2297 Bowl "E," 12½" Cabarette
    Crystal, 1926-1930; $35.00
    Amber, 1926-1930; $40.00
    Green, 1926-1930; $40.00
    Blue, 1926-1927; $45.00
    Canary, 1926; $54.00
    Ebony, 1926-1928; $35.00
    Orchid, 1927-1928; $40.00

Amber 2297½ Deep Bowl D, 2314 Ebony Base; Amber 2297 Deep Bowl C, 2369 Candlesticks, Rivera Decoration

Rose, 1928-1930; $40.00
2297 Bowl "E," 12½", SO
    Amber, 1927-1929; $45.00
    Green, 1927-1929; $45.00
    Blue, 1927; $50.00
    Orchid, 1927-1928; $45.00
    Rose, 1929; $45.00
2305 Base, 4½" Ebony, 1925-1943; $15.00
2309 Flower Block, 3", 3¾", 1925-1943
    Crystal, $15.00
    Green, $20.00
    Amber, $18.00
    Rose, $22.00
    Blue, 1925-1927; $24.00
2309 Flower Block, 5", Green, $24.00
2309 Flower Block, 4½" Oval
    Crystal, 1929-1943; $18.00
    Green, 1929-1939; $24.00
    Amber, 1929-1939; $22.00
    Rose, 1929-1939; $24.00
    Azure; 1929-1934; $30.00
2314 Base, 3½" Ebony; $15.00
2315 Bowl (see Twenty-Three Fifteen)
2320 Bowl "A," 11" Flared, Open Edge
    Amber, 1925-1927; $35.00
    Green, 1925-1927; $35.00
    Blue, 1925-1927; $40.00
    Canary, 1925-1926; $48.00
    Ebony, 1925-1927; $30.00
2320 Bowl "A," 12" Flared, Open Edge
    Amber, 1925-1927; $35.00
    Green, 1925-1927; $35.00
    Blue, 1925-1927; $40.00
    Canary, 1925-1926; $45.00
    Ebony, 1925-1927; $30.00
2320 Bowl "B," 10" Cupped, Open Edge
    Amber, 1925-1927; $35.00
    Green, 1925-1927; $35.00
    Blue, 1925-1927; $40.00
    Canary, 1925-1926; $45.00
    Ebony, 1925-1927; $30.00
2320 Bowl "B," 11" Cupped, Open Edge
    Amber, 1925-1939; $35.00
    Green, 1927-1939; $35.00
    Blue, 1925-1927; $40.00
    Canary, 1925-1926; $45.00
    Ebony, 1929-1938; $30.00
    Rose, 1928-1939; $38.00
2324 Bowl, 10" Footed Console
    Crystal, 1925-1927; $75.00
    Amber, 1925-1927; $78.00
    Blue, 1925-1927; $125.00
    Green, 1925-1927; $85.00
    Canary, 1925-1926; $125.00
    Orchid, 1927; $125.00
2324 Bowl, 12" or 13" Footed Console
    Crystal, 1925-1927; $82.00
    Amber, 1925-1927; $84.00

Green 2329 Oval Centerpiece, Arlington Decoration, 2471 Flower Holder; Green 2333 Bowl; and 8" Candlesticks

    Blue, 1925-1927; $135.00
    Green, 1925-1927; $95.00
2324 Bowl, Small Footed Urn, 7"
    Crystal, 1925-1927; $74.00
    Amber, 1925-1927; $85.00
    Blue, 1925-1927; $125.00
    Green, 1925-1927; $95.00
    Canary, 1925-1926; $135.00
    Orchid, 1927; $125.00
2324 Bowl, Large Footed Urn, 10"
    Amber, 1925-1927; $88.00
    Blue, 1925-1927; $135.00
    Green, 1925-1927; $97.00
2324 Console Sets used 2324 9" and 12" Candlesticks
2329 Centerpiece, 11", used 2324 4" Candles
    Crystal, 1927-1929; $38.00

Green 2443 Ice Tub and Candlesticks shown as a centerpiece (Milbra Long photograph)

Crystal, SO, 1928-1930; $40.00
Amber, 1925-1930; $38.00
Amber, SO, 1927; $40.00
Blue, 1925-1927; $42.00
Blue, SO, 1927; $45.00
Green, 1925-1930; $40.00
Green, SO, 1927; $42.00
Canary, 1925-1926, Plain; $45.00
Ebony, 1926-1930, Plain; $38.00
Rose, 1928-1930; $40.00
Rose, SO, 1928-1930; $42.00
Azure, 1928-1930; $24.00
Azure, SO, 1928-1930; $45.00
Orchid, 1927-1928; $40.00
Orchid, SO, 1927-1928; $45.00
2329 Centerpiece, 13 to 14", use 2324½ 4" Candles
Crystal, 1925-1930; $40.00
Crystal, SO, 1927-1930; $40.00
Amber, 1925-1930; $42.00
Amber, SO, 1927-1930; $42.00
Blue, 1925-1927; $45.00
Blue, SO, 1927; $45.00
Green, 1925-1930; $42.00
Green, SO, 1927-1930; $42.00
Ebony, 1926-1930; $40.00
Rose, 1928-1930; $42.00
Rose, SO, 1928-1930; $44.00
2333 Bowl, 11" Footed Console, used 2333 8" or 11" Candlesticks
Crystal, 1925-1927; $57.00
Amber, 1925-1927; $65.00
Blue, 1925-1927; $75.00
Green, 1925-1927; $68.00
2339 Bowl "D," 7¼" Regular
Crystal, 1925-1927; $30.00
Amber, 1925-1927; $34.00
Green, 1925-1927; $34.00
Blue, 1925-1927; $38.00
Orchid, 1927; $40.00
Canary, 1925-1926; $45.00
2339 Bowl "A," 10½" Flared
Amber, 1925-1927; $35.00
Green, 1925-1927; $35.00
Blue, 1925-1927; $40.00
Orchid, 1927; $40.00
Canary, 1925-1926; $45.00
2339 Bowl "B," 10¾" Cupped
Crystal, 1925-1957; $30.00
Amber, 1925-1927; $35.00
Green, 1925-1927; $35.00
Blue, 1925-1927; $40.00
Orchid, 1927; $40.00
Canary, 1925-1926; $45.00
2339 Bowl "C," 10½" Rolled Edge
Crystal, 1925-1927; $30.00
Amber, 1925-1927; $35.00
Green, 1925-1927; $35.00

Rose 2415 Combination Bowl; Rose June 2495 Bowl and either 3" or 5" 2495½ Candlesticks

Blue, 1925-1927; $40.00
Orchid, 1927; $40.00
Canary, 1925-1926; $45.00
2339 Bowl "E," 12"
Crystal, 1926-1927; $32.00
Amber, 1926-1927; $37.00
Green, 1926-1927; $37.00
Blue, 1926-1927; $40.00
Orchid, 1927; $40.00
Canary, 1926; $48.00
Ebony, 1926-1927; $32.00
2339 Bowl "A," 10½" SO
Amber, 1927-1930; $35.00
Green, 1927-1930; $35.00
Blue, 1927; $40.00
Orchid, 1927; $40.00
Rose, 1929-1930; $40.00
Azure, 1929-1930; $40.00
2342 Bowl "A," 12½" Octagon
Crystal, 1928-1932; $30.00
Amber, 1927-1932; $34.00
Green, 1927-1932; $34.00
Blue, 1927; $40.00
Orchid, 1927; $40.00
Rose, 1928-1932; $38.00
Azure, 1928-1932; $38.00
2342 Bowl, 12" Salad
Amber, 1927-1928; $35.00
Green, 1927-1928; $35.00
Blue, 1927; $40.00

Blue 2329 Centerpiece, SO; 2372 Candle Blocks, SO; Green Vesper 2329 Centerpiece, 2324 Candlestick

Orchid, 1927-1928; $38.00
Rose, 1928; $40.00
2362 Bowl, 12", 2362 3" Candlesticks
  Amber, 1927-1928; $46.00
  Blue, 1927; $64.00
  Green, 1927-1929; $52.00
  Rose, 1928; $60.00
  Orchid, 1927-1928; $60.00
2362 Comport, 11" (used as a Centerpiece), 2362 9"
  Candlesticks
  Crystal, 1927-1928; $65.00
  Amber, 1927-1928; $65.00
  Blue, 1927; $95.00
  Green, 1927-1929; $75.00
  Ebony, 1927; $60.00
  Orchid, 1927-1928; $75.00
2364 Bowl (see Sonata)
2367 Bowl, 7" Bulb
  Amber, 1926-1927; $30.00
  Green, 1926-1927; $30.00
  Blue, 1926-1927; $35.00
  Ebony, 1926-1927; $30.00
2367 Bowl, 8" Bulb
  Amber, 1926-1927; $30.00
  Green, 1926-1927; $30.00
  Blue, 1926-1927; $35.00
  Ebony, 1926-1927; $30.00
2371 Flower Holder (top piece in color; plain glass bottom)
  Crystal, 1928-1930; $35.00
  Rose, 1928-1930; $45.00
  Azure, 1928-1930; $50.00
  Green, 1928-1930; $45.00
  Amber, 1928-1930; $40.00
  Orchid, 1928; $45.00
2371 Centerpiece, 13" Oval, 2372 2" Candle Block
  Crystal, Plain, 1927-1929; $54.00
  Green, 1927-1930; $65.00
  Green, SO, 1927; $65.00
  Amber, 1927-1930; $60.00
  Amber, SO, 1927; $60.00
  Blue, 1927; $70.00
  Orchid, 1927-1928; $65.00
  Orchid, SO, 1927; $65.00
2375 Bowls (see Fairfax)
2375 Berry Set, Fairfax, 8" Nappy and six Fruit Bowls,
  1927-1928
  Crystal; $134.00
  Rose; $165.00
  Azure; $165.00
  Green; $148.00
  Amber; $138.00
  Orchid; $170.00
  Topaz; $153.00
2390 Bowl, 12" Footed
  Amber, 1927-1929; $52.00
  Green, 1927-1929; $58.00
  Rose, 1928-1929; $58.00

2371 Flower Holder and 2309 Flower Block (Milbra Long photograph)

  Azure, 1928-1929; $65.00
  Orchid, 1927-1928; $60.00
2390 Centerpiece, 11", used 2309 3¾" Flower Block, 2390 3"
  Candlesticks
  Amber, 1927-1928; $45.00
  Green, 1927-1928; $48.00
  Orchid, 1927-1928; $50.00
2393 Centerpiece, 12" and 15" SO, Crimped,
  used 2393 Candle, SO, Crimped
  Amber, 1928-1929; $58.00
  Green, 1928-1929; $60.00
  Rose, 1928-1929; $60.00
  Azure, 1928-1929; $65.00
2394 Bowl, 12" Flared, 2394 2" Candlesticks
  Crystal, 1928-1943; $40.00
  Amber, 1928-1939; $45.00
  Regal Blue, 1934-1938; $74.00
  Green, 1928-1939; $48.00
  Burgundy, 1934-1941; $70.00
  Empire Green, 1934-1939; $74.00
  Rose, 1928-1938; $48.00
  Azure, 1928-1939; $48.00
  Orchid, 1928; $56.00
  Topaz/Gold Tint, 1929-1939; $47.00
  Ruby, 1934-1940; $75.00
2394 Bowl D, 7½", 2394 2" Candlesticks

Wisteria 2470½ Bowl and Candlesticks; Wisteria Base 2470 Bowl and Candlesticks

Crystal, 1928-1934; $38.00
Amber, 1928-1934; $40.00
Green, 1928-1934; $43.00
Rose, 1928-1934; $43.00
Azure, 1928-1932; $45.00
Topaz, 1929-1934; $43.00
2395 Bowl, 10", used 2395 3" or 2395½ 5" Candlestick
Crystal, 1928-1938; $57.00
Amber, 1928-1938; $60.00
Green, 1928-1938; $60.00
Ebony, 1928-1938; $60.00
Rose, 1928-1938; $60.00
Azure, 1928-1934; $65.00
Topaz/Gold Tint, 1929-1938; $60.00
2398 Bowl, 11" Cornucopia
Crystal, 1928-1930; $58.00
Amber, 1928-1930; $75.00
Green, 1928-1930; $85.00
Orchid, 1928; $125.00
Rose, 1928-1930; $125.00
Azure, 1928-1930; $125.00
2402 Bowl, 9", used 2402 2" Candlesticks
Crystal, 1933-1938; $22.00
Amber, 1929-1938; $27.00
Green, 1929-1938; $27.00
Ebony, 1929-1938; $27.00
Rose, 1929-1934; $30.00
Azure, 1929-1934; $30.00
Topaz/Gold Tint, 1929-1937; $27.00
2402 Bowl, 11", used 2402 2" Candlesticks
Crystal, 1929-1933; $26.00
Amber, 1929-1934; $30.00
Green, 1929-1938; $30.00
Ebony, 1929-1934; $30.00
Rose, 1929-1934; $32.00
Azure, 1929-1938; $35.00
Topaz, 1929-1933; $32.00
2415 Bowl, Combination
Green, 1929; $55.00
Ebony, 1929; $55.00
Rose, 1929; $55.00
Azure, 1929; $60.00
Topaz, 1929; $55.00
2418 Bowl, 10" Oval Footed (Listed in 1929 in Rose, Azure, Green, and Amber. Not listed again. No picture. Never seen.)
2424 Bowl, 8" RO (Later part of Kent pattern in Crystal only.)
Crystal, 1933-1934 (see Kent); $28.00
Amber, 1933-1934; $42.00
Green, 1933-1934; $42.00
Rose, 1933-1934; $48.00
Topaz, 1933-1934; $48.00
Wisteria, 1933-1934; $75.00
2424 Bowl, 9 to 9½" Flared (Later part of Kent pattern in Crystal only.)
Crystal, 1933-1934 (see Kent); $34.00

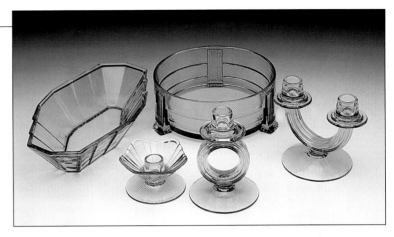

Topaz 2425 Bowl, Azure Candlestick, Topaz 2425 Bowl, Rose 2446 Candlestick, Topaz 2447 Duo Candlestick

Amber, 1933-1934; $44.00
Green, 1933-1934; $44.00
Rose, 1933-1934; $48.00
Topaz, 1933-1934; $48.00
Wisteria, 1933-1934; $75.00
2425 Bowl, 13" Oblong, used 2425 2" Candlesticks
Crystal, 1930-1932; $28.00
Amber, 1930-1932; $34.00
Green, 1930-1932; $34.00
Ebony, 1930-1932; $34.00
Rose, 1930-1932; $38.00
Azure, 1930-1932; $40.00
Topaz, 1930-1932; $37.00
2426 Bowl, 12" Oval, 4113 6" Candlesticks
Regal Blue, 1933-1938; $75.00
Burgundy, 1933-1938; $75.00
Empire Green, 1933-1935; $85.00
2428 Bowl, 7" Round
Amber, 1930-1934; $54.00
Green, 1930-1934; $54.00
Rose, 1930-1934; $58.00
Ebony, 1930-1934; $54.00
Topaz, 1930-1934; $58.00
Wisteria, 1931-1934; $95.00
2430 Bowl (see Diadem)
2434 Bowl, 13"
Amber, 1930-1933; $95.00
Green, 1930-1933; $95.00

Topaz/Gold Tint 2440 Lafayette 10" Bowl B, Azure 2297 Cornucopia Bowl

2432 Bowl, 11"
    Burgundy, 1934-1935; $75.00
    Regal Blue, 1934-1937; $95.00
    Empire Green, 1934-1937; $85.00
2441 Bowl, 12"
    Crystal, 1932-1934; $48.00
    Amber, 1930-1934; $55.00
    Green, 1930-1934; $55.00
    Rose, 1930-1934; $60.00
    Azure, 1930-1934; $60.00
    Topaz, 1930-1934; $58.00
2443 Bowl, 10" Oval, used 2443 4" Candlesticks
    Crystal, 1931-1938; $38.00
    Amber, 1931-1934; $45.00
    Green, 1931-1934; $48.00
    Ebony, 1931-1938; $45.00
    Rose, 1931-1938; $48.00
    Azure, 1931-1934; $55.00
    Topaz, 1933-1934; $55.00
2445 Bowl, 8½"
    Crystal, 1931-1934; $68.00
    Amber, 1931-1934; $77.00
    Green, 1931-1934; $77.00
    Rose, 1931-1934; $85.00
    Azure, 1931-1934; $95.00
    Ebony, 1931-1934; 475.00
    Topaz, 1931-1934; $85.00
2455 Bowl, 11"
    Crystal, 1931-1933; $75.00
    Amber, 1931-1934; $80.00
    Green, 1931-1933; $85.00
    Rose, 1931-1933; $85.00
    Topaz, 1931-1933; $85.00
2458 Bowl, 11½" Flared, 3-toed, 4113 6" Candlesticks
    Regal Blue, 1933-1935; $68.00
    Burgundy, 1933-1935; $68.00
    Empire Green, 1933-1935; $68.00
2466 Plateau, not shown
    Crystal, 1933
    Green, 1933
    Topaz, 1933
    Ebony, 1933
2470/2470½ (see Twenty Four Seventy)
2481 Bowl, 11" Oblong, used 2481 5" Candles
    Crystal, 1933-1938; $38.00
    Amber, 1933-1934; $42.00
    Green, 1933-1934; $42.00
    Ebony, 1933-1938; $40.00
    Rose, 1933-1934; $42.00
    Topaz/Gold Tint, 1933-1938; $40.00
2484 Bowl, 10" Handled (see Baroque)
2496 Bowl (see Baroque)
2527 Bowl, 9" Footed, used 2527 8½" 2-light Candelabra, Crystal, 1936-1938; $58.00
2533 Bowl, 9" Handled, 2533 6¼" Duo or Candelabra with 2527 Bobache, Crystal, 1936-1943; $95.00

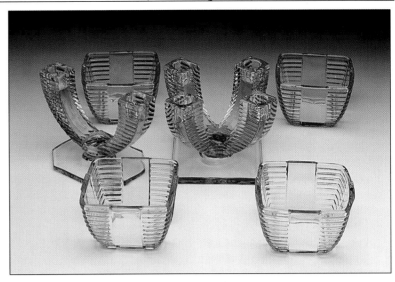

Azure 2546 Quadrangle Candlestick, four Bowls; Crystal Duo Candlestick

2535 Bowl, 7" Cupped, 2535 Candlesticks, Crystal, 1935-1939; $65.00
2535 Bowl, 9" Flared, 2535 Candlesticks, Crystal, 1935-1939; $65.00
2536 Bowl, 9" Handled, used 2535 5½" Candlesticks
    Crystal, 1935-1942; $60.00
    Regal Blue, 1935-1938; $75.00
    Burgundy, 1935-1939; $75.00
    Empire Green, 1935-1939; $75.00
    Ruby, 1935-1940; $75.00
2538 Salad Set, 11" Bowl and six 6" Nappy
    Crystal, 1936-1940; $85.00
    Topaz/Gold Tint, 1936-1937; $110.00
2538 Berry Set, 11" Bowl and six 4½" Nappies
    Crystal, 1936-1940; $85.00
    Topaz/Gold Tint, 1936-1937; $95.00
2545 Bowl (see Flame)
2546 Quadrangle
    Crystal, 1937-1942; $20.00
    Azure, 1937-1942; $25.00
2547 Bowl, 6½" Oblong, 2547 5⅛" Trindle Candlesticks
    Crystal, 1937-1942; $57.00

2639 Ivy Bowl and Duo Candlestick, 2481 Bowl and Candlestick, Midnight Rose etching

Azure, 1937-1939; $65.00
Gold Tint, 1937-1939; $65.00

2563 Bowl, 9½' Handled Viking, 2563 4½" Viking Candlesticks, Crystal, 1939-1943; $95.00

2570 Bowls (see Artisan)

2594 Bowl, 10" Handled, 2594 5½" Single or 8" Trindle Candlesticks, Crystal, 1941-1957; $92.00

2596 Bowl, 7½" Square, 2596 5" Candlesticks, Crystal, 1940-1941; $75.00

2596 Bowl, 11" Shallow, Oblong, 2596 5" Candlesticks, Crystal, 1940-1943; $85.00

2598 Bowl, 11" Oval, 2598 7½" Duo Candle, Crystal, 1940-1943; $85.00

2600 Bowl, 9½" Footed Acanthus, 2600 10" Acanthus Trindle Candle or Candelabra with 2545 Bobache, 18 UDP, Crystal, 1940-1943; $135.00

2601 Bowl, 10½" Lyre, 2601 8" Duo Lyre Candlesticks, Crystal, 1940-1949; $95.00

2634 Bowl, 13" Centerpiece for Mermaid, 1953; $95.00

2639 Bowl, 11" Ivy, 2639 9¾" Duo Candle, Crystal, 1952-1957; $125.00

2639 Bowl, 13½" Oval, 2639 9¾" Duo Candlesticks, Crystal, 1950-1960; $70.00

2640 Garden Center Set, 14" Lily Pond, Flower Block, six Candleholders, Crystal, 1949-1963; $250.00

2651 Bowl, 11" Handled, 2652 5¾" Trindle, Crystal, 1952-1962; $95.00

2652 Bowl, 13½" Handled, 2652 5¾" Trindle, Crystal, 1952-1956; $95.00

2666 Salad Set, 9" Contour
    Crystal, 1952-1970; $80.00
    Ebony, 1954-1958; $95.00

2666 Salad Set, 11" Contour
    Crystal, 1952-1972; $90.00
    Ebony, 1954-1958; $100.00

2667 Bowl, 7", Footed Blown, 1953-1958; $34.00

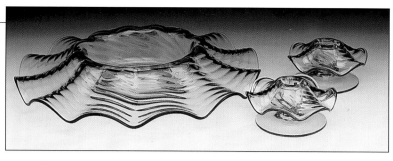

Azure 2393 15" Crimped, Spiral Optic Bowl and Candlestick

2536 Bowl, Corsage etching; Azure June 2394 Bowl and Candlesticks

2667 Bowl, 9¼" Footed Blown, 1953-1958, used 2½" or 6" Candlesticks; $43.00

2697 Flared Bowl, Wood Base, 1957; $24.00

2697 Floating Bowl, Wood Base; 1957; $24.00

2697 Salad Bowl, Wood Base, 1957; $24.00

2703 Bowls (see Artisan)

2706 Salad/Punch Bowl (14" on Ebony Wood Base), 1957-1972; $48.00

2719 Salad Set, 10" Jamestown, Crystal, 1959-1972; $130.00

2722 Table Charms
    Sets 1 and 2: Crystal, 1959-1965; $120.00
                   Pink, 1959-1963; $175.00
                   Yellcw, 1959-1960; $195.00
    Sets 3 and 4: Crystal, 1959-1965; $95.00
                   Pink, 1959-1963; $125.00
                   Yellow, 1959-1960; $150.00

2785 Salad Bowl, 10" Footed, Gourmet, Crystal, 1964-1972; $35.00

2806 Salad/Punch Bowl, 11½" Pebble Beach, 1969-1972; $65.00

4024 Bowl, 10½" (Victorian), 6" Candlesticks
    Regal Blue, 1934-1942; $135.00
    Burgundy, 1934-1943; $125.00
    Empire Green, 1934-1935; $135.00

4171 Bowl, 10¼", Crystal, Charcoal, Bark, and Spruce with Wood Stand, Ebony Finish, 1957; $34.00

6023 Bowl, 9¼" Blown Footed, 2324 4" or 6" Candlesticks, Crystal, 1939-1943; $87.00

Decorated Blue Console Set; Copper Blue Rebecca Console Set (Milbra Long photograph)

Yellow Table Charms as presented by the Cleburne Garden Club (Milbra Long photograph)

2367—7 in. Bulb Bowl.
Made in 7 and 8 in.
Also made in Ebony.
Not made in Orchid.

Table Charms shown in three of the four suggested uses: with three yellow Flora Candles and one Peg Vase, with three Pink Peg Vases and Candle, and with three Yellow Peg Vases and one Flora Candle

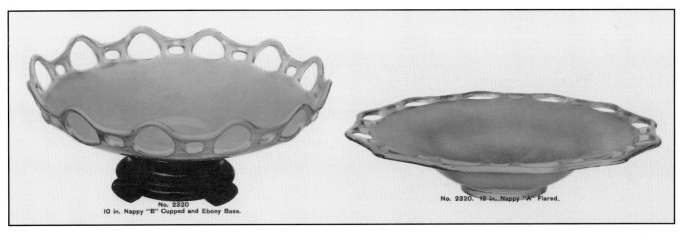

No. 2320
10 in. Nappy "B" Cupped and Ebony Base.

No. 2320. 12 in. Nappy "A" Flared.

2297—12 in. Deep Bowl "A".
Made plain or in spiral optic.
Made Shallow in plain only.

2297—7½ in. Deep Bowl "D".
Made plain or in spiral optic.
Crystal not made in spiral optic.
Made Shallow in plain only.

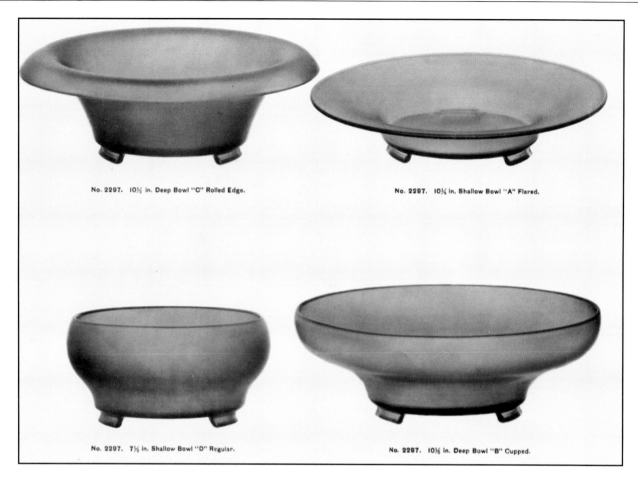

No. 2297. 10½ in. Deep Bowl "C" Rolled Edge.

No. 2297. 10¼ in. Shallow Bowl "A" Flared.

No. 2297. 7½ in. Shallow Bowl "D" Regular.

No. 2297. 10½ in. Deep Bowl "B" Cupped.

No. 2339. 7 in. Console Bowl "D" Regular.

No. 2339. 10 in. Console Bowl "C" Rolled Edge.

No. 2339
10½ in. Console Bowl "A" Flared with Ebony Base.

No. 2439
10½ in. Console Bowl "B" Cupped with Ebony Base.

2342—12 in. Bowl.

No. 2342—12 in. Salad Bowl.

No. 2333. 11 in. Candle.
No. 2333. 8 in. Candle.
(Made in Crystal and Amber only)

No. 2333. 11 in. Console Bowl.
(Made in Crystal and Amber only)

No. 2333. 11 in. Candle.
(Made in Crystal and Amber only)

No. 2372—Candle.
Also made in Spiral Optic.
Patent Applied For.

No. 2371—13 in. Centerpiece (oval).
No. 2371—Flower Holder.
Patent Applied For.

No. 2372—Candle.
Also made in Spiral Optic.
Patent Applied For.

No. 2362—3 in. Candle.
Made in 3 and 9 in.

No. 2362—12 in. Bowl.
No. 2309—3¾ in. Flower Block.
Bowl not made in crystal.
Flower block not made in orchid.
Patent Applied For Bowl.

No. 2362—3 in. Candle.
Made in 3 and 9 in.

59

2432—11 in. Oval Bowl
Height 2⅞ in.

2667—9¼ in.
Footed Bowl
Height 5¾ in.

2667—7 in.
Footed Bowl
Height 6½ in.

2428 7-in. Bowl
Ro-Gr-Am-Eb-Tz-Wis
Priced on page 45

2445 8½" Bowl
Ro-Az-Gr-Am-Eb-Crys-Tz

2455-11" BOWL

No 2297½
7½ in. Deep Bowl "D" Regular with Ebony Base.
Replaced by 2339 Bowl, Page 72

No. 2297½
9¾ in. Shallow Bowl "C" Rolled Edge with Ebony Base.
Replaced by 2339 Bowl, Page 72

No. 2297½
9¾ in. Shallow Bowl "B" Cupped with Ebony Base.
Replaced by 2339 Bowl, Page 72

No. 2297½
12 in. Deep Bowl "A" Flared with Ebony Base.
Replaced by 2339 Bowl, Page 72

315—Thin Bowl
See Price List For Sizes

CUT STAR B
Beaded Edge With 24 Point Star
All Polished. Illustrated

Cut Star A
24 Point Star. Polished. Plain Edge
See Price List For Complete List of Sizes Made
in Both of Above Designs

2398—11 in. Bowl.
Ro-Az-Gr-Am-Crys.
Design Patent No. 76,878.

2394 7½-in. Bowl "D"
Ro-Az-Gr-Am-Crys-Tz
Priced on page 45

2390—12 in. Bowl.

2390—3 in. Candle.

2390—11 in. Centerpiece.
2309—3¾ in. Flower Block.

2390—3 in. Candle.

No. 2275
9 in. Candlestick.

No. 2267
10 in. Deep Footed Bowl, Rolled Edge.

No. 2275
9 in. Candlestick.

2324—4 in. Candle.
Made in 2, 4, 6, 9 and 12 in.
12 in. not made in orchid.
Patent No. 71,646.

2329—11 in. Round Centerpiece.
Made in 11 and 13 in.
Made Plain or in Spiral Optic.

2324—4 in. Candle.
Made in 2, 4, 6, 9 and 12 in.
12 in. not made in orchid.
Patent No. 71,646.

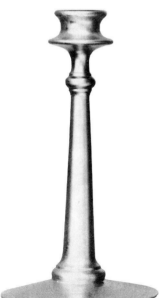

2324—9 in. Candle.
Made in 2, 4, 6, 9 and 12 in.
12 in. not made in orchid.
Patent No. 68,057.

2324—Small Urn.
Top Diameter, 7 inches.
Also made in large size.
Top diameter 10 in.
Large size not made in orchid.

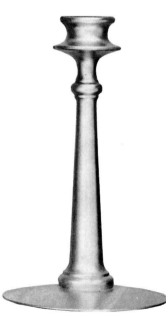

2324—9 in. Candle.
Made in 2, 4, 6, 9 and 12 in.
12 in. not made in orchid.
Patent No. 68,057.

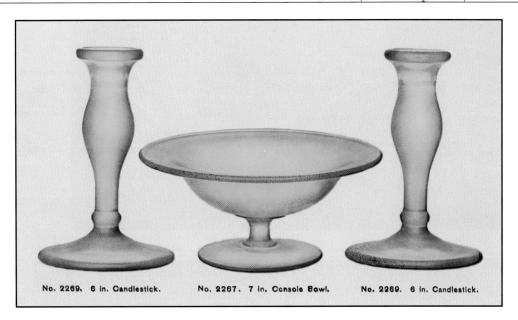

No. 2269. 6 in. Candlestick.　　No. 2267. 7 in. Console Bowl.　　No. 2269. 6 in. Candlestick.

2639
Duo Candlestick
Height 9¾ in.　Spread 5¾..in.

2639
Oval Bowl
Height 4 in.　Length 13¼ in.

No. 2639
11 in. Ivy Bowl
Height 3¾ in.

2594
Trindle Candlestick
Height 8 in.　Spread 6½ in.

2594
10 in. Handled Bowl
Height 3 in.
Length overall 13½ in.

2594
5½ in. Candlestick

2601
10½ in. Lyre, Oval Bowl
Height 2¾ in.　Width 8¼ in.

2601
Lyre Duo Candlestick
Height 8 in.　Spread 5¾ in.

2570—9 in. Bowl
Height 4⅜ in.

2570—11½ in. Bowl
Height 3⅜ in.

2425 2-in. Candlestick
Ro-Az-Gr-Am-Eb-Crys-Tz
Priced on page 44

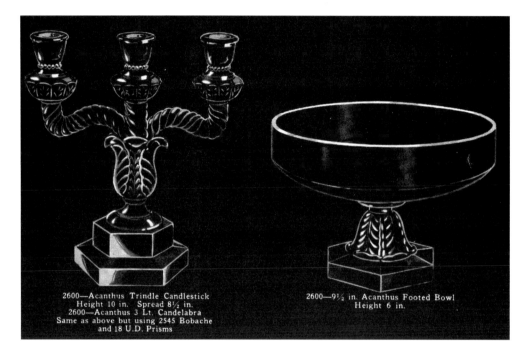

2600—Acanthus Trindle Candlestick
Height 10 in.   Spread 8½ in.
2600—Acanthus 3 Lt. Candelabra
Same as above but using 2545 Bobache
and 18 U.D. Prisms

2600—9½ in. Acanthus Footed Bowl
Height 6 in.

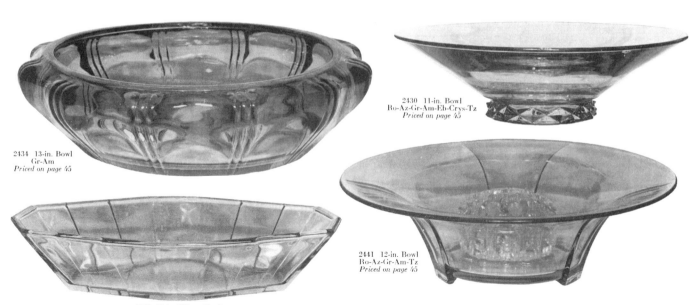

2434 13-in. Bowl
Gr-Am
Priced on page 45

2430 11-in. Bowl
Ro-Az-Gr-Am-Eb-Crys-Tz
Priced on page 45

2425 13-in. Oblong Bowl
Ro-Az-Gr-Am-Eb-Crys-Tz
Priced on page 45

2441 12-in. Bowl
Ro-Az-Gr-Am-Tz
Priced on page 45

2395—10 in. Bowl
Ro-Az-Gr-Am-Eb-Crys-Tz

2395½—5 in. Candlestick
Ro-Az-Gr-Am-Eb-Crys-Tz

2443—4 in. Candlestick
Ro-Az-Gr-Am-Eb-Crys-Tz

2443—10 in. Oval Bowl
Ro-Az-Gr-Am-Eb-Crys-Tz

2424—9 in. Bowl, Fld.
Ro-Gr-Am-Crys-Tz-Wis
2424—8 in. Bowl, Reg.
Ro-Gr-Am-Crys-Tz-Wis

2481—11 in. Oblong Bowl
Ro-Gr-Am-Eb-Crys-Tz

2481—5 in. Candlestick
Ro-Gr-Am-Eb-Crys-Tz

2535—9 in. Bowl, Flared
Height 3⅝ in.

4113—6 in. Candlestick

2535—7 in. Bowl, Cupped
Height 4⅛ in.

2535
5½ in. Candlestick

2536—9 in. Handled Bowl
Height 3¼ in.

2535
5½ in. Candlestick

2527—2 Light Candelabra, 16 U. D. P.
using 2527 Bobache
Height 8½ in.   Spread 7½ in.

2527—2 Light Candelabra, 16 U. D. P.
using 2527 Bobache
Height 8½ in.   Spread 7½ in.

2527—9-in. Footed Bowl
Height 4¼ in.

2364—12 in. Lily Pond
Height 2¼ in.

2596—7½ in. Square Bowl
Height 2½ in.

2596—5 in. Candlestick

2596—11 in. Oblong Shallow Bowl
Height 2 in.

2598—11 in. Oval Bowl
Height 2¾ in.

2598—Duo Candlestick
Height 7½ in.   Spread 7⅛ in.

4024—6 in. Candlestick

4024—6 in. Candlestick

4024—10½ in. Footed Bowl
Height 4⅛ in.

2533—Duo Candlestick
Height 6¼ in. Spread 6½ in.
To make 2533—2 Light
Candelabra, with 16 U. D. P.
use No. 2527 Bobache

2533—Duo Candlestick
Height 6¼ in. Spread 6½ in.
To make 2533—2 Light
Candelabra, with 16 U. D. P.
use No. 2527 Bobache

2533—9 in. Handled Bowl
Height 4⅝ in.

2472—Duo Candlestick
Use with 2470½—10½ in. Bowl
Height 4⅞ in. Spread 8 in.

2482—Trindle Candlestick
Use with 2470½—10½ in. Bowl
Height 6¾ in. Spread 8¼ in.

2447—Duo Candlestick
Height 5 in. Spread 6½ in.

2538—9 Piece Salad Set
Consisting of
1/12 Doz. 2538 11 in. Nappy
2/3 Doz. 2538 6 in. Nappy

2440—3 Piece Salad Set
Height 4¼ in.
Consisting of
1/12 Doz. 2440—12 in. Salad Bowl
1/12 Doz. 2440—13 in. Torte Plate
1/12 Doz. Salad Fork and Spoon, Wood

2056—3 Piece Salad Set
Height 5 in.
Consisting of
1/12 Doz. 2056— 10 in. Deep Nappy
1/12 Doz. 2056— 14 in. Torte Plate
1/12 Doz. Salad Fork and Spoon, Wood

2496—3 Piece Salad Set
Height 4¼ in.
Consisting of
1/12 Doz. 2496—10½ in. Salad Bowl
1/12 Doz. 2496—14 in. Torte Plate
1/12 Doz. Salad Fork and Spoon, Wood

2510—3 Piece Salad Set
Height 4¾ in.
Consisting of
1/12 Doz. 2510—12 in. Salad Bowl
1/12 Doz. 2510—16 in. Flat Plate
1/12 Doz. Salad Fork and Spoon, Wood

2545—2 in. "Flame" Candlestick

2545—12½ in. "Flame" Oval Bowl
Height 2⅞ in.

2545—4½ in. "Flame" Candlestick

2394—2 in. Candlestick

2394—12 in. Bowl, A
Height 3¾ in.
2309—3¾ in.
Flower Block

2394—2 in. Candlestick

2324—6 in. Candlestick

6023—Footed Bowl, Blown
Height 4¼ in.   Diameter 9¼ in.

2324—4 in. Candlestick

2563—4½ in. Viking Candlestick

2563—Handled Viking Bowl
Length 9½ in.   Width 7⅜ in.
Height 3⅛ in.

2297—12 in. Bowl, A
Ro-Gr-Am-Eb-Crys

2324—4 in. Candlestick
Ro-Az-Gr-Am-Eb-Crys

2309—3¾ in.
Flower Block
Ro-Gr-Am-
Eb-Crys

2394—12 in. Bowl, A
Ro-Az-Gr-Am- Crys-Tz-Wis

2394—2 in. Candlestick
Ro-Az-Gr-Am-Crys-Tz-Wis

2183—12 in. Cabarette
Ro-Az-Gr-Am

2402—2 in. Candlestick
Ro-Az-Gr-Am-Eb-Crys-Tz

2320—11 in. Bowl, B
Ro-Gr-Am-Eb

2402— 9 in. Bowl
Ro-Az-Gr-Am-Eb-Crys-Tz
2402—11 in. Bowl
Ro-Az-Gr-Am-Eb-Crys-Tz

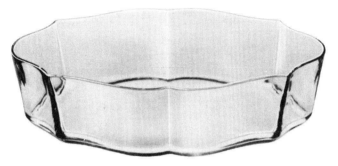

2426—12 in. Oval Bowl
RB-Bur-Emp.

2458—11½ in. Flared Bowl
RB-Bur-Emp.

No. 2651
11 in. Handled Bowl
Height 3-⅝ in.

No. 2653
Trindle Candlestick
Height 6¼ in. Spread 9 in.

No. 2652
Trindle Candlestick
Height 5-¾ in. Spread 9 in.

No. 2652
13-½ in. Handled Bowl
Height 3-¼ in.

2640
8 pc. Garden Center Set
Consisting of:
1/12 doz. 2640 Lily Pond
1/12 doz. 2640 Flower Block
½ doz. 2640 Candleholder
Height 7⅝ in.

2640
Candleholder

2640 — 14 in.
Lily Pond
Height 2 in.

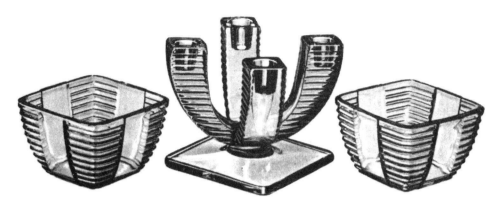

2546—Quadrangle Candlestick
Height 4¾ in.   Spread 7¼ in.

2546—4½ in. Quadrangle Bowl
Height 2¾ in.   4½ in. Square

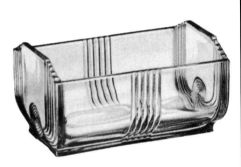

2547—6½ in. Oblong Bowl
Height 3½ in.—Width 4½ in.

Fostoria's Fashionable New Crystal Console Set "Quadrangle"

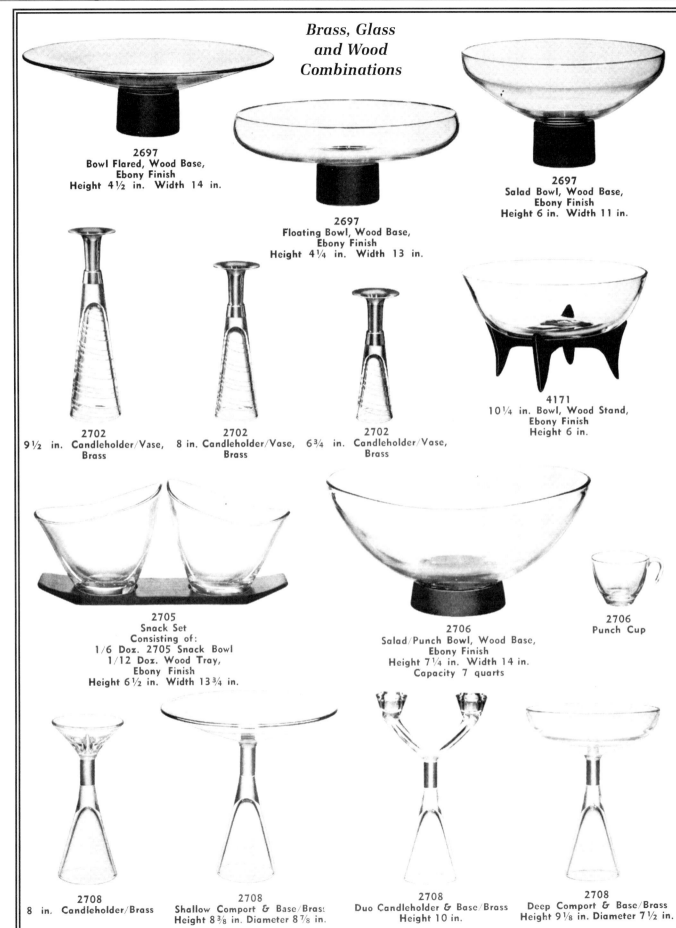

**Brass, Glass
and Wood
Combinations**

2697
Bowl Flared, Wood Base,
Ebony Finish
Height 4½ in. Width 14 in.

2697
Floating Bowl, Wood Base,
Ebony Finish
Height 4¼ in. Width 13 in.

2697
Salad Bowl, Wood Base,
Ebony Finish
Height 6 in. Width 11 in.

2702
9½ in. Candleholder/Vase,
Brass

2702
8 in. Candleholder/Vase,
Brass

2702
6¾ in. Candleholder/Vase,
Brass

4171
10¼ in. Bowl, Wood Stand,
Ebony Finish
Height 6 in.

2705
Snack Set
Consisting of:
1/6 Doz. 2705 Snack Bowl
1/12 Doz. Wood Tray,
Ebony Finish
Height 6½ in. Width 13¾ in.

2706
Salad/Punch Bowl, Wood Base,
Ebony Finish
Height 7¼ in. Width 14 in.
Capacity 7 quarts

2706
Punch Cup

2708
8 in. Candleholder/Brass

2708
Shallow Comport & Base/Brass
Height 8⅜ in. Diameter 8⅞ in.

2708
Duo Candleholder & Base/Brass
Height 10 in.

2708
Deep Comport & Base/Brass
Height 9⅛ in. Diameter 7½ in.

2722/460
Flora Candle/Snack Bowl
Height 3" Spread 5"

2722/334
Trindle Candle Arm
Height 2¼" Spread 7½"

2722/312
Peg Vase
Height 8"

2722/364
Table Charms, Set No. 1
Consisting of:

1 2722/334 Trindle Candle Arm
1 2722/312 Peg Vase
3 2722/460 Flora Candle/Snack Bowl
    Height 10" Spread 11"

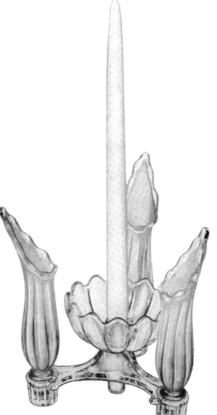

2722/364
Table Charms, Set No. 2
Consisting of:

1 2722/334 Trindle Candle Arm
3 2722/312 Peg Vase
1 2722/460 Flora Candle/Snack Bowl
    Height 10" Spread 9"

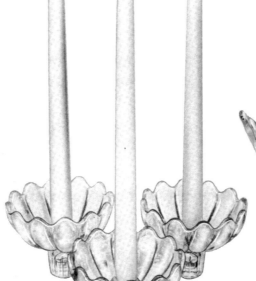

2722/364
Table Charms, Set No. 3
Consisting of:

1 2722/334 Trindle Candle Arm
3 2722/460 Flora Candle/Snack Bowl
    Height 10" Spread 11"

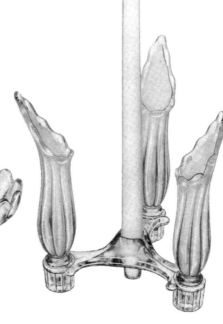

2722/364
Table Charms, Set No. 4
Consisting of:

1 2722/334 Trindle Candle Arm
3 2722/312 Peg Vase
    Height 10" Spread 9"

CANDLESTICKS, CANDELABRA, LUSTRES, and CANDLE LAMPS

2453 Lustres in Topaz, Wisteria; 2436 Lustre, Wisteria Base, UDP; 2436 Lustre, Ebony Base, Tear Drop Prisms; 2453 Lustres in Amber, Ebony

Candlesticks had been an on-going popular bestseller for the Fostoria Glass Company from its beginning in 1887. The elaborate three to seven arm candelabra, easily dubbed the "statesmen of the evening," are reminiscent of a time gone by, seeming to hold the romantic evening captive in their elegant designs. In 1924 many of the earliest candlesticks still were being offered. Even though electric lights eventually replaced the need for candles, it was not until after World War II that a noticeable decline in production was evident. After the war, only a few candlesticks independent of pressed patterns were offered.

Even though we cannot show pictures of all the candlesticks made by the Fostoria Glass Company, we have tried to present as complete a listing as possible. Additionally, candlesticks which were discontinued before 1924 are not priced, but are given dates when possible. The lustre was a single candlestick with bobache and prisms; a candelabra was a two-light or more candlestick with bobache and prisms for each light. Parts for lustres, candelabra, and candle lamps will be found at the end of the listings.

The Fostoria Glass Company first made candle lamps and hurricane lamps in the late 1930s. Candle lamps have been popular since some ingenious soul thought of the idea of a shade around the candle flame to keep it from being extinguished by a puff of wind. Early ones were called fairy lights or courting lamps. Oftentimes the base held the candle; however, many styles had a candle cup that fit inside or over the base and the globe or chimney rested on this piece. The smaller ones were called candle lamps and the larger, taller ones were referred to as hurricane lamps. They were used in nurseries, dim corners, to light hallways, and as some have speculated, to create a romantic atmosphere.

In 1939 both a candle lamp and a hurricane lamp were made in the popular American pattern. The candle lamp had three pieces and is a difficult item to find with all the parts. The delicate blown shade was easily broken on any of these lamps so bases will be seen more often. The part that holds the chimney was like an insert as it had a peg that fit into the candle base. The No. 26 was called a Candle Lamp Base but it is more like an insert with a peg on the bottom. Fostoria catalogs suggested that this base could be used in any single candlestick. Certainly it was made to fit any standard Fostoria candlestick even though it was marketed with the American, Spool, and Flame bases. Sometimes these were offered with a wax pot which was a small metal pot to hold the candle.

In 1963 an exquisite rope twist in pure, clear crystal was the big attraction. The 9" base was used with short and tall shades and also with a wired bobache with 10 flat 4" prisms. An elegant site indeed! The last candle lamp made by Fostoria was for the Virginia pattern which was still being made in 1986. Candlesticks are priced each unless noted.

Canary 2311 Lustre, Green 2311 Lustre with flat prisms, 2311 Bobache, 2311 Canary Candlestick

No. 1 Candelabra, 3-light, 26", circa 1888, used 7" Vase for top bobache, plain arms

No. 1 Candelabra, 4-light, circa 1888; 1934 through 1940; $395.00

No. 2 Candelabra, 4-light, 1889-1905

No. 3 Candelabra, 7-light, Banquet, 1889-1916

No. 3 Candelabra, 4-light, Banquet, 1889-1905

No. 4 Lustre Candlestick, 1889-1909; 1934-1940; $75.00

No. 5 Candlestick, Single Handled, circa 1889

No. 5A Candelabra, 2-light, 1888-1916; 1924-1942; $225.00

No. 6 Candlestick, Single Ribboned, 1889-1905

No. 7 Candelabra, 5-light, 1889-1942; $395.00

No. 7, Candelabra, 4-light, 1889-1916; 1934-1937; $300.00

No. 7 Candelabra, 3-light, 1889-1916; 1934-1937; $275.00

No. 7 Candelabra, 6-light, 1889-1916; 1934-1937; $425.00

No. 7 Candelabra, 7-light, 1889-1916

No. 8 Candelabra, Crucifix, 3-light, 1888-1896

No. 8 Candelabra, Crucifix, 4-light, 1888-1896

No. 9 Candelabra, 4-light, 1889-1904

No. 10 Candelabra, 6-light, 1889-1903

No. 11 Candelabra, Floral, 1889-1904

No. 12 Candelabra, Arabian Light, 1889-1897

No. 13 Candelabra, 3-light, circa 1889

No. 13 Candelabra, 4-light, circa 1889

No. 13 Candelabra, 5-light, 1889-1925, 1934; $395.00

No. 13 Candelabra, 6-light, circa 1889

No. 13 Candelabra, 7-light, circa 1889

No. 13 Candelabra, low 4-light, Pink holders, circa 1889

No. 13 Candelabra, low 5-light, Pink holders, circa 1889

No. 13 Candelabra, low 6-light, Pink holders, circa 1889

No. 14 Candelabra, low 6-light, 1889-1905

No. 15 Candelabra, 2-light, 1889-1925; 1934-1942; $225.00

No. 16 Candelabra, 4-light, 1888-1902

No. 16 Candelabra, 5-light, 1888-1902

No. 16 Candelabra, 6-light, 1888-1902

No. 16 Candlestick, Cut Star and Fan, 1888-1902

No. 17 Candlestick, circa 1888

No. 17 Candelabra, 5-light, 1888-1925; 1934-1937; $375.00

No. 17 Candelabra, 4-light, 1888-1916

No. 17 Candelabra, 3-light, 1888-1916

No. 17 Candelabra, 6-light, 1888-1916

No. 17 Candelabra, 7-light, 1888-1916

No. 18 Candlestick, Single, circa 1890

No. 18 Candelabra, 4-light, 1890-1925; $350.00

No. 19 Candlestick, Single Column, 10", 12", 15" 18", 1890-1916; 7" 1925; $65.00 - $165.00

No. 19 Candlestick, Single Handled, circa 1890

No. 21 Lustre Candlestick, 1890-1925; 1934-1936; $95.00

No. 22 Candelabra, 2-light, 1889-1925; 1934-1940; $165.00

No. 23 Candelabra, 3-light, 1889-1925; 1934-1940; $200.00

No. 24 Candelabra, 4-light, 21" Prisms, 1890-1924; 1934-1940; 1960-1980; $250.00

1490 Candlestick, Etched; 1963 Candlestick, Deep Etched; Number 19 Candlestick, 15" Cut; 1495 Candlestick, Etch B, 9½" and 8"

No. 25 Candelabra, 5-light, 24" Prisms, 1890-1925; 1960-1973; $300.00

No. 25½ Candelabra, 5-light, etched, with Spearhead and Colonial Prisms, 1890-1925; $350.00

No. 26 Candle Lamp Parts (see Parts, Lustres, Candelabra, Candle Lamps)

No. 32, Candelabra, 2-light, with Candle Lamps and shades, 1909, 1916

2245 Deep Etched Candlestick, 2324 9" Decorated Candlestick, 2244 Deep Etched 6" Candlestick

No. 33 Candelabra, 3-light, with Candle Lamps and shades, 1909, 1916

No. 34 Candelabra, 4-light, with Candle Lamps and shades, 1909,1916

No. 35 Candelabra, 5-light, with Candle Lamps and shades, 1909, 1916

(No. is assumed)

112 Candlestick, 9", 1888; 1924-1925; $54.00

112 Candelabra with mirror, 3-light, 1888-1920

121 Bobache (see Parts, Lustres, Candelabra, Candle Lamps)

122 Bobache (see Parts, Lustres, Candelabra, Candle Lamps)

140 Candlestick, Chamber, 1888-1896

161 Candlestick, Single, 6½", 7", 1889-1925; $47.00

188 Bobache or Candle Drip (see Parts, Lustres, Candelabra, Candle Lamps)

737 Candlestick, Single, 1898-1905

1064 Candlestick, 8" Single, 1909-1925; $58.00

1081 Candlestick, 8" Single, 1909-1925; $58.00

1103 Candlestick, 9½" Single, 1909-1928; $67.00

1103 Candlestick, 14½" Lustre, 1916-1928; 1934 through 1940 (called 2412 Queen Anne in Amber, Green and Blue, 1926-1927; see Queen Anne); $125.00

1103 Candlestick, 18½" Lustre, 1916-1928; $175.00

1103 Candlestick, 22½" Lustre, 1916-1928; $235.00

1204 Candlestick, 8½" Single, 1909-1925, 1928; $75.00

1204 Candlestick, 8½", Deep Etched "D," 1909-1925; $75.00

1205 Candlestick, 8" Single, 1909-1925; $68.00

1218 Candlestick, 8" Single, 1909-1925, 1928; $68.00

1218 Candlestick, 8", Deep Etched "A," Cut 72; $75.00

1372 Candlesticks (See Coin)

1453 Candlestick, 11" Single, 1909-1925; $95.00

1485 Candlestick, 8" Single, Etched "B," 1909-1925; 1928; 1933-1938; $67.00

1485 Candlestick, 8" Lustre, 1933-1938; $120.00

1485 Candlestick, 9½" Single, 1909-1925; 1928; $85.00

1485 Candlestick, 11" Single, 1909-1925, 1928; $95.00

1485 Candlestick, 8" Cut 160; $72.00

1490 Candlestick, 8" Single, 1909-1928; $67.00

1490 Candlestick, 15" Single, Plain or Etched, 1924-1927; $95.00

1490 Candlestick, Plain or Etched Prisms, 15" Lustre, 1925-1927; $150.00

1490 Candlestick, 8", Cutting 162; $72.00

1490 Candlestick, 8", Etched C-2; $75.00

1490 Candlestick, 15", Etched; $125.00

1513 Candlestick, Single Saucer, 1909-1925; $36.00

1513 Candlestick, Chamber, 1909-1925; $45.00

1612 Candlestick, 5" Christmas, 1909-1925; $34.00

1639 Candlestick, 8" Single, 1909-1928; $68.00

1639 Candlestick, 8", Deep Etched "D"; $75.00

1640 Candlestick, 8½" Single, 1909-1925; $75.00

1640 Candlestick, 11½" Lustre, Plain or Etched Colonial Prisms, 1909-1925; $150.00

1642 Candlestick 8" Single, 1909-1925; $67.00

2601 Lyre Duo Candlestick, 2600 Acanthus Trindle Candelabra, 2594 Trindle Candlestick, 2527 Duo Candelabra with 2527 Bobeches

1643 Candlestick, 9" Single, 1909-1916

1666 Candlestick, Chamber, 1909-1925; $45.00

1842 Candlestick, 8½" Single, 1916-1925; $68.00

1843 Candle Lamp, Single Handled with or without shade, 1916

1856 Candlestick, 8" Single, Plain or Etched, 1909-1928; $67.00

1856 Candlestick, 8", Cutting 163; $72.00

1856 Candlestick, 8", Deep Etched; $85.00

1962 Candlestick, 9", 2-handled, Single, Plain, or Etched, 1909-1928; $125.00

1962 Candlestick, 9", Deep Etched, $125.00

1963 Candlestick, 9" Single, Plain or Etched, 1909-1928; $75.00

2652 Trindle Candlestick, 2547 Trindle Candlestick, 2653 Trindle Candlestick

963 Candlestick, 9", Deep Etched, $95.00

964 Candlestick, 9" Single, Plain, or Etched, 1909-1928; $75.00

964 Candlestick, 9", Deep Etched, $95.00

965 Candlestick, 8" Single, Plain, or Etched, 1909-1928; $67.00

965 Candlestick, 8", Cutting 164; 1909-1924; $65.00

965 Candlestick, 8", Deep Etched, $85.00

2056 Candlesticks (see American)

2063 Candlestick, 2³⁄₁₆" Chamber
  Crystal, 1916-1928; $32.00
  Amber, 1924-1928; $38.00
  Green, 1924-1928; $40.00
  Blue, 1926-1927; $48.00

2080 Candlestick, 6½" Single, 1916-1928; $58.00

2108 Candlestick, Single, 1916-1918

2183 Candlestick, 1955-1958 (see Milk Glass); $24.00

2183 Hurricane Lamp, 1955-1958 (see Milk Glass); $38.00

2183 Flora Candle (see Heirloom)

2244 Candlestick, 6" Single, Etched "D," 1909-1928; $65.00

2244 Candlestick, 6", Deep Etched, $67.00

2244 Candlestick, 8" Single, Cut 165, Etched "D," 1909-1928; $77.00

2244 Candlestick, 8", Deep Etched, $85.00

2244 Candlestick, 8¼" Single, Decorations 12, 17, 20, 21, 31, and 32, 1924-1928; $85.00

2245 Candlestick, 6" Single
  Crystal, 1909-1928; $52.00
  Amber, 1924-1927; $55.00
  Canary, 1924-1926; $85.00
  Green, 1924-1927; $60.00
  Blue, 1925-1927; $85.00
  Ebony, 1925; $70.00
  Also Deep Etched and Decorated

2245 Candlestick, 6", Deep Etched, $62.00

2245 Candlestick, 8" Single
  Crystal, 1909-1928; $58.00
  Amber, 1924-1927; $65.00
  Canary, 1924-1926; $95.00
  Green, 1924-1927; $70.00
  Blue, 1925-1927; $95.00
  Ebony, 1925; $75.00
  Also Deep Etched and Decorated

2245 Candlestick, 8¼", Deep Etched; $85.00

2246 Candlestick, 8¼" Single, 1909-1928; $52.00

2246 Candlestick, 8¼", Deep Etched; $85.00

2247 Candlestick, 8½" Single, 1924-1925; $58.00

2268 Candlestick, 6" Single, Deep Etched, 1924-1928; $68.00

2269 Candlestick, 6" Single
  Crystal, 1924-1928; $45.00
  Amber, 1924-1928; $52.00
  Green, 1924-1928; $56.00
  Canary, 1924-1926; $65.00
  Blue, 1925-1927; $60.00
  Ebony, 1925-1927; $52.00
  Also Deep Etched and Decorated

2535 Candlestick in Crystal and Ruby, 2536 Duo Candlestick

2269 Candlestick, 6", Deep Etched, $55.00

2275 Candlestick, 7½" Single
  Crystal, 1924-1927; $45.00
  Amber, 1924-1927; $52.00
  Green, 1924-1927; $56.00
  Canary, 1924-1926; $65.00
  Blue, 1925-1927; $60.00
  Ebony, 1925-1927; $52.00
  Also Deep Etched and Decorated

2275 Candlestick, 9" Single
  Crystal, 1924-1927; $50.00

Amber 2430 Diadem Candlestick, 2372 Duo Candlestick, 2269 Candlestick, 2324½ Candlesticks (note the larger candle cup); 2390 Candlestick

Amber, 1924-1927; $56.00
Green, 1924-1927; $58.00
Canary, 1924-1926; $68.00
Blue, 1925-1927; $65.00
Ebony, 1925-1927; $55.00
Also Deep Etched
2275 Candlestick, 9", Deep Etched, $90.00
2279 Candleholder/Bobache, 4½" Diameter, Pegged, with prisms 1924-1928, 1933-1934; $20.00
2297 Candlestick, 7" Single
Crystal, 1924-1928; $45.00
Amber, 1924-1927; $45.00
Green, 1924-1927; $54.00
Blue, 1925-1927; $65.00
Canary, 1924-1926; $65.00
Ebony, 1925-1927; $50.00
2298 Candlestick, 3½" Single
Crystal, 1924-1927; $20.00
Amber, 1924-1927; $22.00
Green, 1924-1927; $25.00
Canary, 1924-1926; $30.00
Blue, 1925-1927; $30.00
Ebony, 1925-1927; $22.00
2299 Candlestick, 5" Single (oval base)
Crystal, 1924-1927; $30.00
Amber,1924-1927; $32.00
Green, 1924-1927; $34.00
Canary, 1924-1926; $38.00
Blue, 1925-1927; $38.00
Ebony,1925-1927; $30.00
2311 Candlestick, 7" Single
Crystal, 1924-1927; $45.00
Amber, 1924-1927; $50.00
Green, 1924-1927; $60.00
Canary, 1924-1926; $75.00
2311 Candlestick, 9" Lustre
Canary with Crystal Bobache, 1924; $150.00
All Amber, 1924-1927; $135.00
All Green 1924-1927; $145.00
2311 Candleholder, Bobache with 4" Colonial or U Drop Prisms
Crystal, 1924; $75.00
Amber, 1924-1926; $85.00
Green, 1924-1926; $85.00
2324 Candlestick, 2"
Crystal, 1926-1932; $15.00
Amber, 1926-1932; $18.00
Green, 1926-1932; $20.00
Canary, 1926; $26.00
Blue, 1926-1927; $25.00
Ebony, 1926-1932; $18.00
2324 Candlestick, 4" Single
Crystal, 1925-1982; $15.00
Amber, 1925-1940; $18.00
Green, 1925-1937; $20.00
Canary, 1925-1926; $30.00
Blue, 1925--1927; $28.00

Green 2383 Trindle Candlestick, 2324 9" Candlestick, 2844 Sea Shells Flora Candlestick, 2443 Candlestick

Orchid, 1926-1927; $28.00
Rose, 1928-1940; $22.00
Azure, 1928-1938; $24.00
Ebony, 1925-1937; $18.00
2324 Candlestick, 4", Etched, $20.00
2324 Candlestick, 9" Single
Crystal, 1925-1929; $20.00
Amber, 1925-1929; $23.00
Green, 1925-1929; $25.00
Canary, 1925-1926; $37.00
Blue, 1925-1927; $35.00
Ebony, 1925-1929; $23.00
2324 Candlestick, 9", Etched, $95.00
2324 Candlestick, 12" Single
Crystal, 1925-1929; $26.00
Amber, 1925-1929; $30.00
Green, 1925-1929; $34.00
Ebony, 1925-1929; $30.00
2324 Candlestick, 12", Etched, $125.00
2324½ Candlestick, 4" (Candle socket is 1½" diameter for larger candle.)

Wisteria 2447 Duo Candlestick, Rose 2482 Trindle Candlestick, Romance 6023 Duo Candlestick

Crystal, 1924-1926; $32.00
Amber, 1924-1926; $35.00
Green, 1924-1926; $38.00
Canary, 1924-1926; $45.00
Blue, 1924-1926; $45.00
Ebony, 1924-1926; $35.00
2324 Candlestick, 6" Single
Crystal, 1926-1929; 1939-1965;
1981-1982; $18.00
Amber, 1926-1929; $20.00
Green, 1926-1929; $22.00
Canary, 1926; $32.00
Blue, 1926-1927; $30.00
Orchid, 1927-1928; $30.00
Ebony, 1929; $20.00
Light Blue, 1981-1982; $25.00
2326 Candle Vase (see Lead Crystal Giftware)
2333 Candlestick, 8" Single
Amber, 1924-1928; $54.00
Green, 1924-1928; $58.00
Blue, 1924-1927; $65.00
2333 Candlestick, 11" Single
Amber, 1924-1926; $65.00
2352 Candlestick, Lily
Crystal, 1927-1928; $34.00
Amber, 1927-1928; $36.00
Green, 1927-1928; $40.00
Blue, 1927; $45.00
Orchid, 1927; $45.00
2362 Candlestick, 3" Single
Green, 1927-1929; $20.00
Blue, 1927; $27.00
Orchid, 1927-1928; $25.00
2362 Candlestick, 9" Single
Green, 1927-1929; $57.00
Blue, 1927; $65.00
Orchid, 1927-1928; $60.00
2372 Candlestick, 2" Block, Plain or Spiral Optic
Crystal, 1927-1929; $15.00
Amber, 1927-1929; $18.00
Green, 1927-1929; $20.00
Blue, 1927; $24.00
Orchid, 1927-1928; $22.00
Rose, 1928-1929; $22.00
2375 Candlestick, 3" (see Fairfax)
Crystal, 1927-1959; $12.50
Amber, 1927-1940; $15.00
Green, 1927-1940; $17.50
Orchid, 1927-1928; $17.50
Rose, 1928-1940; $17.50
Azure, 1928-1940; $17.50
Topaz/Gold Tint, 1929-1939; $17.50
Ebony, 1930-1941; $15.00
2375½ Candlestick (Mushroom)
Crystal, 1928-1932; $20.00
Amber, 1928-1932; $22.50
Green, 1928-1932; $25.00

Amber, Blue, and Green 2352 "Lily" Candlesticks; 2545 Flame Lustre in Gold Tint; 2484 Lustre

Orchid, 1928; $32.50
Rose, 1928-1932; $25.00
Azure, 1928-1932; $25.00
Topaz, 1929-1932; $25.00
2383 Candlestick, Trindle
Crystal, 1928-1935; $45.00
Amber, 1928-1939; $48.00
Green, 1928-1935; $54.00
Rose, 1928-1934; $54.00
Azure, 1928-1939; $54.00
Topaz/Gold Tint, 1929-1939; $50.00
Ebony, 1928-1939; $48.00
2390 Candlestick, 3"
Amber, 1927-1929; $22.00
Green, 1927-1929; $25.00
Rose, 1929; $35.00
Azure, 1929; $35.00
Orchid, 1927-1928; $40.00
2393 Candlestick, 2" Crimped, Spiral Optic
Amber, 1928-1930; $25.00

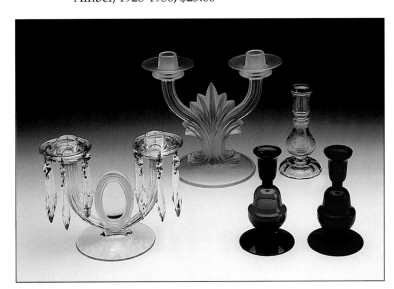

2510 Glacier Duo Candlestick; Silver Mist 2484 Duo Candlestick with Candle Drips; 4113 Candlesticks in Burgundy and Regal Blue, 4024 Candlestick with Vintage Etching

Green, 1928-1930; $30.00
Rose, 1928-1930; $30.00
Azure, 1928-1930; $34.00
2394 Candlestick, 2" (3-toed)
Crystal, 1928-1940; $20.00
Amber, 1928-1940; $22.00
Green, 1928-1940; $25.00
Orchid, 1928; $32.00
Rose, 1928-1938; $30.00
Azure, 1928-1940; $30.00
Topaz/Gold Tint, 1929-1940; $28.00
Wisteria, 1931-1936; $38.00
Regal Blue, 1934-1938; $45.00
Burgundy, 1934-1939; $45.00
Empire Green, 1934-1939; $45.00
2395 Candlestick, 3"
Crystal, 1930-1932; $25.00
Amber, 1930-1932; $28.00
Green, 1930-1932; $30.00
Rose, 1930-1932; $30.00
Azure, 1930; $45.00
Ebony, 1930-1932; $28.00
2395½ Candlestick, 5½"
Crystal, 1929-1938; $35.00
Amber, 1929-1939; $38.00
Green, 1929-1939; $45.00
Rose, 1929-1937; $45.00
Azure, 1929-1934; $50.00
Topaz/Gold Tint, 1929-1939; $45.00
Ebony, 1929-1939; $40.00
2402 Candlestick, 2"
Crystal, 1933-1939; $12.00
Amber, 1929-1935; $15.00
Green, 1929-1935; $18.00
Rose, 1929-1939; $18.00
Azure, 1929-1934; $20.00
Topaz/Gold Tint, 1929-1939; $18.00
Ebony, 1929-1934; 1953-1957; $15.00
2424 Candlestick (see Kent)
2425 Candlestick, 2"
Crystal, 1929-1932; $20.00
Amber, 1930-1932; $22.00
Green, 1930-1932; $24.00
Rose, 1930-1932; $24.00
Azure, 1930-1932; $26.00
Topaz, 1930-1932; $24.00
Ebony, 1930-1932; $22.00
2430 Candlesticks (see Diadem)
2433 Candlestick (see Twenty Four Thirty Three and
    Bowls, Centerpieces, and Console Bowls)
2436 Candlestick, 9" Lustre
Crystal, 1930-1940; $58.00
Amber, 1930-1934; $65.00
Green, 1930-1934; $70.00
Rose, 1930-1932; $85.00
Topaz, 1930-1934; $70.00
Ebony, 1931-1934; $70.00

2402 Ebony Candle, 2433 Ebony Base Candlestick, 2668 Ebony Candlestick, 2667 6" Candlestick, 2667 Candles in Ebony and Crystal, 2638 Contour Candlestick, 2752 Gold Facets Candlestick

Wisteria, 1931-1933; $95.00
2443 Candlestick, 4"
Crystal, 1931-1939; $20.00
Amber, 1931-1934; $22.00
Green, 1931-1934; $24.00
Rose, 1931-1938; $24.00
Azure, 1931-1937; $25.00
Topaz/Gold Tint, 1931-1938; $24.00
Ebony, 1931-1937; $24.00
Wisteria, 1931-1936; $38.00
Ruby, 1935; $45.00

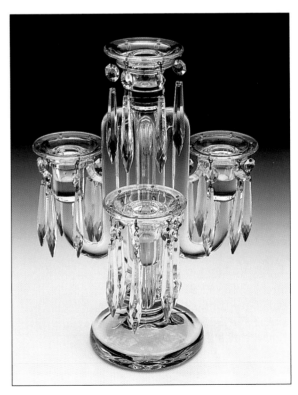

2655 four-light Candelabra

2446 Candlestick
Crystal, 1931-1935; $25.00
Amber, 1931-1934; $28.00
Green, 1931-1934; $30.00
Rose, 1931-1934; $30.00
Azure, 1931-1934; $34.00
Topaz, 1931-1935; $34.00
Ebony, 1931-1935; $30.00

2447 Candlestick, Duo
Crystal, 1931-1939; $30.00
Amber, 1931-1938; $35.00
Green, 1931-1938; $38.00
Rose, 1931-1935; $38.00
Azure, 1931-1933; $45.00
Topaz/Gold Tint, 1931-1938; $35.00
Ebony, 1931-1938; $35.00

2449 Candlestick, 6" (see Hermitage)

2453 Candlestick, 7½" Lustre
Crystal, 1933-1940; 1953-1957; $75.00
Amber, 1933-1934; $87.00
Green, 1933-1934; $95.00
Topaz, 1933-1934; $90.00
Ebony, 1953-1957; $95.00
Wisteria, 1933-1934; $125.00

2455 Candlestick, 6"
Crystal, 1931-1933; $45.00
Amber, 1931-1933; $48.00
Green, 1931-1933; $56.00
Rose, 1931-1933; $56.00
Topaz, 1931-1932; $56.00

2466 Candlestick, 3", listed in 1933, not shown
Crystal, 1933; $15.00
Amber, 1933; $18.00
Green, 1933; $20.00
Topaz, 1933; $20.00
Ebony, 1933; $18.00

2470 Candlestick (see Twenty Four Seventy)

2470½ (see Twenty Four Seventy)

2472 Candlestick, Duo
Crystal 1932-1958; $40.00
Amber, 1932-1939; $45.00
Green, 1932-1939; $47.00
Rose, 1932-1939; $47.00
Topaz/Gold Tint, 1932-1939; $45.00
Ebony, 1932-1934; $45.00

2481 Candlestick, 5"
Crystal, 1933-1938; $40.00
Amber, 1933-1934; $45.00
Green, 1933-1934; $47.00
Rose, 1933-1934; $47.00
Topaz/Gold Tint, 1933-1938; $45.00
Ebony, 1933-1936; $45.00

2482 Candlestick, Trindle (also offered with 1 or 2 Bobeches and called a Candelabra in Crystal)
Crystal, 1933-1973; $54.00
Amber, 1933-1935; $58.00
Green, 1933-1938; $65.00
Rose, 1933-1937; $65.00

2767 Candle Lamp Lustre

Topaz, 1933-1939; $65.00
Ebony, 1933-1939; $58.00

2484 Candlesticks (see Baroque)

2496 Candlesticks (see Baroque)

2510 Candlesticks (see Sunray)

2521 Bird Candleholder (see Lead Crystal Giftware)

2527 Candelabra, 2-light, 2527 Bobache, 16 UDP, 1935-1940; $125.00

2533 Candlestick, Duo, 1935-1940; $58.00

2533 Candelabra, Duo with 2527 Bobache, 2" B Prisms, Crystal, 1936-1939; $97.00

2535 Candlestick, 5½" Single
Crystal, 1935-1940; $45.00
Regal Blue, 1935-1939; $65.00
Burgundy, 1935-1939; $65.00
Empire Green, 1935-1939; $65.00
Ruby, 1935-1939; $65.00

2545 Candlesticks (see Flame)

2546 Candlestick, Duo, 1937-1939; $58.00

2546 Candelabra, Duo with Square Bobache, 7 B Prisms, 1937-1939; $200.00

2546 Candlestick, Quadrangle
Crystal, 1937-1939; $95.00
Azure, 1937-1939; $125.00

2546 Candelabra, Quadrangle, Square Bobache, B Prisms
Crystal, 1937-1939; $400.00/market
Azure, 1937-1939; $425.00/market

2547 Candlestick, Trindle
Crystal, 1937-1939; $85.00
Azure, 1937; $125.00
Gold Tint, 1937-1939; $110.00

2636 Plume Candlesticks, 2629 Chanticleer. An innovative suggestion from the authors for a festive table.

2550 Candlesticks (see Spool)
2560 Candlesticks (see Coronet)
2563 Candlestick, 4½" Viking, 1939-1943; $47.00
2574 Candlesticks (see Raleigh)
2592 Candlesticks (see Myriad)
2596 Candlestick, 5", 1940-1943; $47.00
2594 Candlestick, 5½", 1941-1957 (see Bowls, Centerpieces, and Console Bowls); $52.00
2594 Candlestick, Trindle, 1941-1957 (see Bowls, Centerpieces, and Console Bowls); $75.00
2598 Candlestick, Duo, 1940-1943; $95.00
2600 Candlestick, Acanthus Trindle, 1940-1943; $125.00
2600 Candelabra, 3-light, 2545 Bobache, UDP, 1940; $250.00
2601 Candlestick, Duo, Lyre, 1942-1948; $75.00
2620 Candlestick, (see Wistar)
2636 Candlestick, Plume, 1949-1958; $85.00
2636 Candlestick, Duo, Plume, 1950-1957; $115.00
2638 Candlestick (see Contour, Ebony Glass)
2639 Candlestick, Duo, 1950-1957; $115.00
2640 Garden Center, 1949-1963; $250.00
2652 Candlestick, Trindle, 1951-1957; $95.00
2653 Candlestick, Trindle, 1951-1955; $95.00
2655 Candlestick, 4-light, 1951-1955; $125.00
2655 Candelabra, 3- or 4-light, 2527 Bobache, 1951-1955; $250.00
2666 (see Contour)
2667 Candlestick, 2½"
    Crystal, 1953-1960; $18.00
    Ebony, 1953-1961; $20.00
2667 Candlestick, 6", 1953-1958; $32.00
2668 Candlestick
    Crystal, 1953-1964; $32.00
    Ebony, 1953-1961; $35.00
2668 Hurricane Lamp Complete: 2668 Candlestick, 2668 Hurricane Lamp Chimney
    Crystal, 1953-1963; $55.00
    Ebony Base, 1953-1961; $65.00
2702 Candleholder/Vase, 6¾", Brass and Glass, 1956-1962; $22.00 (see Vases, p. 212)
2702 Candleholder/Vase, 8", Brass and Glass, 1956-1962; $25.00 (see Vases, p. 212)
2702 Candleholder/Vase, 9½", Brass and Glass, 1956-1962; $28.00 (see Vases, p. 212)
2708 Candleholder/Brass, 8", 1957-1962; $35.00
2708 Candleholder, Duo, 1958-1961; $40.00
2722 Table Charms (see Bowls, Centerpieces, and Console Bowls)
2742 Candlestick (see Sculpture)
2749 Candlesticks (see Crown)
2752 Candlestick (see Facets)
2757 Candle Twist (see Sculpture)
2761 Candlestick, 10½" Lustre, 8 5" Flat Prisms, 1963-1973; $125.00
2762 Candelabra, 2-light, 12", 2762 Bobache with 8 4" Flat Prisms, 1963-1969; $150.00
2763 Candlestick, 9", 1963-1974; $110.00
2763 Candle Lamp, 13½": 2763 9" Candlestick, 2763 5" Candle Lamp Shade, 1963-1974; $135.00

2765 Candelabra, 3-light, 11¼", 2765 Bobache, 10 4" Flat Prisms, 1963-1969; $175.00
2767 Candle Lamp, 17½": 2763 Candlestick, 2767 9" Shade, 1964-1973; 1981-1982; $157.00
2767 Candlestick, 9" Lustre, 2769 Bobache with 10 Flat Prisms, 1964-1973; $135.00
2767 Candle Lamp Lustre, 17½": 2763 9" Candlestick, 2769 Bobache wired with 10 4" Flat Prisms, 2767 9" Shade, 1964-1973; $200.00
2768 Candlestick, 3-light, 1964-1982; $150.00
2768 Candelabra, 3-light, 12": 2768 Candlestick, 2765 Bobache (3), 30 Spearhead Prisms, 1964-1982; $290.00
2776/2777 Candlesticks (see Henry Ford Museum)
2782 Candleholder, 3½", 1964-1974; $20.00
2782 Candle Lamp, 12¼", 1970-1974; $40.00
2864 Candleholder B, 1975-1981; $7.00 (see Lead Crystal)
2883 Candlestick, 6", 1974-1981; $10.00 (see Lead Crystal)
3008 Candlestick (see Holly and Ruby Giftware)
4024 Candlestick, 6"
    Crystal, 1933-1939; $34.00
    Regal Blue Bowl, 1933-1937; $65.00
    Burgundy Bowl, 1933-1938; $65.00
    Empire Green Bowl, 1933-1938; $65.00
4113 Candlestick, 6"
    Regal Blue, 1933-1938; $65.00
    Burgundy, 1933-1938; $65.00
    Empire Green, 1933-1938; $65.00
6023 Candlestick, Duo, 1940-1963; $35.00
(see also Candlestick Collection, Candle Vase Collection, Light Show Collection, Lotus Giftware, Maypole Giftware, Morning Glory Giftware, and Virginia Giftware)

323 7" Candlestick, Transition Candlestick, Coronation Candlestick (see Vases), Ruby Bird Candle, 314 (Kent reintroduction) 3" Candlestick, Glacier Brown Candlestick

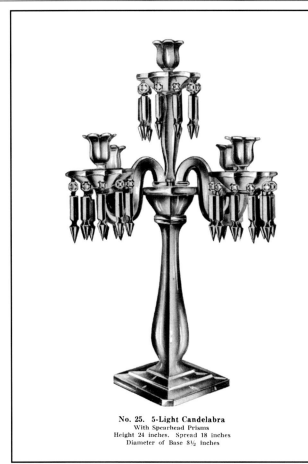

No. 25. 5-Light Candelabra
With Spearhead Prisms
Height 24 inches. Spread 18 inches
Diameter of Base 8½ inches

No. 17. 5-Light Candelabra
With U Drop Prisms
Height 23 inches. Spread 15 inches
Diameter of Base 8 inches

No. 24. 4-Light Candelabra
With Spearhead Prisms
Height 21 inches. Spread 14 inches
Diameter of Base 6½ inches

No. 23. 3-Light Candelabra
With Spearhead Prisms
Height 22 inches. Spread 15 inches
Diameter of Base 6½ inches

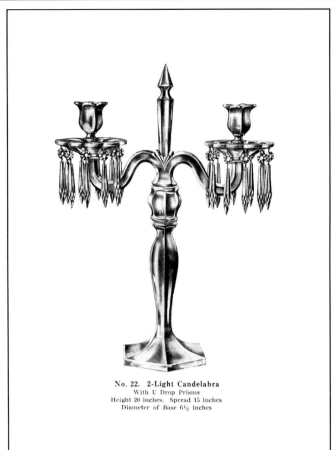

No. 22. 2-Light Candelabra
With U Drop Prisms
Height 20 inches. Spread 15 inches
Diameter of Base 6½ inches

No. 13. 5-Light Candelabra
With U Drop Prisms
Height 18 inches. Spread 15 inches
Diameter of Base 7 inches

No. 7. 5-Light Candelabra
With U Drop Prisms
Height 23 inches. Spread 15 inches
Diameter of Base 7 inches

No. 1. 4-Light Candelabra
With U Drop Prisms
Height 21 inches. Spread 12 inches
Diameter of Base 6 inches

No. 15. 2-Light Candelabra
With U Drop Prisms
Height 13 inches. Spread 14 inches
Diameter of Base 7 inches

No. 5A. 2-Light Candelabra
With U Drop Prisms
Height 16 inches. Spread 14 inches
Diameter of Base 6 inches

No. 21. Lustre Candlestick
With Spearhead Prisms
Height 12½ in. Diameter of Base 5½ in

No. 4. Lustre Candlestick
With U Drop Prisms
Height 10 in. Diameter of Base 5 in.

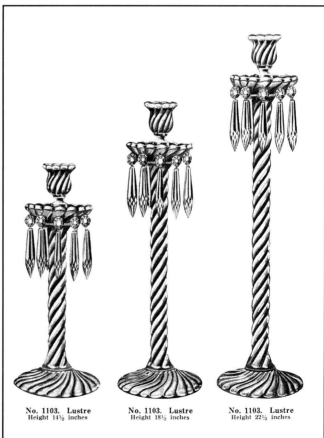

No. 1103. Lustre
Height 14½ inches

No. 1103. Lustre
Height 18½ inches

No. 1103. Lustre
Height 22½ inches

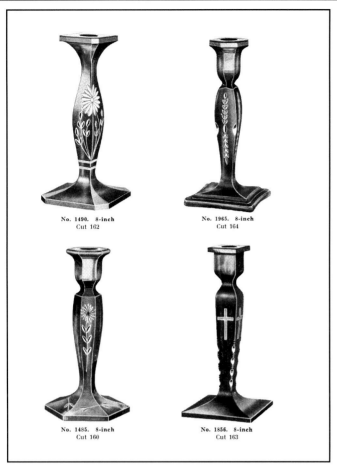

No. 1490. 8-inch
Cut 162

No. 1965. 8-inch
Cut 164

No. 1485. 8-inch
Cut 160

No. 1856. 8-inch
Cut 163

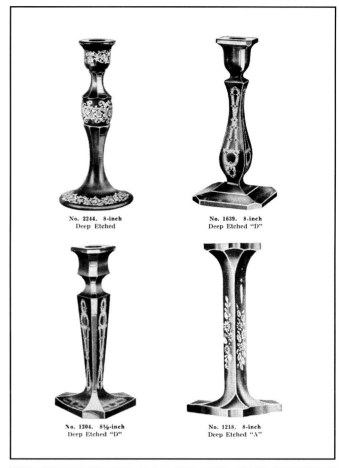

No. 2244. 8-inch
Deep Etched

No. 1639. 8-inch
Deep Etched "D"

No. 1204. 8½-inch
Deep Etched "D"

No. 1218. 8-inch
Deep Etched "A"

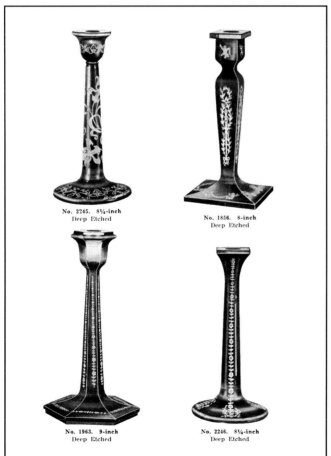

No. 2245. 8¼-inch
Deep Etched

No. 1856. 8-inch
Deep Etched

No. 1963. 9-inch
Deep Etched

No. 2246. 8¼-inch
Deep Etched

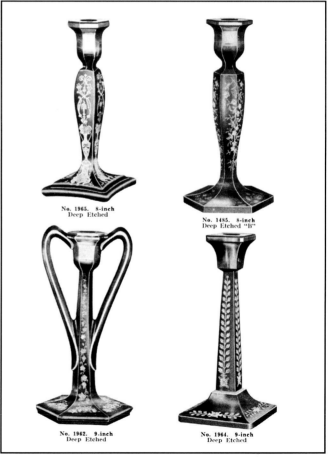

No. 1965. 8-inch
Deep Etched

No. 1485. 8-inch
Deep Etched "B"

No. 1962. 9-inch
Deep Etched

No. 1964. 9-inch
Deep Etched

No. 2324. 4-inch
Etched

No. 2324. 12-inch
Etched

No. 2324. 9-inch
Etched

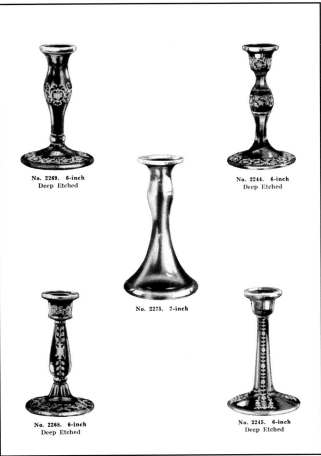

No. 2269. 6-inch
Deep Etched

No. 2244. 6-inch
Deep Etched

No. 2275. 7-inch

No. 2268. 6-inch
Deep Etched

No. 2245. 6-inch
Deep Etched

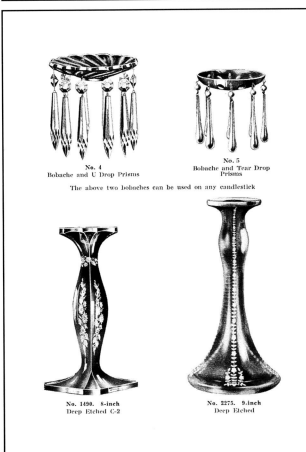

No. 4
Bobache and U Drop Prisms

No. 5
Bobache and Tear Drop Prisms

The above two bobaches can be used on any candlestick

No. 1490. 8-inch
Deep Etched C-2

No. 2275. 9-inch
Deep Etched

No. 2299. 5-inch

No. 2298. 3½-inch

No. 2279. Candleholder and
Bobache Combined
Diameter 4½ inches
This can be used on any
candlestick

No. 1640. 11½-inch Lustre
With Fostoria 6-inch Prisms

No. 2311. 9-inch Lustre
With Fostoria 4-inch Prisms

No. 2324. 12-inch

No. 2333. 8-inch

No. 2333. 11-inch

No. 2324. 4-inch

No. 2324. 9-inch

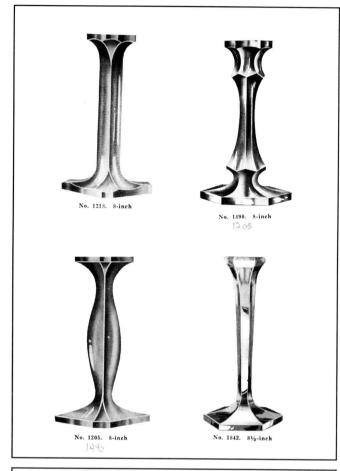

No. 1218. 8-inch

No. 1490. 8-inch

1205

No. 1205. 8-inch

No. 1842. 8½-inch

1490

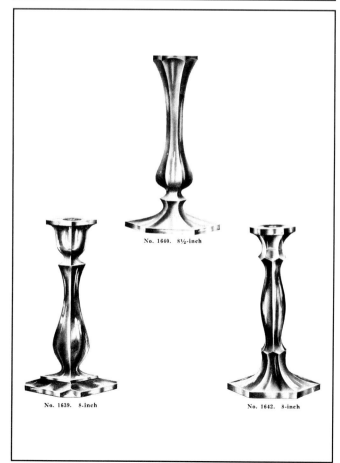

No. 1640. 8½-inch

No. 1639. 8-inch

No. 1642. 8-inch

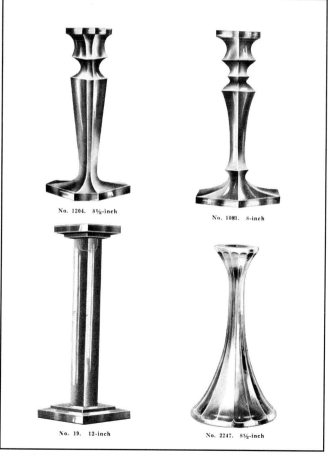

No. 1204. 8½-inch

No. 1081. 8-inch

No. 19. 12-inch

No. 2247. 8½-inch

No. 1064. 8-inch

No. 161. 7-inch

No. 112. 9-inch

No. 1103. 9½-inch

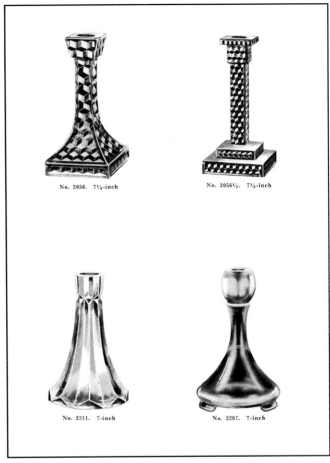

No. 2056. 7¼-inch

No. 2056½. 7¼-inch

No. 2311. 7-inch

No. 2297. 7-inch

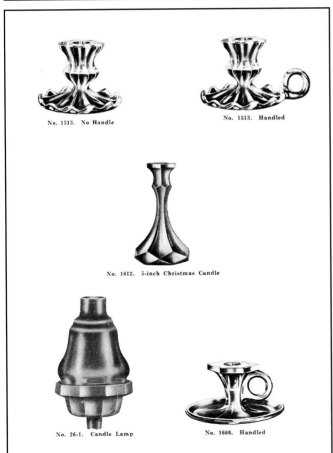

No. 1513. No Handle

No. 1513. Handled

No. 1612. 5-inch Christmas Candle

No. 26-1. Candle Lamp

No. 1666. Handled

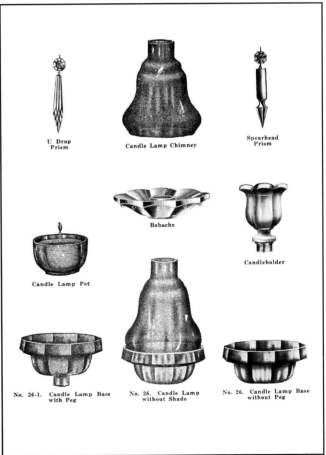

U Drop Prism

Candle Lamp Chimney

Spearhead Prism

Bobache

Candleholder

Candle Lamp Pot

No. 26-1. Candle Lamp Base with Peg

No. 26. Candle Lamp without Shade

No. 26. Candle Lamp Base without Peg

No. 3   7-Light Banquet Candelabra
With U Drop Prisms
Height 30 inches. Spread 20 inches
Diameter of Base 8 inches
Price as illustrated $20.00. One Vase extra included

No. 18   4-Light Candelabra
With U Drop Prisms
Height 21 inches. Spread 12 inches
Diameter of Base 8 inches
Price as illustrated $7.60

No. 25½   5-Light Candelabra Etched
With Spearhead Prisms and Eight Colonial Prisms
Height 27 inches. Spread 18 inches
Diameter of Base 8½ inches
Price as illustrated $18.00   Price without Etching $15.50

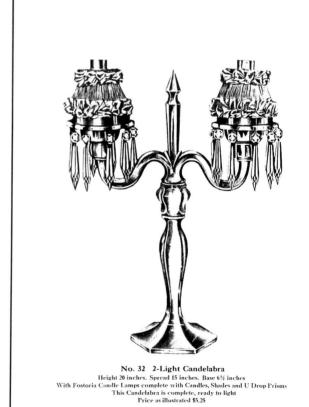

No. 32   2-Light Candelabra
Height 20 inches. Spread 15 inches. Base 6½ inches
With Fostoria Candle Lamps complete with Candles, Shades and U Drop Prisms
This Candelabra is complete, ready to light
Price as illustrated $5.25

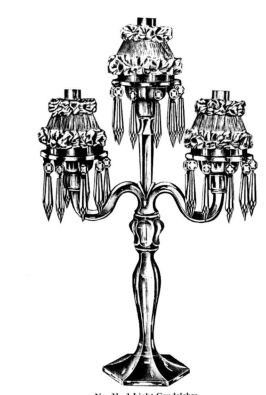

No. 33 3-Light Candelabra
Height 25 inches. Spread 15 inches. Base 6½ inches
With Fostoria Candle Lamps complete with Candles, Shades and U Drop Prisms
This Candelabra is complete, ready to light
Price as illustrated $7.00

No. 34 4-Light Candelabra
Height 25 inches. Spread 14 inches. Base 6½ inches
With Fostoria Candle Lamps complete with Candles, Shades and U Drop Prisms
This Candelabra is complete, ready to light
Price as illustrated $7.75

No. 35 5-Light Candelabra
Height 26 inches. Spread 18 inches. Diameter of Base 8 inches
With Fostoria Candle Lamps complete with Candles, Shades and U Drop Prisms
This Candelabra is complete, ready to light
Price as illustrated $10.50

16 Candelabra.
Made in 4, 5 and 6 Light.   Height 20 inches.   Diameter of Base 6½ inches.

No. 2 Candelabra. 4 Lights

737 Candlestick.

4 Lustre Candlestick.
Packed 2½ doz. in bbl.

No. 26 Candle Lamp
With Shade and Candle
40 cents each

2372—2 in. Candle Block.
Made plain or in spiral optic.

4024—10½ in. Footed Bowl
Height 4⅛ in.

4024—6 in. Candlestick

2453—7½ in. Lustre
Gr-Am-Crys-Tz-Wis

2484—2 Light Candelabra
Height 8 in.
Crys-Tz
2484—Bobache and Prisms
Crystal

2436—9 in. Lustre
Gr-Am-Crys-Eb-Tz-Wis

2482—Trindle Candlestick
Ro-Gr-Am-Eb-Crys-Tz

2472—Duo Candlestick
Ro-Gr-Am-Eb-Crys-Tz

2447—Duo Candlestick
Ro-Az-Gr-Am-Eb-
Crys-Tz-Wis

1485—8 in. Candlestick
2279—Bobache and Prisms
Crystal

2279—Bobache and Prisms
Crystal

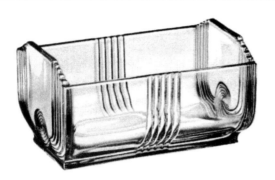

2547—6½ in. Oblong Bowl
Height 3½ in.—Width 4½ in.

2547—Trindle Candlestick
Height 5⅛ in.—Spread 7⅛ in.

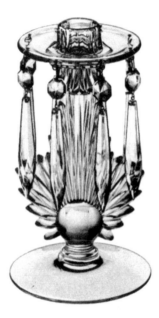

2545—"Flame" Lustre
8 U Drop Prisms
Height 7½ in.

2546—Square Bobache and 7 B Prisms
2⅝ in. Square

2546 Duo Candlestick
Height 4¾ in.—Spread 7 in.

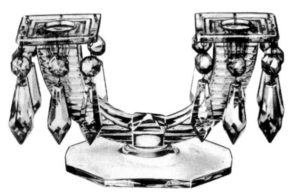

2546—2 Light Candelabra, 14 B Prisms
Using 2546 Square Bobache
Height 5 in.   Spread 8¼

2546—4 Light Candelabra, 28 B Prisms
Using 2546 Square Bobache
Height 5 in.   Spread 8¼ in.

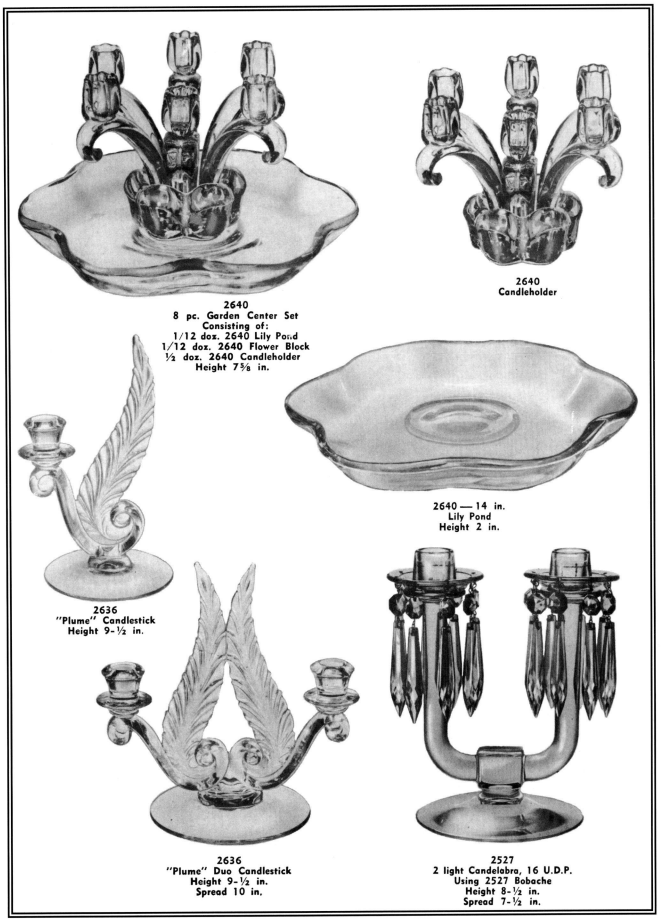

2640
Candleholder

2640
8 pc. Garden Center Set
Consisting of:
1/12 doz. 2640 Lily Pond
1/12 doz. 2640 Flower Block
½ doz. 2640 Candleholder
Height 7⅝ in.

2640 — 14 in.
Lily Pond
Height 2 in.

2636
"Plume" Candlestick
Height 9-½ in.

2636
"Plume" Duo Candlestick
Height 9-½ in.
Spread 10 in.

2527
2 light Candelabra, 16 U.D.P.
Using 2527 Bobache
Height 8-½ in.
Spread 7-½ in.

2375 3-in. Candlestick

2375½ Candlestick

2383 Trindle—3-Light Candlestick
Ro-Az-Gr-Am-Eb-Crys-Tz
Priced on page 44

2436 9-in. Lustre
with U. D. Prisms
Ro-Gr-Am-Eb-Crys-Tz-Wis
Priced on page 44

2443 4-in. Candlestick
Ro-Az-Gr-Am-Eb-Crys-Tz
Priced on page 44

2447 Duo Candlestick
Ro-Az-Gr-Am-Eb-Crys-Tz-Wis
Priced on page 44

2446 Candlestick
Ro-Az-Gr-Am-Eb-Crys-Tz
Priced on page 44

2443 10-in. Oval Bowl
Ro-Az-Gr-Am-Eb-Crys-Tz
Priced on page 45

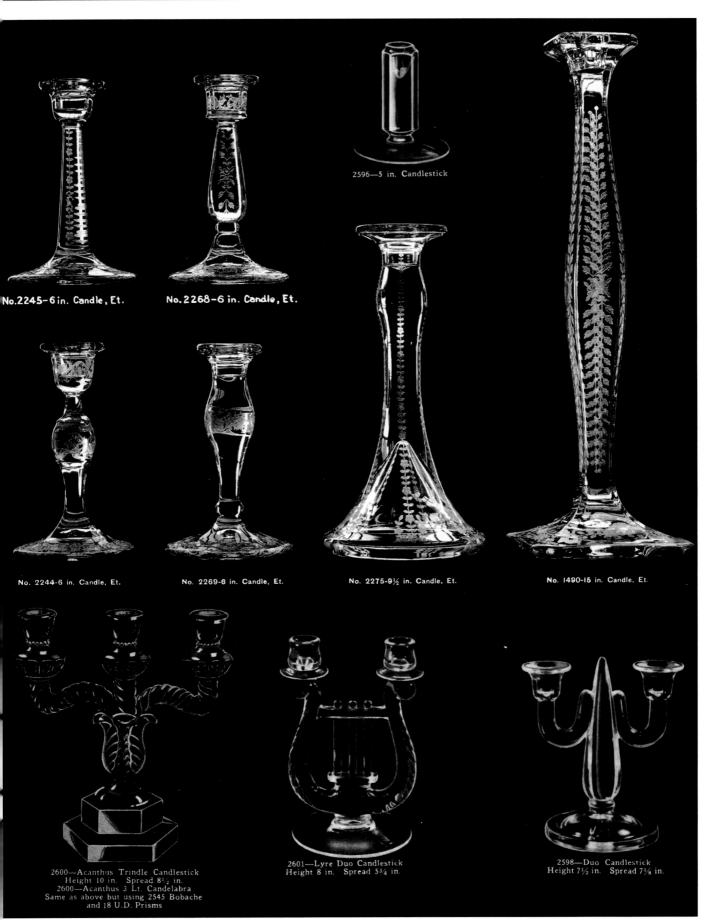

No.2245-6 in. Candle, Et.

No.2268-6 in. Candle, Et.

2596—5 in. Candlestick

No. 2244-6 in. Candle, Et.

No. 2269-6 in. Candle, Et.

No. 2275-9½ in. Candle, Et.

No. 1490-15 in. Candle, Et.

2600—Acanthus Trindle Candlestick
Height 10 in.   Spread 8½ in.
2600—Acanthus 3 Lt. Candelabra
Same as above but using 2545 Bobache
and 18 U.D. Prisms

2601—Lyre Duo Candlestick
Height 8 in.   Spread 5¾ in.

2598—Duo Candlestick
Height 7½ in.   Spread 7⅛ in.

2455-6" CANDLESTICK

4113—6 in. Candlestick
RB-Bur-Emp.

2063—Candle.
Not made in ebony.

2352—Candle.
Also made in orchid.
Not made in ebony.

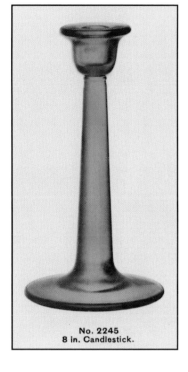

No. 2245
8 in. Candlestick.

No. 2653
Trindle Candlestick
Height 6¼ in. Spread 9 in.

No. 2652
Trindle Candlestick
Height 5-¾ in. Spread 9 in.

2430 9½-in. Candlestick
Ro-Az-Gr-Am-Eb-Crys-Tz
Priced on page 44

2470—5½ in. Candlestick
Solid Crystal
Gr-Am-Wis Base with Crys. Bowl
Crystal Base with Ro-Tz Bowl

2470½—5½ in. Candlestick
Ro-Gr-Am-Crys-Tz-Wis

2443—4 in. Candlestick
Ro-Az-Gr-Am-Eb-Crys-Tz

2481—5 in. Candlestick
Ro-Gr-Am-Eb-Crys-Tz

100

2425 2-in. Candlestick
Ro-Az-Gr-Am-Eb-Crys-Tz

2433 3-in. Candlestick
Solid Crystal
Gr-Am-Eb Base with Crys Bowl
Crys Base with Ro-Az-Tz-Wis Bowl

2563—4½ in. Viking Candlestick

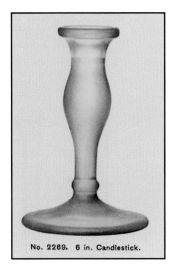

No. 2269. 6 in. Candlestick.

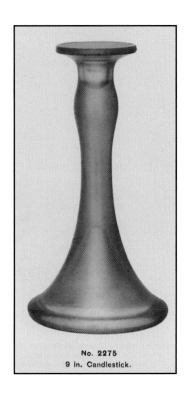

No. 2275
9 in. Candlestick.

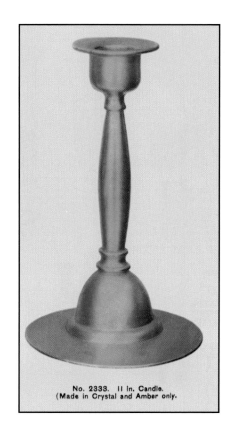

No. 2333. 11 in. Candle.
(Made in Crystal and Amber only.

2668
Hurricane Lamp, Complete
Height 11¾ in.
Consisting of:
1/12 Doz. 2668—Candlestick
1/12 Doz. 2668 Hurricane Lamp
Chimney

2667—6 in.
Candlestick

2668
Candlestick
Height 2½ in.

2667—2½ in.
Candlestick

6023
Duo Candlestick
Height 5½ in. Spread 6 in.

2324—4 in. Candlestick
Ro-Az-Gr-Am-Eb-Crys

2394—2 in. Candlestick
Ro-Az-Gr-Am-Crys-Tz-Wis

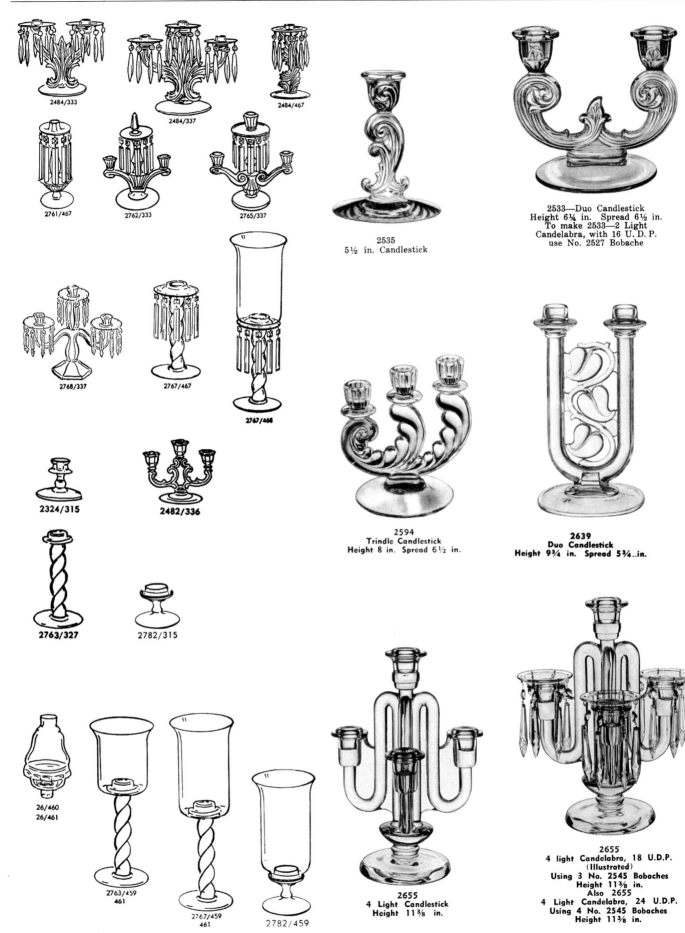

2484/333

2484/337

2484/467

2761/467

2762/333

2765/337

2535
5½ in. Candlestick

2533—Duo Candlestick
Height 6¼ in. Spread 6½ in.
To make 2533—2 Light
Candelabra, with 16 U. D. P.
use No. 2527 Bobache

2768/337

2767/467

2767/468

2324/315

2482/336

2594
Trindle Candlestick
Height 8 in. Spread 6½ in.

2639
Duo Candlestick
Height 9¾ in. Spread 5¾ in.

2763/327

2782/315

26/460
26/461

2763/459
461

2767/459
461

2782/459

2655
4 Light Candlestick
Height 11⅜ in.

2655
4 light Candelabra, 18 U.D.P.
(Illustrated)
Using 3 No. 2545 Bobaches
Height 11⅜ in.
Also 2655
4 Light Candelabra, 24 U.D.P.
Using 4 No. 2545 Bobaches
Height 11⅜ in.

PARTS

for Candlesticks, Candelabra, Lustres, and Candle Lamps

Most of the prisms used after 1924 were U Drop, Colonial Flat, or "B" prisms. The bobache was used plain as a candle drip, or wired for prisms on candelabra. Tear Drop prisms are shown in 1925 on the No. 5 Bobache, but no candlestick or lustre is listed using them until 1931 (the 2436 Lustre). More than likely the prisms were interchangeable as the 2436 Lustre is shown with U Drop Prisms after 1932. The 2545 Bobache was called 2545 when used with Flame, but when used to make the 2527 Candelabra, was called the 2527 Bobache.

4 Bobache, UDP (see p. 89); $50.00

5 Bobache, Cut, Tear Drop Prisms(see p. 89); $40.00

21 Candle Holder with Metal threaded peg to screw into candelabra candle arms; $36.00

21 Bobache, Wired, 4¹³⁄₁₆" outside; ⅞" inside; $25.00

26 Candle Lamp Base (see p. 91); $20.00

*26 Candle Lamp Base with peg (see p. 91); $25.00

26 Candle Lamp Chimney (see p. 91); $65.00

26 Candle Lamp Pot; $5.00

26 Ferrule (used to adapt); $10.00

26 Candle Lamp Shade (see p. 94); market

121 Bobache with U Drop prisms; $50.00

122 Bobache with U Drop prisms; $50.00

188 Bobache with U Drop prisms; $50.00

1640 Bobache, Wired, uses 6" Colonial Prisms, plain, cut, or etched; $50.00

1941 Bobache or Candle Drip; $15.00

2279 Candleholder/Bobache in Crystal (will fit any Fostoria candlestick, see p. 89 & 95); $15.00

2308 Bobache, Wired, Amber and Green, 1924-1926; $65.00

2311 Candleholder/Bobache/Lustre (see p. 89)
Amber, Green, and Crystal with 4" Colonial Prisms
Crystal, 1924; $75.00
Amber, 1924-1926; $85.00
Green, 1924-1926; $85.00

2482 Bobache wired for 8 prisms, 3⅞" outside; 1⅜" inside; $35.00

2482½ Candle Drip, 3¼"; $20.00

2484½ Candle Drip, Crystal or Silver Mist, 3½"; $20.00

2484 Bobache, wired for 8 UDP, 4¼" outside; 1⁷⁄₁₆" inside; $45.00

2527 Bobache and UDP or 2" "B" Prisms (same as 2545 Bobache); $45.00

2545 Bobache, UDP or B Prisms, $45.00

2546 Bobache, Square with 7 "B" Prisms (see p. 96); $75.00

2762 Bobache, wired for 8 UDP, 3¾" outside; 1⅛" inside; $60.00

2763 Candle Lamp Shade, 5"; $20.00

2765 Bobache, wired for 10 UDP, 4½" outside; 1¾" inside; $60.00

2767 Candle Lamp Shade, 9"; $30.00

2769 Bobache, wired for 10 Prisms, 4⅞" outside; 2¾" inside; $50.00

30 Spearhead Prism; $3.50

35 U Drop Prism (UDP); $2.50

40 Colonial or Flat Prisms (may be cut or etched); $6.00

"B" Prism, 2" (always more expensive than UDP); $4.00

Tear Drop Prism; $4.00

*With the pegged base, these can be used in any standard candlestick. In the early 1900s they were used on any or all candelabra.

No. 121 Bobache. Top View.   No. 188 Bobache. Top View.   No. 122 Bobache. Top View.

No. 121 Bobache.   No. 188 Bobache.   No. 122 Bobache.

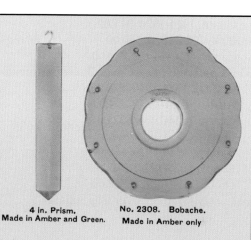

4 in. Prism. Made in Amber and Green.   No. 2308. Bobache. Made in Amber only

35/981   30/981   40/981   41/981   21/929   2482/132   2484/132   2765/132   2769/132

OUTSIDE DIA.   INSIDE DIA.

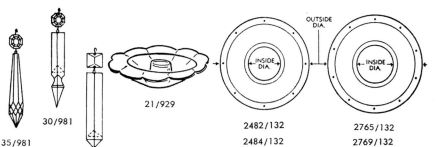

CANDY JARS and CANDY BOXES

Fostoria designers did not overlook the importance of providing attractive, useful containers for serving all kinds of goodies for the sweet tooth. The hostess was offered an array of shapes and colors from which to choose. In earlier years, Fostoria offered candy trays, and later bon bons and sweetmeats were offered with most major patterns. By 1924, these servers for sweets were called Candy Jars or Candy Boxes for the most part. The 2496 Baroque, and the 2331 three-part candy boxes were used extensively with cut, etched, and decorated patterns. Interestingly, the 2331 candy box was offered from 1924 through 1926 without the compartments. The 2456 candy jar blends very nicely with the Lafayette pattern. We did not find it listed in Topaz, but since we have one in the color, we assume that some were made.

The 2413 Urn and Cover was a puzzler at first because of the name. When we found the picture, and then, later, the actual piece, we could see that the top part is the 2380 Confection and Cover resting on a 2324 Candlestick. One wonders why it was not called the 2380½ Footed Confection and Cover. The 2394 Candy Jar and Cover was not listed in the ¼ lb. size. Finding one in Rose suggests that others may have been made.

Pieces from other lines such as American and Sonata may be found in the earlier volumes of this series. SO, LO, and RO refer to optics (spiral optic, loop optic, regular optic).

June 1924 Good Housekeeping

1229 Frisco (see Milkglass and Centennial II)
1372 Coin (see Coin Glass)
1904 Bon Bon and Cover, Pre 1924-1930; $65.00
2056 American (see American)
2136 Bon Bon and Cover, 5"
    Crystal, Pre 1924-1926; $35.00
    Amber, 1924-1925; $45.00
    Green, 1924-1926; $45.00
    Blue, 1925-1926; $55.00
    Canary, 1924-1926; $55.00
2219 Candy Jar, Footed, and Cover
    Crystal, 1924-1930; $35.00

    Amber, 1924-1929; $45.00
    Green, 1924-1929; $47.00
    Blue, 1925-1927; $54.00
    Canary, 1924-1926; $58.00
2250 Candy Jar and Cover , ¼, ½, and 1 pound sizes
    Crystal, 1924-1929; $35.00
    Amber, 1924-1930; $40.00
    Green, 1924-1930; $45.00
    Blue, 1925-1927; $50.00
    Canary, 1924-1926; $50.00
2328 Candy Box, 7" Oblong, and Cover
    Crystal, 1925; $34.00
    Amber, 1925; $40.00
    Green, 1925; $47.00
    Blue, 1925; $55.00
    Canary, 1925; $65.00
2331 Candy Box and Cover, no compartments
    Crystal, 1924-1926; $34.00
    Amber, 1924-1926; $40.00
    Green, 1924-1926; $45.00
    Blue, 1924-1926; $50.00
    Canary, 1924-1926; $60.00
2331-3 Candy Box and Cover, 3 compartments
    Crystal, 1924-1940; $28.00
    Amber, 1924-1937; $34.00
    Green, 1924-1934; $37.00
    Blue, 1925-1927; $45.00
    Canary, 1924-1926; $60.00
    Ebony, 1925-1928; $34.00
    Orchid, 1927-1928; $48.00
2364 Candy Jar and Cover (see Sonata)

Decorated ¼ lb. Candy Jar, Woodland ½ lb. Candy Jar, Blue 2250 1 lb. Candy Jar

2380 Confection and Cover, Plain or SO
    Crystal, 1925-1929, Plain; $34.00
    Amber, 1925-1930, Plain; $36.00
    Amber, 1928-1930, SO; $38.00
    Green, 1925-1930, Plain; $36.00
    Green, 1928-1930, SO; $35.00
    Blue, 1925-1927, Plain; $45.00
    Orchid, 1927-1928, Plain; $45.00
    Rose, 1928-1930, Plain or SO; $45.00
    Azure, 1928-1930, Plain; $45.00
2394 Candy Jar and Cover, ½ pound
    Crystal, 1929-1932; $42.00
    Amber, 1929-1933; $45.00
    Green, 1929-1934; $45.00
    Rose, 1929-1934; $45.00
    Azure, 1929-1934; $48.00
    Topaz, 1929-1932; $45.00
2395 Confection, Oval, and Cover
    Amber, 1929-1932; $48.00
    Green, 1929-1932; $50.00
    Rose, 1929-1932; $50.00
    Azure, 1929-1932; $54.00
    Topaz, 1929-1932; $50.00
2412 Colony (see Colony)
2413 Urn, Footed, and Cover
    Amber, 1929-1930; $58.00
    Green, 1929-1930; $62.00
    Rose, 1929-1930; $62.00
    Azure, 1929-1930; $65.00
2424 Kent (see Kent)
2430 Diadem (see Diadem)
2456 Candy Jar and Cover
    Crystal, 1933-1934; $55.00
    Amber, 1933-1934; $58.00
    Green, 1933-1934; $65.00
    Rose, 1933-1934; $65.00
    Ebony, 1933-1934; $58.00
2496 Baroque (see Baroque)
2510 Sunray (see Sunray)
2513 Grape Leaf (see Grape Leaf)
2545 Flame (see Flame)
2546 Quadrangle Candy Box and Cover
    Crystal, 1937-1942; $40.00
    Azure, 1937-1942; $48.00
    Gold Tint, 1937-1942; $48.00
2592 Myriad (see Myriad)
2616 Candy Box, Oval, and Cover, 1942-1943; $85.00
2630 Century (see Century)
2711 Diamond Sunburst (see Milk Glass)
2712 Berry (see Milk Glass)
2713 Vintage (see Milk Glass)
4095 Candy Jar and Cover, ½ pound (5" Nappy),
    pound (6" Nappy)
    Amber, 1926-1927, LO; $75.00
    Amber Foot, 1926-1927, LO; $70.00
    Green, 1926-1927, SO; $85.00

Amber (cutting unknown) and Orchid Grape 2331 three-part Candy and Cover

    Green Foot, 1926-1927, SO; $80.00
    Blue, 1926-1927, RO; $95.00
    Blue Foot, 1926-1927, RO; $90.00
4095½ Candy Jar and Cover, Tall, ½ pound
    Amber, 1926-1927, LO; $75.00
    Amber Foot, 1926-1927, LO; $70.00
    Green, 1926-1927, SO; $85.00
    Green Foot, 1926-1927, SO; $80.00
    Blue, 1926-1927, RO; $95.00
    Blue Foot, 1926-1927, RO; $90.00
4099 Candy Jar and Cover
    Crystal, 1934-1942; $64.00
    Regal Blue, 1934-1942; $125.00
    Burgundy, 1934-1942; $125.00
    Empire Green, 1934-1942; $125.00
4117 Bubble Candy Jar and Cover
    Crystal, 1934-1939; $60.00
    Ruby, 1934-1936; $95.00
    Regal Blue, 1934-1939; $87.00
    Burgundy, 1934-1936; $90.00
    Empire Green, 1934-1936; $90.00

Ruby American Footed Candy and Cover, Regal Blue 4099 Candy and Cover, American Candy and Cover, Empire Green 4099 Candy and Cover

5084 Candy Jar and Cover, RO
Crystal, 1926-1929; $72.00
Amber, 1926-1929; $85.00
Amber Foot, 1926-1927; $80.00
Green, 1926-1929; $90.00
Green Foot, 1926-1927; $85.00
Blue, 1926-1927; $125.00
Blue Foot, 1926-1927; $95.00

Rose ¼ lb. Candy and Cover, Topaz June 2394 ½ lb. Candy and Cover, Azure ½ lb. Candy and Cover

Blue 2328 Candy and Cover, Victory Etching Candy and Cover, Blue 2219 ½ lb. Candy and Cover,

Frisco Candy and Cover, Camelia Candy and Cover, Colony Candy and Cover, Aqua 2513 Vintage Candy Box, Sunray Candy and Cover

Gold Tint Quadrangle 2546 Candy and Cover, Green Minuet 2430 Candy and Cover, Baroque Candy and Cover, Topaz Legion 2456 Candy and Cover

Blue 2380 Confection and Cover, Plain and Spiral Optic, Azure 2545 Flame Candy and Cover, Azure 2413 Urn and Cover, 2395 Oval Confection

2510
½-lb. Candy Jar and Cover
Height 7¾ in.

4099
½ lb. Candy Jar and Cover
Height 6 in.

4117
½ lb. Bubble Candy Jar
and Cover
Height 5¼ in.

2513—½-lb. Candy Jar
and Cover
Height 6¼ in.

2546—Candy Box and Cover
Height 4 in.

4095—5 in. Nappy and Cover.
Spiral Optic.

2394 ½-lb. Candy Jar and Cover
Ro-Az-Gr-Am-Crys-Tz

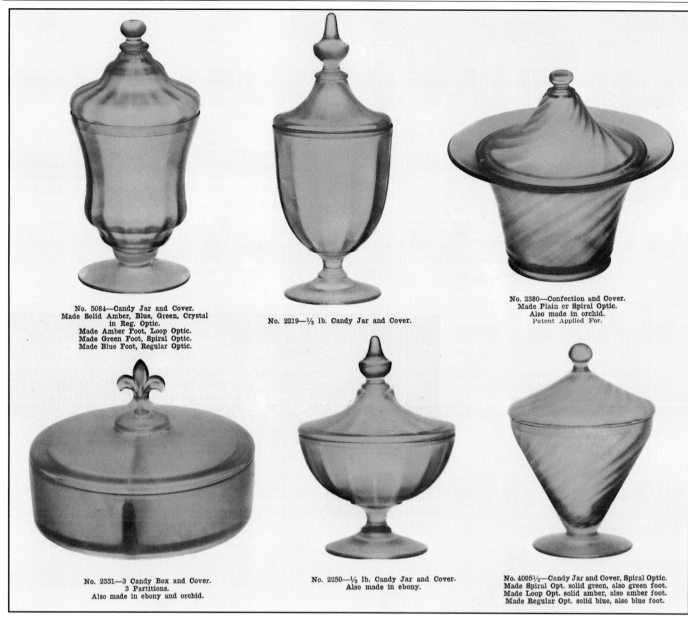

No. 5084—Candy Jar and Cover.
Made Solid Amber, Blue, Green, Crystal
in Reg. Optic.
Made Amber Foot, Loop Optic.
Made Green Foot, Spiral Optic.
Made Blue Foot, Regular Optic.

No. 2219—½ lb. Candy Jar and Cover.

No. 2380—Confection and Cover.
Made Plain or Spiral Optic.
Also made in orchid.
Patent Applied For.

No. 2331—3 Candy Box and Cover.
3 Partitions.
Also made in ebony and orchid.

No. 2250—½ lb. Candy Jar and Cover.
Also made in ebony.

No. 4095½—Candy Jar and Cover, Spiral Optic.
Made Spiral Opt. solid green, also green foot.
Made Loop Opt. solid amber, also amber foot.
Made Regular Opt. solid blue, also blue foot.

2395—Oval Confection and Cover.
Ro-Az-Gr-Am-Tz.

2413—Urn and Cover.
Ro-Az-Gr-Am.

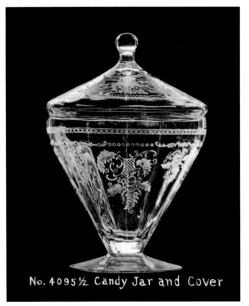

No. 4095½ Candy Jar and Cover

No. 2250-½ Lb. Candy Jar and Cover. No. 2250-¼ Lb. Candy Jar and Cover.

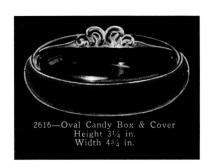

2616—Oval Candy Box & Cover
Height 3¼ in.
Width 4¾ in.

1934 House and Garden

2496—3 Part Candy Box and Cover
Height 2½ in.—Width 6¼ in.

2430—½ Lb. Candy Jar
and Cover
Ro-Az-Gr-Am-Eb-Crys-Tz

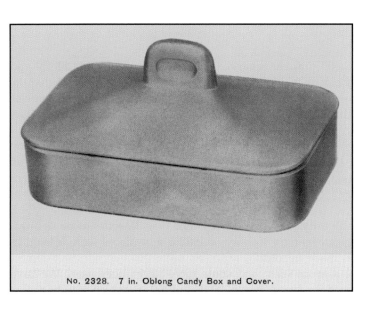

No. 2328. 7 in. Oblong Candy Box and Cover.

2456—½ Lb. Candy Jar and Cover
Ro-Gr-Am-Eb-Crys

CARVINGS

2501 Rosette, Intaglio Carving

Waterfowl, Carving 1

Ski, Carving 2

Colonial, Carving 5

Aztec, Carving 6

Carnival, Carving 7

Yachting, Carving 8

Skater, Carving 9

Stallion, Carving 10

King George, Carving 11

Morning Glory, Carving 12

Brocade, Carving 13

Stars, Carving 14

Nineteenth Hole, Carving 15

Hollyhock, Carving 16

Narcissus, Carving 17

Tiger Lily, Carving 18

Lily of the Valley, Carving 19

Hunt, Carving 34

Oil and Vinegar, Carving 38

Cornucopia, Carving 46

Stars and Bars, Carving 47

Orchid, Carving 48

Dog Show, Carving 49

Toy, Decoration 620

Nightmare, Decoration 621

Carved Decorative Group

Carved Smoking Accessories

Special Carvings

Between 1938 and 1943 the Fostoria Glass Company produced numerous carved designs on crystal glass. Floral and animal themes seemed to be the most popular, with sports and nature well represented. It was during this period that the Eagle Bookends were made with carved stars on the base. Smoker items received a lot of attention. The Kent pattern was used for many of the designs doubtless because it was heavy, thick crystal with plain surface. Fostoria made a special line of heavy vases for carvings.

The carved design was achieved by directing a small stream of sand particles, under high pressure from a compressor, onto the design. The sand acted as an abrasive cutting away the glass to the desired depth, sometimes as much as an eighth of an inch. Heavy glass blanks were needed to accommodate the depth of these designs. An excellent description of the carving process may be found in *Fostoria Factories* by Henry J. Liebmann, available from the Fostoria Glass Society of America, P.O. Box 826, Moundsville, West Virginia, 26041.

The Morning Glory pattern is seen most often as it was the only carved pattern, other than Rosette, to be re-introduced after the War. Several pieces were made 1953 – 1957. From January to May of 1982 a few pieces were offered in Crystal and Blue as Giftware. These were the only carved pieces made in color.

Pricing at this point is difficult. Most of the carvings are seldom seen, and some have never been seen. We have observed some of the larger vases with the special carvings priced for as much as $200.00 to $250.00, which may be realistic for these unique designs. Now that more information is available, interest may be sparked in this short-lived category of Fostoria designs.

2501 ROSETTE
Intaglio Carving
1970 – 1972

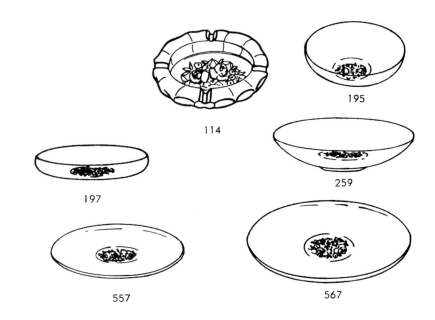

114

195

197

259

557

567

The earlier offering of Rosette (see *Fostoria Tableware: 1924 – 1943*, pages 97 and 98) borrowed pieces from the pressed patterns of that time. The same is true for this reintroduction of the line which used pieces from the 2364 Sonata line. Oddly enough, the earlier pieces are seen more often than these later ones.

2364/195 Bowl, 9" Salad; $35.00
2364/197 Bowl, 9" Lily Pond; $35.00
2364/259 Bowl, 13" Fruit; $50.00
2364/557 Plate, 11" Sandwich; $40.00
2364/567 Plate, 14" Torte; $55.00
2371/114 Ash Tray, 7½" Round; $28.00

WATERFOWL
Carving 1
1938 – 1943

2550 Ash Tray, Round, Swan; $18.00
2391 Cigarette Box and Cover, Swan; $42.00
4132 Decanter, Gull; $95.00
4132 Ice Bowl, Goose; $64.00
2337 Plate, 7", Swan; $12.00
4132 Tumbler, 1½ oz. Whiskey, Gull; $18.00
4132 Tumbler, Old Fashioned Cocktail, Goose; $18.00
4132 Tumbler, 5 oz., Duck; $18.00
4132 Tumbler, 9 oz., Swan; $18.00
4132½ Tumbler, 9 oz. Scotch and Soda, Duck; $18.00
4132 Tumbler, 12 oz., Crane; $22.00
4132 Tumbler, 14 oz., Crane; $22.00

SKI
Carving 2
1938 – 1943

2550 Ash Tray, Round; $18.00
2391 Cigarette Box and Cover; $42.00
4132 Decanter; $95.00
4132 Ice Bowl; $64.00
2337 Plate, 7"; $12.00
4139 Tumbler, Whiskey; $18.00
4139 Tumbler, Old Fashioned Cocktail; $18.00
4139 Tumbler, 5 oz.; $18.00
4139 Tumbler, 9 oz. Water; $18.00
4139 Tumbler, 10 oz.; $20.00
4139 Tumbler, 12 oz.; $20.00
4139 Tumbler, 14 oz.; $22.00
4139 Tumbler, 16 oz.; $22.00

4132—14 oz. Tumbler, Sham
Height 5⅜ in.
4132—12 oz. Tumbler, Sham
Height 4⅞ in.

4132½—9 oz. Scotch &
Soda, Sham
Height 4⅝ in.

4132—9 oz.
Tumbler, Sham
Height 3¾ in.

4132—5 oz.
Tumbler, Sham
Height 3⅝ in.

2550—Round Ash Tray
Diameter 3¼ in.

4132—7½ oz.
Old Fashioned Cocktail, Sham
Height 3⅛ in.

4132—Decanter and Stopper
Capacity 24 oz.
Height 9¾ in.

4132—Ice Bowl
Height 4¾ in.

2391—Large Cigarette and Cover
Length 4¾ in.—Width 3½ in.

4132—1½ oz.
Whiskey, Sham
Height 2⅛ in.

SKI DESIGN
CARVING No. 2

4139—9 oz.
Water Tumbler, Sham
Height 3½ in.

4139—7 oz.
Old Fashioned
Cocktail, Sham
Height 2¾ in.

4139—1¾ oz.
Whiskey, Sham
Height 1⅞ in.

4139—16 oz. Tumbler, Sham
Height 5⅜ in.
4139—14 oz. Tumbler, Sham
Height 6¼ in.
4139—12 oz. Tumbler, Sham
Height 5⅝ in.

4139—10 oz.
Tumbler, Sham
Height 5¼ in.
4139—5 oz.
Tumbler, Sham
Height 4 in.

2550—Round Ash Tray
Diameter 3¼ in.

4132—Decanter and Stopper
Capacity 24 oz.
Height 9¾ in.

2391—Large Cigarette and Cover
Length 4¾ in.—Width 3½ in.

4132—Ice Bowl
Height 4¾ in.

COLONIAL

Carving 5

1938 – 1943

26/1 Candle Lamp, Complete; $50.00

AZTEC

Carving 6

1938 – 1942

1895½ Vase, 10"; $125.00

CARNIVAL

Carving 7

1938 – 1943

4128½ Vase, 5"; $55.00

YACHTING

Carving 8

1938 – 1943

4132½ Vase, 8"; $75.00

SKATER

Carving 9

1938 – 1943

4132½ Vase, 8"; $85.00

STALLION

Carving 10

1938 – 1943

2567 Vase, 7½"; $75.00

Colonial Design
Carving No. 5
26/1 Candle Lamp
with 2545—2 in. "Flame" Candlestick
Height 7 in.

Aztec Design
Carving No. 6
1895½—10 in. Vase

Carnival Design
Carving No. 7
4128½—5 in. Vase

Yachting Design
Carving No. 8
4132½—8 in. Vase

Skater Design
Carving No. 9
4132½—8 in. Vase

Stallion Design
Carving No. 10
2567—7½ in. Vase

KING GEORGE

Carving 11

2424 Plate, 12", 1939 – 1940; $135.00

In 1939 Fostoria offered a 12" plate from the Kent pattern with the King George Carving. This plate was to commemorate the visit of King George and Queen Elizabeth of England to the United States in the summer of 1939. On every other panel around the plate were carved emblems representing England, Ireland, Wales, and Scotland. The center of the plate has a carving of the King and Queen. The words on the the ribbon say "June 1939 George VI and Elizabeth, United States Visit." It was made through 1940.

MORNING GLORY

Carving 12

1939 – 1943 (All pieces)

Reintroduced in 1953 – 1957 as indicated with an asterisk (*). See also Morning Glory, *Fostoria Tableware: 1944 – 1986,* for pieces offered in Blue.

*2427 Ash Tray, Oblong; $10.00
*2516 Ash Tray; $14.00
*2518 Ash Tray, 4" Square; $14.00
*2518 Ash Tray, 4½" Oblong; $15.00
315 Bowl, 7"; $24.00
315 Bowl, 9"; $30.00
*2364 Bowl, 9" Salad; $30.00
*2364 Bowl, 10½" Salad; $45.00
6023 Bowl, Footed; $65.00
2596 Bowl, 11" Oblong Shallow; $95.00
*2364 Bowl, 12" Flared; $52.00
*2364 Bowl, 12" Lily Pond; $52.00
*2364 Bowl, 13" Fruit; $60.00
*2596 Candlestick, 5½" (Pair); $80
*2324 Candlestick, 6" (Pair); $80.00
*6023 Candlestick, Duo (Pair); $95.00
2427 Cigarette Box and Cover; $68.00
*2618 Cigarette Box and Cover; $57.00
*2364 Cheese and Cracker; $70.00
4132 Ice Bowl; $50.00
*2364 Mayonnaise, Plate, Ladle; $65.00
*2337 Plate, 7"; $12.00
*2337 Plate, 8"; $12.00
2419 Plate, Cake; $50.00
*2364 Plate, 11" Sandwich; $50.00
*2364 Plate, 14" Torte; $65.00
*2364 Plate, 16" Torte; $65.00
*2364 Salad Set, 9", 4 pieces, $95.00
*2364 Salad Set, 10½"; $110.00
*2364 Tray, Handled Lunch; $55.00
4128½ Vase, 5"; $55.00

Morning Glory Lily Pond and 6023 Duo Candlesticks

2577 Vase, 5½" Wide; $65.00
2577 Vase, 6"; $65.00
2577 Vase, 8½"; $75.00
2577 Vase 15"; $125.00
2619½ Vase, 6", Ground Bottom; $65.00
2619½ Vase, 7½", Ground Bottom; $75.00
2619½ Vase, 9½" , Ground Bottom; $85.00
4143½ Vase, 6" Footed; $65.00
4143½ Vase, 7½" Footed; $75.00
4132½ Vase, 8"; $80.00
5100 Vase, 10"; $95.00
4126½ Vase, 11"; $110.00
2612 Vase, 13"; $125.00
2591 Vase, 15"; $150.00

2618—4½ in. Oblong Ash Tray

2618—4 in. Square Ash Tray

2364—Mayonnaise & Plate & Ladle
Mayo. Height 2½ in.
Mayo. Diameter 5 in.
Plate, Diameter 6¾ in.

2619½—6 in. Vase, Ground Bottom
2619½—7½ in. Vase, Ground Bottom
2619½—9½ in. Vase, Ground Bottom

2618—Cigarette Box & Cover
Length 5½ in.
Width 4¼ in.
Height 1½ in.
Cigarette Capacity 40

2596—11 in. Oblong Bowl
Height 2 in.

2596—5½ in. Candlestick

2364—Cheese & Cracker
Height 3¼ in.
Cheese Diameter 5¾ in.   Height 2⅞ in.
Plate Diameter 11¼ in.

2577—15 in. Vase

2364—Handled Lunch Tray
Diameter 11¼ in.

2612—13 in. Vase

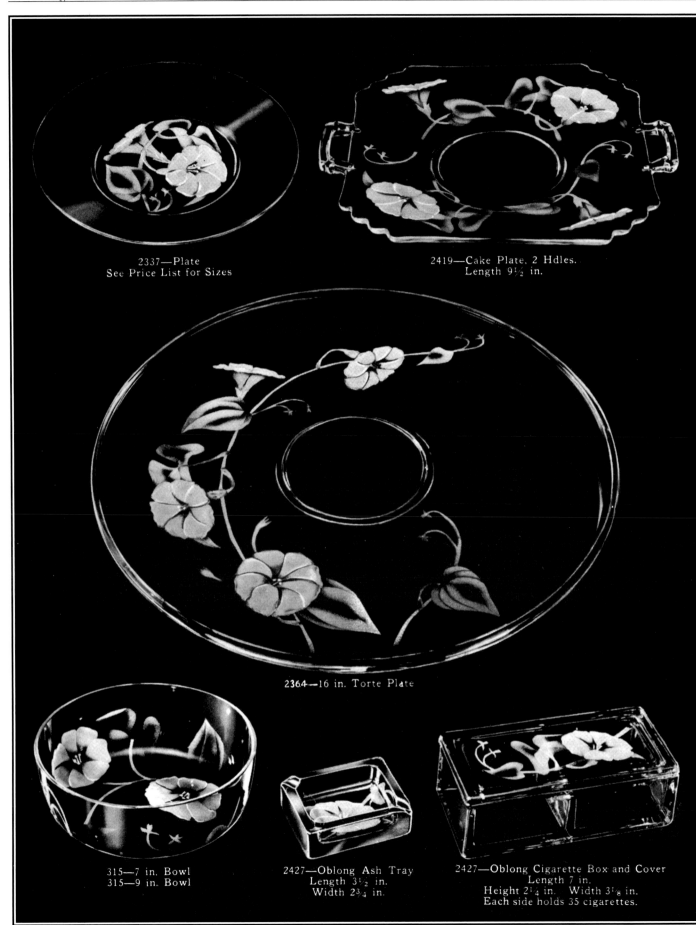

2337—Plate
See Price List for Sizes

2419—Cake Plate, 2 Hdles.
Length 9½ in.

2364—16 in. Torte Plate

315—7 in. Bowl
315—9 in. Bowl

2427—Oblong Ash Tray
Length 3½ in.
Width 2¾ in.

2427—Oblong Cigarette Box and Cover
Length 7 in.
Height 2¼ in.   Width 3⅛ in.
Each side holds 35 cigarettes.

2324—6 in. Candlestick

6023—Footed Bowl
Diameter 9¼ in.
Height 4¼ in.

4132—Ice Bowl
Height 4¾ in.
Top Diameter 6 in.

4132½—8 in. Vase, Heavy

4128½—5 in. Vase, Heavy

5100—10 in. Vase

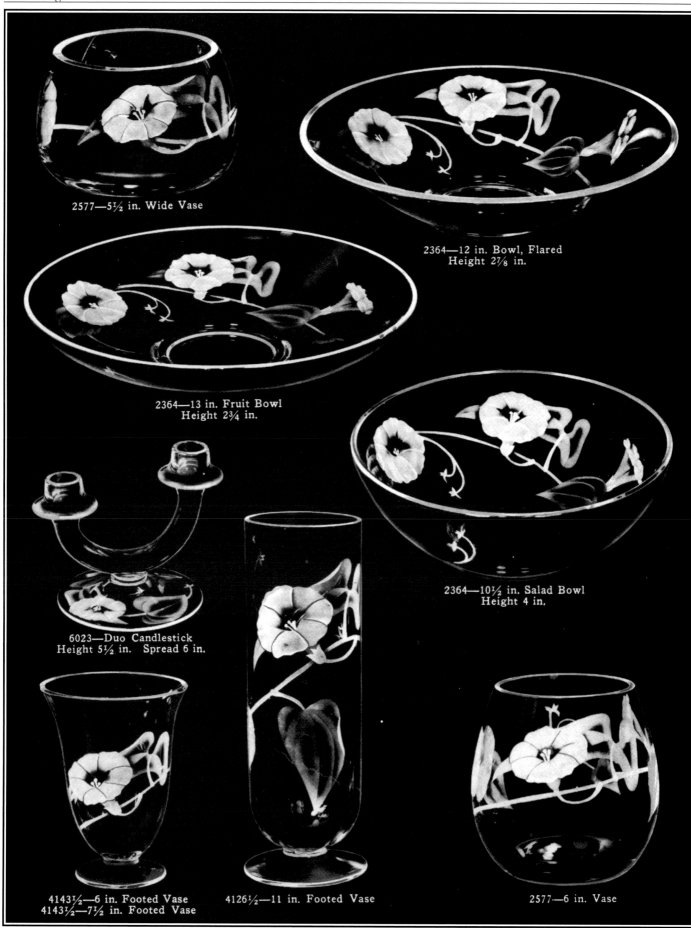

2577—5½ in. Wide Vase

2364—12 in. Bowl, Flared
Height 2⅞ in.

2364—13 in. Fruit Bowl
Height 2¾ in.

2364—10½ in. Salad Bowl
Height 4 in.

6023—Duo Candlestick
Height 5½ in.   Spread 6 in.

4143½—6 in. Footed Vase
4143½—7½ in. Footed Vase

4126½—11 in. Footed Vase

2577—6 in. Vase

2364—12 in. Lily Pond
Height 2¼ in.

2516
Ash Tray

2364—9 in
3 Piece Salad Set (Illustrated)
Consisting of:
1/12 Doz. 2364—9 in.
Salad Bowl Ht. 2⅝ in.
1/12 Doz. 2364—11 in.
Sandwich Plate
1/12 Doz. 2364
Salad Fork and Spoon (Wood)

2364—10½ in.
3 Piece Salad Set
Consisting of:
1/12 Doz. 2364—10½ in.
Salad Bowl Ht. 4 in.
1/12 Doz. 2364—14 in.
Torte Plate
1/12 Doz. 2364
Salad Fork and Spoon (Wood)

2591—15 in. Vase

2577—8½ in. Vase

2083—Salad Dressing Bottle
Marked Oil and Vinegar
Carving 38

STARS

Carving 14

1940 – 1943

2518 Eagle Bookend (Pair); $250.00

BROCADE

Carving 13

1939 – 1943

Brocade Candy Jar and Cover

All pieces are shown with the Kent pattern,
Fostoria Tableware: 1924 – 1943, pages 65 – 67.

2424 Ash Tray; $20.00
2516 Ash Tray; $20.00
2424 Bowl, 8" Regular; $35.00
2424 Bowl, 9½" Flared; $45.00
2424 Bowl, 11½" Fruit; $68.00
2424 Candlestick, 3½" (Pair); $65.00
2424 Candlestick, Duo (Pair); $85.00
2424 Candy Jar and Cover; $85.00
2424 Cigarette Box and Cover; $85.00

2424 Comport, 5"; $50.00
2424 Comport and Cover, 5"; $65.00
2424 Mayonnaise, Plate, Ladle; $65.00
2424 Plate, 12"; $50.00
2424 Sweetmeat; $35.00
2424 Vase, 5" Footed Urn, Flared; $55.00
2424 Vase, 5 ½" Footed Urn, Regular; $60.00
2424 Vase, 6½" Footed Urn, Flared; $65.00
2424 Vase, 7½" Footed Urn, Regular; $75.00

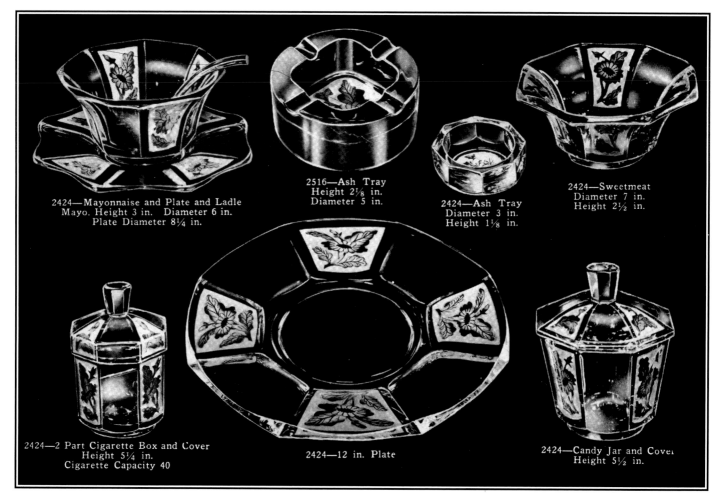

2424—Mayonnaise and Plate and Ladle
Mayo. Height 3 in. Diameter 6 in.
Plate Diameter 8¼ in.

2516—Ash Tray
Height 2⅛ in.
Diameter 5 in.

2424—Ash Tray
Diameter 3 in.
Height 1⅛ in.

2424—Sweetmeat
Diameter 7 in.
Height 2½ in.

2424—2 Part Cigarette Box and Cover
Height 5¼ in.
Cigarette Capacity 40

2424—12 in. Plate

2424—Candy Jar and Cover
Height 5½ in.

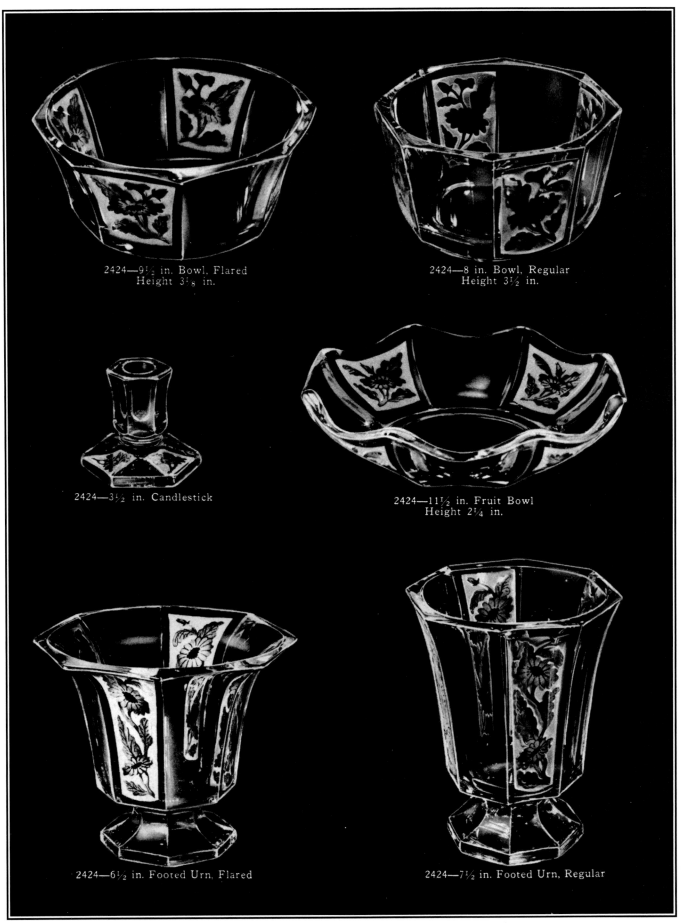

2424—9½ in. Bowl, Flared
Height 3⅛ in.

2424—8 in. Bowl, Regular
Height 3½ in.

2424—3½ in. Candlestick

2424—11½ in. Fruit Bowl
Height 2¼ in.

2424—6½ in. Footed Urn, Flared

2424—7½ in. Footed Urn, Regular

NINETEENTH HOLE

Carving 15

1940 – 1943

2419 Ash Tray, Approaching; $18.00
2427 Ash Tray, Putting; $18.00
2391 Cigarette Box and Cover, Driving; $45.00
4132 Decanter, Driving; $95.00
4132 Ice Bowl, Putting; $65.00

4132 Tumbler, Whiskey, Approaching; $18.00
4132 Tumbler, Old Fashioned Cocktail, Putting; $18.00
4132 Tumbler, 5 oz. Exploding; $20.00
4132½ Tumbler, 9 oz. Scotch and Soda, Exploding; $22.00
4132 Tumbler, 12 oz., Driving; $24.00

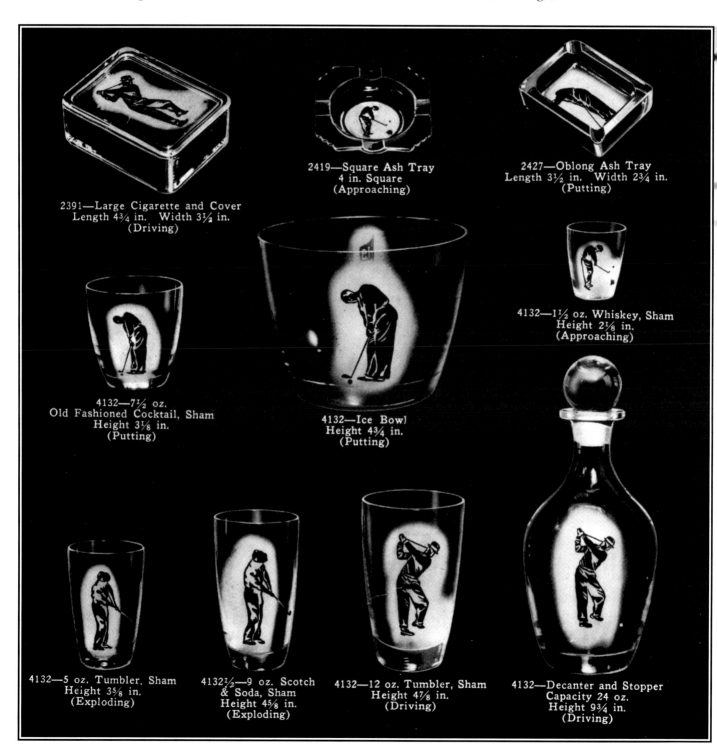

2391—Large Cigarette and Cover
Length 4¾ in.   Width 3½ in.
(Driving)

2419—Square Ash Tray
4 in. Square
(Approaching)

2427—Oblong Ash Tray
Length 3½ in.   Width 2¾ in.
(Putting)

4132—7½ oz.
Old Fashioned Cocktail, Sham
Height 3⅛ in.
(Putting)

4132—Ice Bowl
Height 4¾ in.
(Putting)

4132—1½ oz. Whiskey, Sham
Height 2⅛ in.
(Approaching)

4132—5 oz. Tumbler, Sham
Height 3⅝ in.
(Exploding)

4132½—9 oz. Scotch
& Soda, Sham
Height 4⅝ in.
(Exploding)

4132—12 oz. Tumbler, Sham
Height 4⅞ in.
(Driving)

4132—Decanter and Stopper
Capacity 24 oz.
Height 9¾ in.
(Driving)

HOLLYHOCK

Carving 16

1940 – 1943

1895½ Vase, 10"; $110.00
5100 Vase, 10"; $110.00
4126½ Vase, 11"; $125.00

4126½—11 in. Vase   5100—10 in. Vase   1895½—10 in. Vase

4126½—11 in. Vase   4143½—6 in. Footed Vase   2577—6 in. Vase
                      4143½—7½ in. Footed Vase

NARCISSUS

Carving 17

1940 – 1943

2577 Vase, 6"; $75.00
4143½ Vase, 6"; $75.00
4143½ Vase, 7½"; $85.00
4126½ Vase, 11"; $125.00

TIGER LILY

Carving 18

1940 – 1943

4132 Vase, 5"; $65.00
2577 Vase, 5½" Wide; $70.00
2577 Vase, 6"; $75.00

4132—5 in. Vase   2577—6 in. Vase   2577—5½ in. Wide Vase
(Ice Bowl)

LILY OF THE VALLEY

Carving 19

1940 – 1943

4143½ Vase, 6" Footed; $85.00
4143½ Vase, 7½" Footed; $95.00
4132½ Vase, 8"; $110.00
2568 Vase, 9" Footed; $125.00

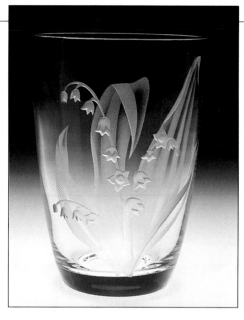

Lily of the Valley 4132½ Vase

HUNT

Carving 34

1940 – 1943

4146 Cordial, 1 oz.; $18.00
4146 Cocktail, 4 oz.; $18.00
4146 Scotch and Soda, 9 oz.; $20.00
4146 Above Set, Nested; $56.00

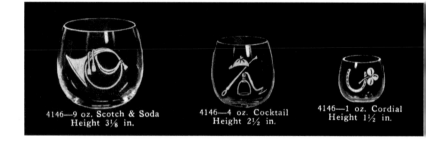

OIL AND VINEGAR

Carving 38

1940 – 1943
See Morning Glory Carving for Catalog picture, p. 119.

2083 Salad Dressing Bottle
Price depends on color and pattern.
See Salad Dressing Bottles, p. 178.

Garland Salad Dressing Bottle

ORCHID

Carving 48

This pattern was made from 1941 to 1943 and is featured in *Fostoria Stemware*, page 40. Since this is the only stemware pattern that was carved, the authors could not resist the temptation to include the original catalog page.

892—11 oz. Goblet
Height 6½ in.

892—7 oz. Saucer
Champagne
Height 5⅛ in.

892—6½ oz. Low Sherbet
Height 4 in.

892—4 oz. Cocktail
Height 4½ in.

892—4 oz. Claret
Height 4⅞ in.

892—3 oz. Wine
Height 4¾ in.

892—5 oz. Footed Tumbler
Height 3⅞ in.

892—12 oz. Footed Tumbler
Height 5½ in.

892—4½ oz. Oyster Cocktail
Height 2⅞ in.

2337—Plate
See Price List for Sizes

1769—Finger Bowl
Height 2 in.
Diameter 4⅛ in.

CORNUCOPIA

Carving 46

1941 – 1943

2364 Bowl, 12" Lily Pond; $75.00
2364 Bowl, 13" Fruit; $75.00
6023 Candlestick, Duo (Pair); $95.00

2364 Plate, 14" Torte; $85.00
2364 Plate, 16" Torte; $85.00
2577 Vase, 8½"; $125.00

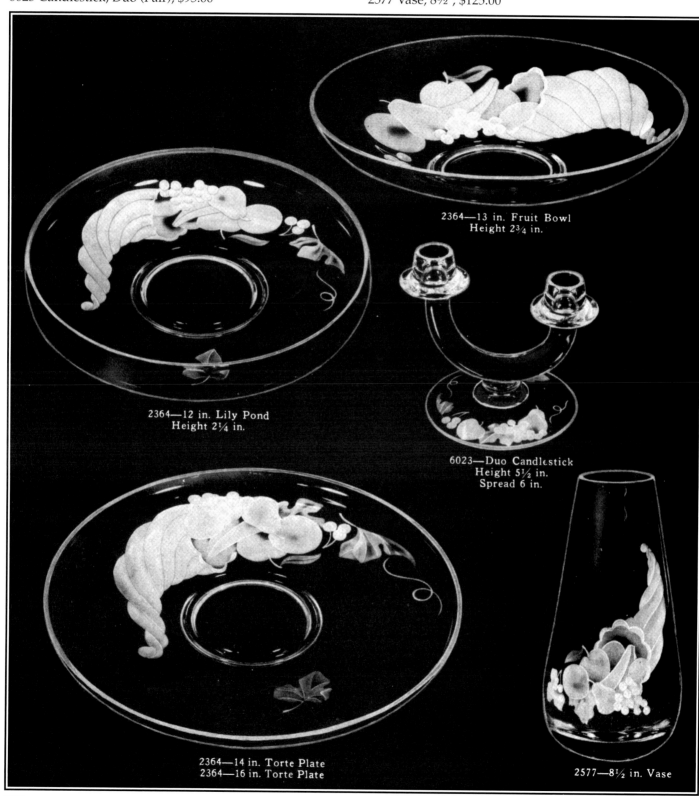

2364—13 in. Fruit Bowl
Height 2¾ in.

2364—12 in. Lily Pond
Height 2¼ in.

6023—Duo Candlestick
Height 5½ in.
Spread 6 in.

2364—14 in. Torte Plate
2364—16 in. Torte Plate

2577—8½ in. Vase

Stars and Bars Ash Tray

STARS AND BARS

Carving 47

1940 – 1943

2596 Ash Tray, 4" Square; $25.00
2596 Bowl, 11" Oblong, Shallow; $95.00
2596 Candlestick, 5" (Pair); $95.00
2596 Cigarette Box and Cover; $65.00
2596 Bowl, 7½" Square; $75.00

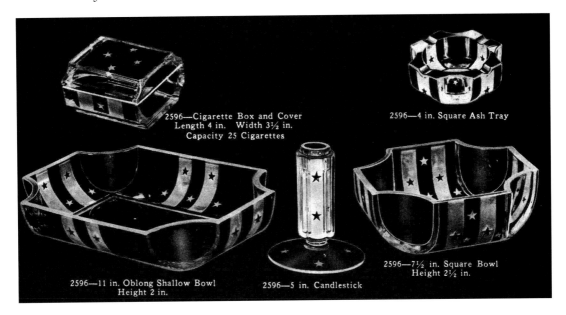

2596—Cigarette Box and Cover
Length 4 in.   Width 3½ in.
Capacity 25 Cigarettes

2596—4 in. Square Ash Tray

2596—11 in. Oblong Shallow Bowl
Height 2 in.

2596—5 in. Candlestick

2596—7½ in. Square Bowl
Height 2½ in.

DOG SHOW

Carving 49

1940 – 1943

2427 Ash Tray, Oblong; $18.00
4132 Decanter; $95.00
4139 Tumbler, 1¾ oz. Whiskey; $18.00
4139 Tumbler, 5 oz.; $18.00
4139 Tumbler, 7 oz. Old Fashioned Cocktail; $20.00
4139 Tumbler, 10 oz.; $20.00
4139 Tumbler, 12 oz.; $22.00
4139 Tumbler, 14 oz.; $22.00

TOY

Carving 33, Decoration 620

Enamel decoration on Carving 33
1940 – 1943

4146 Scotch and Soda, 9 oz.; $25.00-$35.00
4146 Cocktail, 4 oz.; $15.00-$25.00
4146 Cordial, 1 oz.; $20.00-$30.00
4146 Set, 3 piece nested
2306 Smoker Set, 4 piece:
2306 Ash Tray, 2¾"; $15.00
2306 Ash Tray, 3"; $17.50
2306 Ash Tray, 3½"; $20.00
2306 Ash Tray, 4"; $25.00

4146—9 oz. Scotch & Soda Height 3⅛ in.
4146—4 oz. Cocktail Height 2½ in.
4146—1 oz. Cordial Height 1½ in.
2306—2¾ in. Ash Tray
2306—4 in. Ash Tray
2306—3½ in. Ash Tray
2306—3 in. Ash Tray

4146—9 oz. Scotch & Soda Height 3⅛ in.
4146—4 oz. Cocktail Height 2½ in.
4146—1 oz. Cordial Height 1½ in.
2306—2¾ in. Ash Tray
2306—4 in. Ash Tray
2306—3½ in. Ash Tray
2306—3 in. Ash Tray

NIGHTMARE

Carving 39, Decoration 621

Enamel decoration on Carving 39
1940 – 1943

4146 Scotch and Soda, 9 oz.; $25.00-$35.00
4146 Cocktail, 4 oz.; $15.00-$25.00
4146 Cordial, 1 oz.; $20.00-$30.00
4146 Set, 3 piece nested
2306 Smoker Set, 4 piece:
2306 Ash Tray, 2¾"$15.00
2306 Ash Tray, 3"; $17.50
2306 Ash Tray, 3½"; $20.00
2306 Ash Tray, 4"; $25.00

CARVED DECORATIVE GROUP

ARCHER

Carving 24

1940 – 1942

315 Bowl, 9"; $45.00

GREYHOUNDS

Carving 25

1940 – 1943

2577 Vase, 5½" Wide; $65.00

THREE GEESE

Carving 26

1940 – 1943

4132½ Vase, 8"; $85.00

DOLPHIN

Carving 27

1940 – 1943

2577 Vase, 8½"; $110.00

BUBBLE BABY

Carving 28

1940 – 1943

4116½ Vase, 5" Ball; $65.00

4116½—5 in. Ball
Bubble Baby Carving 28

2577—5½ in. Wide Vase
Greyhounds Carving 25

315—9 in. Bowl
Archer Carving 24

2577—8½ in. Vase
Dolphin Carving 27

4132½—8 in. Vase
Three Geese Carving 26

CARVED SMOKING ACCESSORIES

LYRE
Carving 30
1940 – 1943
2427 Ash Tray, Oblong; $18.00
2427 Cigarette Box and Cover; $70.00

HORSE
Carving 35
1940 – 1943
4148 Ash Tray, 2½" Individual; $18.00
4148 Cigarette Holder; $30.00

ELEPHANT
Carving 36
1940 – 1943
4148 Ash Tray, 2½" Individual; $18.00
4148 Cigarette Holder; $30.00

ROOSTER
Carving 37
1940 – 1943
4148 Ash Tray, 2½" Individual; $18.00
4148 Cigarette Holder; $30.00

THOROUGHBRED
Carving 40
1940 – 1943
2516 Ash Tray; $20.00

CHANTICLEER
Carving 41
1940 – 1943
2516 Ash Tray; $20.00

SNOW CRYSTAL
Carving 42
1940 – 1943
2427 Ash Tray, Oblong; $18.00
2427 Cigarette Box and Cover, Oblong; $55.00

GROS POINT
Carving 43
1940 – 1943
2427 Ash Tray, Oblong; $18.00
2427 Cigarette Box and Cover, Oblong, $55.00

4148—2½ in.
Ind. Ash Tray, Blown
Horse Carving 35

4148—2½ in.
Ind. Ash Tray, Blown
Elephant Carving 36

4148—2½ in.
Ind. Ash Tray, Blown
Rooster Carving 37

4148—2¼ in.
Cigarette Holder
Blown
Horse Carving 35
Top Diameter 2 in.

4148—2¼ in.
Cigarette Holder
Blown
Elephant Carving 36
Top Diameter 2 in.

4148—2¼ in.
Cigarette Holder
Blown
Rooster Carving 37
Top Diameter 2 in.

2427—Oblong Ash Tray
Snow Crystal Carving 42
Length 3½ in.   Width 2¾ in.

2427—Oblong Cigarette Box and Cover
Gros Point Carving 43
Length 7 in.
Height 2¼ in.   Width 3⅛ in.
Each side holds 35 Cigarettes

2427—Oblong Cigarette Box and Cover
Snow Crystal Carving 42
Length 7 in.
Height 2¼ in.   Width 3⅛ in.
Each side holds 35 Cigarettes

2427—Oblong Ash Tray
Gros Point Carving 43
Length 3½ in.   Width 2¾ in.

2516—Ash Tray
Chanticleer Carving 41
Height 2¼ in.   Diameter 5 in.

2516—Ash Tray
Thoroughbred Carving 40
Height 2⅛ in.   Diameter 5 in.

2427—Oblong Cigarette Box and Cover
Lyre Carving 30
Length 7 in.   Height 2¼ in.
Width 3⅛ in.
Each side holds 35 Cigarettes

2427—Oblong Ash Tray
Lyre Carving 30
Length 3½ in.
Width 2¾ in.

SPECIAL CARVINGS

POLAR BEAR
Carving 29
1941 – 1943
2577 Vase, 6"; $95.00

HERON
Carving 31
1941 – 1943
2591 Vase, 15"; $225.00

SPREAD EAGLE
Carving 32
1941 – 1943
4143½ Vase, 6"; $125.00
4143½ Vase, 7½"; $145.00

USA MAP
Carving 44
1941 – 1943
2577 Vase, 6"; $125.00

BANNER
Carving 45
1941 – 1943
2577 Vase, 8½"; $175.00

2577—6 in. Vase
Polar Bear Carving 29

2577—6 in. Vase
U.S.A. Map Carving 44

4143½—6 in. Footed Vase
4143½—7½ in. Footed Vase
Spread Eagle Carving 32

2591—15 in. Vase
Heron Carving 31

2577—8½ in. Vase
Banner Carving 45

CHRISTMAS NATIVITY

The Holy Family was the first in a series of three sculptures depicting the Nativity. Each sculpture is signed, dated, numbered, and gift boxed as shown. Limited to 3,000 for each edition, these are of extremely fine crystal and weigh several pounds each. Each edition originally sold for $125.00.

The Holy Family, First Edition, 1979; $250.00
The Magi, Second Edition, 1980; $250.00
The Shepherds, Third Edition, 1981; $250.00

*The three pieces comprising
the Christmas Nativity*

CHRISTMAS ORNAMENTS

Christmas Tree, 1976; $15.00
Snowflake, 1976; $15.00
True Holly, 1976; $15.00
Wreath, 1976; $15.00
Bells, 1978; $15.00
Partridge, Crystal Mist, 1978; $18.00
Sphere, 1978; $15.00
Turtle Doves, Crystal Mist, 1978; $18.00

*Wreath, Christmas Tree,
and Bells Ornaments*

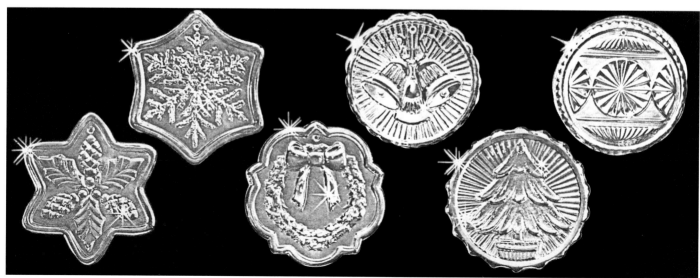

CLOCK SETS

These are the only clock sets Fostoria made. Production had a short run so these sets are seldom seen. The 2298 style may be found with several decorations. The 2299 candlesticks have an oval base and were found listed with Decorations 52, 53, and 57; however, the 2299 clock was not found listed with any decoration. Even though most of the clocks no longer work, these sets remain popular with collectors.

2298 Clock Set, St. Clair, Clock and two 3½"
Candlesticks
Blue, 1925-1927; $275.00
Amber, 1925-1927; $235.00
Green, 1925-1927; $250.00
Canary, 1925-1926; $325.00
Ebony, 1925-1927; $235.00

2298 Ebony Clock Set with Decoration 57, Waveland; Amber

2299 Clock Set, St. Alexis, Clock and two 5"
Candlesticks, oval base
Blue, 1925-1927; $350.00
Amber, 1925-1927; $300.00
Green, 1925-1927; $300.00
Canary, 1925-1926; $450.00
Ebony, 1925-1927; $300.00

2299 Clock Set in Canary

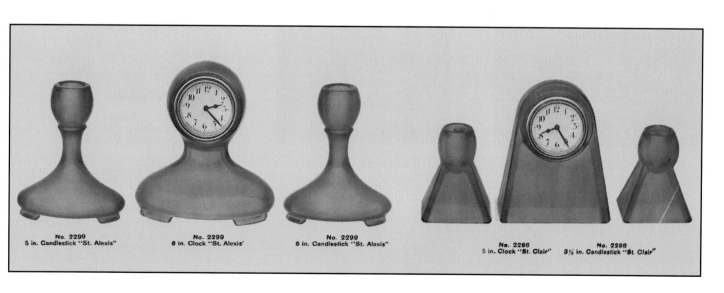

No. 2299
5 in. Candlestick "St. Alexis"

No. 2299
6 in. Clock "St. Alexis"

No. 2299
5 in. Candlestick "St. Alexis"

No. 2298
5 in. Clock "St. Clair"

No. 2298
3½ in. Candlestick "St. Clair"

COASTERS

Coasters did not seem to create much interest at the Fostoria Company. A few had been offered before 1924, and one that lasted until 1927 is pictured. The Utility Coaster with spoon rest was an innovation of 1939 and was popular for a long time. Several pressed patterns included a coaster, and the reader is referred to the pattern for more information. During the Lead Crystal period, several coasters were made and are featured in *Fostoria Tableware: 1944 – 1986*

1590 Coaster, pre 1924-1927; $8.00
2056 Coaster (see American)
2106 Coaster
    Crystal, 1931-1940; $5.00
    Amber, 1931-1934; $6.00
    Green, 1931-1941; $6.00
2272 Coaster
    Amber, 1927-1939; $5.00
    Green, 1927-1936; $5.00
    Blue, 1927; $8.00
    Rose, 1928-1939; $5.00
    Azure, 1928-1934; $7.00
    Topaz/Gold Tint, 1930-1937; $5.00
    Orchid, 1927-1928; $7.00

2442 Coaster
    Crystal, 1931-1943; $6.00
    Amber, 1931-1936; $7.00
    Green, 1931-1939; $7.00
    Rose, 1931-1940; $7.00
    Ebony, 193-1939; $6.00
    Topaz/Gold Tint, 1931-1943; $7.00
2510 Coaster (see Sunray)
2584 Coaster, 1939-1976; $6.00
2650 Coaster (see Horizon)
2803 Coaster (see Sea Shells)
4186 Coaster (see Mesa)
See also Lead Crystal

Ridged Lead Crystal Coaster, 2584 Utility Coaster, Utility Coaster, Blue Mesa Coaster, 2272 Coasters in Blue, Amber and Azure

No.1590-3½ in. Coaster Cut 171.

2584—Utility Coaster
Length 4¾ in.
Coaster Diameter 3⅜ in.

2442—Coaster
Diameter 4 in.
Ro-Gr-Am-Eb-Crys-Tz

2272—Coaster
Diameter 4¼ in.
Ro-Az-Gr-Am-Crys-Tz

2106 Coaster
Gr-Am-Crys

COMPORTS, NAPPIES, and JELLIES

Comports were offered with most dinnerware lines and are shown with the patterns in both *Fostoria Tableware: 1924 – 1943* and *Fostoria Tableware: 1944 – 1986*. Several comports were used over and over to complement numerous lines and are shown here. Most of the early comports were blown with a pulled or very plain stem making it difficult to distinguish those made by Fostoria. The 2327 twisted stem comport in 1925 was the first of several which employed pressed stems, some of unique design, making identification easier. Sometimes comports were measured from top to bottom (height) and other times the measurement given referred to diameter of the bowl. Most of the comports used in etched and crystal patterns during the 1920s belonged to the 803 or 5078 lines. Both lines are shown in *Fostoria Tableware: 1924 – 1943*.

Nappy was another name for bowl. Nappies or comports were sometimes designated as jellies, and it can be difficult to see any difference between a piece called a comport and pieces called a nappy or a jelly.

766 Nappy, 5" Footed, 1924-1927; $15.00
803 Nappy, 5" Footed
    Regal Blue, 1933-1935; $15.00
    Empire Green, 1933-1935; $15.00
    Burgundy, 1933-1935; $15.00
803 Nappy, 6" Footed
    Regal Blue, 1933-1934; $18.00
    Empire Green, 1933-1934; $18.00
    Burgundy, 1933-1934; $18.00
803 Nappy, 7", pre 1924-1928; $15.00
825 Jelly and Cover, pre 1924-1928; $20.00
1372 Jelly, Nappies (See Coin)
1861½ Jelly
    Crystal, 1925-1932; $30.00
    Amber, 1925-1932; $32.00
    Blue, 1925-1927; $35.00
    Green, 1925-1932; $32.00
    Canary, 1925-1926; $40.00
    Rose, 1928-1932; $35.00
    Azure, 1928-1932; $35.00
2056 Comport, Nappy, Jelly (See American)
2183 Comport, Nappies, Jelly (See Colonial Prism)
2327 Comport, 7" Regular
    Crystal, 1925-1932; $30.00
    Blue, 1926-1927; $38.00
    Canary, 1925-1926; $45.00
    Orchid, 1927-1928; $38.00
    Rose, 1928-1934; $38.00
    Azure, 1928; $38.00
    Green, 1925-1934; $35.00
    Amber, 1925-1933; $35.00
    Ebony, 1925-1927; $30.00
2327 Comport, 7" Salver
    Blue, 1925-1927; $45.00
    Canary, 1925-1926; $54.00
    Green, 1925-1927; $40.00
    Amber, 1925-1927; $40.00
2350 8" Comport (See Pioneer)
2362 Comport, 11" (See Bowls, Centerpieces,
    and Console Bowls)
    Crystal, 1927-1928; $65.00
    Blue, 1927; $95.00
    Orchid, 1927-1928; $75.00
    Green, 1927-1928; $75.00
    Amber, 1927-1928; $75.00
    Ebony, 1927; $60.00

Blue 2327 Salver, Vesper Comport, Royal 1861½ Jelly

2364 Comport (See Sonata)
2374 Comport, 6" (see Small Bowls, Mints, and Nuts)
    Crystal, 1933-1934; $24.00
    Rose, 1933-1934; $28.00
    Azure, 1933-1934; $28.00
    Amber, 1933-1934; $25.00
    Green, 1933-1934; $25.00
2375 7" Comport (See Fairfax)
2400 Comport, 6"
    Crystal, 1929-1943; $20.00
    Topaz/Gold Tint, 1929-1943; $25.00
    Rose, 1929-1932; $30.00

Woodland 825 Jelly, no cover; 1300 Heavy Drape Comport; 803 Footed Nappy, Chrysanthemum Cutting; 6030 Blown Comport

Azure, 1929-1934; $30.00
Green, 1929-1938; $28.00
Amber, 1929-1934; $25.00
Ebony, 1929-1934; $25.00
Wisteria, 1931-1932; $35.00
2400 Comport, 8"
  Crystal, 1928-1932; $32.00
  Rose, 1928-1932; $38.00
  Azure, 1928-1932; $40.00
  Green, 1928-1932; $38.00
  Amber, 1928-1932; $35.00
  Orchid, 1928; $38.00
2412 Comport, Jelly (See Colony)
2419 Comport, Jelly (See Mayfair)
2424 Comport (See Kent)
2430 Jelly (See Diadem)
2433 Comports (See Twenty-Four Thirty-Three)
2449 Comport (See Hermitage)
2470 Comports (See Twenty-Four Seventy)
2496 Comport, Jelly, Nappies (See Baroque)
2510 Comport, Jelly, (See Sunray)
2538 Nappy, 4½"
  Crystal, 1936-1940; $8.00
  Topaz/Gold Tint, 1936-1937; $10.00
2538 Nappy, 6" (see Bowls, Centerpieces, and Console Bowls)
  Crystal, 1936-1940; $10.00
  Topaz/Gold Tint, 1936-1937; $12.00
2538 Nappy, 11" (see Salad Sets)
  Crystal, 1936-1943; $35.00
  Topaz/Gold Tint, 1936-1937; $45.00
2550 Comport, Handled Nappy (See Spool)
2560 Comport (See Coronet)
2574 Comport (See Raleigh)
2592 Jelly (See Myriad)
2620 Nappies (See Wistar)
2630 Comport (See Century)
2650 Nappy (See Horizon)
2667 Comport, 6" Blown, Crystal, 1953-1956; $26.00
2692/388 Comport, 6½"
  Crystal, 1971 only; $22.00
  Ruby, 1971 only; $26.00
2708 Comport, Shallow and Deep, Brass and Glass (see p. 74), 1957-1962; $34.00
2718 Jelly (see Fairmont)
2788 Comport (see Henry Ford Museum)
2719 Jelly (See Jamestown)
4024 Comport, 5"
  Crystal, 1934-1939; $36.00
  Regal Blue, 1934-1940; $47.00
  Burgundy 1934-1937; $47.00
  Empire Green, 1934-1936; $48.00
  Ruby, 1935-1937; $48.00
4095 Nappy, 4½" with or without Cover
  (no Cover offered after 1927)
  Crystal, RO, 1925-1936; $6.00
  Amber Foot, LO, 1925-1938; $7.00

2470 Comport, Wisteria Foot, Wisteria 2400 6" Comport, Topaz 5098 Comport, Rose 5098 Nappy

Green, SO, 1925-1938; $8.00
Green Foot, SO, 1925-1927; $7.00
Blue Foot, RO, 1925-1927; $10.00
Rose Bowl, RO, 1928-1934; $15.00
Azure Bowl, RO, 1928-1936; $16.00
Green Bowl, RO, 1928-1937; $14.00
4095 Nappy, 5" with or without Cover
  Crystal, 1926-1927; $7.00
  Amber Foot, LO, 1926-1927; $7.00
  Green Foot, SO, 1926-1927; $8.00
  Blue Foot, RO, 1926-1927; $10.00
4095 Nappy, 6" with or without Cover
  Crystal, 1926-1927; $7.00
  Amber Foot, LO, 1926-1927; $8.00
  Green Foot, SO, 1926-1927; $10.00
  Blue Foot, RO, 1926-1927; $12.00
4095 Nappy, 7" with or without Cover
  Crystal, 1926-1927; $9.00

2433 Tall Comport, Amber Base; Low Comport, Green Base

Amber Foot, LO, 1926-1927; $10.00
Green Foot, SO, 1926-1927; $12.00
Blue Foot, RO, 1926-1927; $15.00
4119 Nappy, 4" Footed
    Regal Blue, 1934-1938; $42.00
    Empire Green, 1935-1938; $40.00
    Burgundy, 1935-1938; $42.00
5078 Comport, 5" and Cover, pre 1924-1928; $10.00
5078 Comport, 6", pre 1924-1928; $6.00
5078 Nappy, Low Foot, with or without cover, 5",
    6", 7", 8", pre 1924-1928; $14.00
5098 Comport, 5"
    Crystal, 1929-1934; $37.00
    Rose, 1928-1937; $48.00
    Azure, 1928-1938; $50.00
    Topaz, 1929-1934; $45.00
    Amber, 1930-1937; $38.00
    Green, 1928-1938; $40.00

Buttercup 2364 Sonata 8" Comport, Green 2350 8" (diameter) Comport, Green 2400 Comport

Azure Baroque 5½" Comport, Topaz 2419 Mayfair Comport, Spool Nappy, Gold Tint Baroque 6½" Comport

6013 Comport, 5", colored bowl
    Crystal, 1935-1939; $40.00
    Regal Blue, 1935-1937; $75.00
    Burgundy, 1935-1940; $65.00
    Ruby, 1935-1939; $75.00
6023 5" Blown Comport, Crystal, 1939-1943;
    $35.00
6030 5" Blown Comport, Crystal, 1942-1943;
    $40.00

5098 Nappy, 6"
    Crystal, 1929-1930; $38.00
    Amber, 1929-1930; $47.00
    Green, 1929-1930; $75.00
    Rose, 1929-1930; $75.00
    Azure, 1929-1930; $84.00
    Topaz, 1929-1930; $65.00
5099 Comport, 6"
    Topaz, 1929-1934; $47.00
    Rose, 1929-1935; $50.00
    Azure, 1929-1935; $54.00
    Green, 1929-1934; $50.00

Azure 2375 Comport, 5099 6" Comport

2430   7-in. Jelly
Ro-Az-Gr-Am-Eb-Crys-Tz
Priced on page 41

2400   6-in. Comport
Ro-Az-Gr-Am-Eb-Crys-Tz-Wis
2400   8-in. Comport
Ro-Az-Gr-Am-Crys
Priced on page 41

5099   6-in. Comport
Ro-Az-Gr-Tz
Priced on page 41

5098   5-in. Comport
Ro-Az-Gr-Am-Crys-Tz
Priced on page 41

2433   6-in. Tall Comport
Solid Crystal
Gr-Am-Eb Base with Crys Bowl
Crys Base with Ro-Az-Tz-Wis Bowl
Priced on page 43

2327   7-in. Comport
Ro-Gr-Am-Crys
Priced on page 41

2433   6-in. Low Comport
Solid Crystal
Gr-Am-Eb Base with Crys Bowl
Crys Base with Ro-Az-Tz Bowl
Priced on page 43

1861½   Jelly
Ro-Az-Gr-Am-Crys
Priced on page 41

No. 2362—11 in. Comport.
Also made in crystal.
Patent Applied For.

No. 2327. 7 in. Comport. Salver Shape.

4095—5 in. Nappy and Cover.
Spiral Optic.

4095—5 in. Nappy, Loop Optic.
Made in 4½, 5, 6 and 7 in.

2374—6 in. Comport
Ro-Az-Gr-Am-Crys

4119
4-in. Footed Nappy
Height 2⅜ in.

6013
5 in. Comport
Height 6 in.

2667—6 in.
Footed Comport
Height 4½ in.

4024—5 in. Comport
Height 3½ in.

5098—6 in. Nappy.
5298—6 in. Nappy.

803—5 in. Footed
Nappy
803—6 in. Footed
Nappy
RB-Bur-Emp.

No. 5078-5 in. Nappy.

No. 5078-6 in. Nappy.

No. 5078-6 in. Comport.

No. 803-7 in. Nappy.

No. 825. Jelly and Cover.

No. 5078-5 in. Comport and Cover.

6030—5 in. Comport
Blown Bowl

6023—5 in. Blown Comport
Height 4¾ in.

2538—11 in. Nappy
2538—6 in. Nappy
2538—4½ in. Nappy

2692/388

DISPLAY and SHOW WINDOW PLATES and STANDS

Fine jewelry and department stores knew the importance of presenting items tastefully. They looked to the Fostoria Glass Company for ways to create attractive and appealing show windows to display their wares. We found some of the display plates and stands they made for this purpose listed in 1924. Several candlesticks were made flat on top to be used for stands or shelf supports. Large plates were used to display jewelry and even shoes. We have seen the No. 19 candle column (see Candlesticks, Candelabra, Lustres, and Candle Lamps for photograph), but have not identified a plate or stand or shoe rest, and have not found any catalog pages to illustrate this information. We also know that the 1103 Pedestal was the twisted candlestick with no hole to serve as a candle cup. Doubtless the list of items was made over a much longer period of time. Prices will vary depending on whether the owner has identified the item as Fostoria.

Shoe
1103½ Plate and Stand, 17", 21", 25" sizes
1739½ Plate and Stand, 10", 13", 15", 18" sizes
1981 Shoe Rest
1981½ Shoe Rest
2205 Shoe Rest

Jewelry
1738 Plate and Stand, 10½", 13" and 16" sizes

Candle Column or Pedestal
No. 19 Candle, 7", 10", 12", 15", 18" sizes
No. 1103 Pedestal, 11", 15", 19" flat only

FIGURALS

There were three main periods of figural production. In 1935 a group of four animal figures called Table Ornaments were made in Crystal, Topaz, and Silver Mist. The Topaz color is more difficult to find. By 1943 these were all discontinued. Standing and reclining colts and deer were also made at this time in Crystal and Silver Mist. The owl, horse, seahorse, and elephant were also used as bookends, and are listed in that category. From 1943 to 1950 no figurals were made with the exception of the horse bookend.

From 1950 to around 1960 a group of figures was offered in brilliant Crystal. One of the grandest was the huge rooster, appropriately called "Chanticleer," which was also offered in Ebony with gold decoration (see Ebony Glass). It was during this period that an attempt was made to make the Chanticleer in milk glass. This never proved successful even though the mold was reworked to fill in the space between tail feathers. Only a few were produced, and they were not offered as a production item. The 4165 Santa Claus was listed, but only shown on a small brochure.

The last group of figures appeared in 1971 and were made in Silver Mist colors as well as the colors of the period. The Ebony bases for the religious group could be lighted. The squirrel set and duck set were made again at this time.

In 1987 the Fostoria Glass Society of America purchased the pelican mold and each year produces a different color as a souvenir for club members. These pelicans are all marked with "FGSA" and the year of manufacture, except for the first one which was made in Amber.

A cardinal head in Silver Mist and a Ruby that was closer to cranberry in color was made as a special order for the Frederick Crawford Museum's Western Reserve Historical Society over a six-year period (1980 – 1986). Used as trophies in the Concours d' Elegance competitions, they were made to fit either a Model T or Model A radiator cap. Jon Saffell, former head of the Fostoria Design Department has recalled that he worked with Bill Bradford to create the model for the mold. Information from the Frederick Crawford Museum and Mr. Frank Fenton of the Fenton Art Glass Company indicates that after Fostoria closed in 1986, the Fenton Company continued to make a few in the same colors. The cardinal head was never listed by Fostoria as a production item. (See photograph, p. 147.)

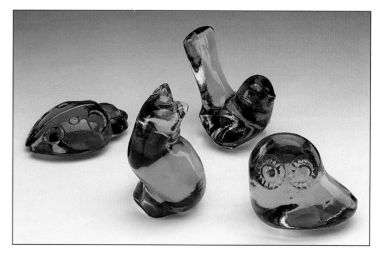

Lemon Lady Bug, Blue Cat, Lemon Bird, and Blue Owl (The bird was not listed, but is signed "Fostoria.")

2497 Seafood Cocktail (see Appetizers)
2521 Bird (see Shakers and Open Salts)
2531 Penguin
   Crystal, 1935-1943; $65.00

141

Topaz/Gold Tint, 1935-1938; $95.00
Silver Mist, 1936-1943; $75.00
2531 Pelican
    Crystal, 1935-1943; $65.00
    Topaz/Gold Tint, 1935-1938; $95.00
    Silver Mist, 1936-1943; $75.00
2531 Polar Bear
    Crystal, 1935-1943; $65.00
    Topaz/ Gold Tint, 1935-1938; $110.00
    Silver Mist, 1936-1943; $75.00
2531 Seal
    Crystal, 1935-1943; $65.00
    Topaz, 1935-1938; $110.00
    Silver Mist, 1935-1943; $75.00
2566 Fish Ash Tray (see Smoker Items)
2589 Colt, Standing
    Crystal, 1940-1943; $45.00
    Silver Mist, 1940-1943; $48.00
2589½ Colt, Reclining
    Crystal, 1940-1943; $45.00
    Silver Mist, 1940-1943; $48.00
2589 Deer, Standing
    Crystal, 1940-1943; $45.00
    Silver Mist, 1940-1943; $48.00
    Milk Glass, 1954-1958; $45.00
2589½ Deer, Reclining
    Crystal, 1940-1943; $45.00
    Silver Mist, 1940-1943; $48.00
    Milk Glass, 1954-1958; $45.00
2595 Sleigh (see Milk Glass)
2629 Chanticleer
    Crystal, 1950-1958; $300.00
    Ebony, 1953-1957; $500.00
    Decoration 522, Ebony with Gold, 1954-1957; $700.00
2631 Squirrels A & B, 2 pieces
    Crystal, 1950-1958; $47.00
    Amber, 1965-1973; $55.00
    Olive Green, 1965-1973; $55.00
    Cobalt, 1965-1973; $65.00
    Amber Mist, 1965-1973; $64.00
    Olive Green Mist, 1965-1973; $64.00
    Cobalt Mist, 1965-1973; $65.00
2623 Duckling Set: Mama Duck, Ducklings A (Head Back), B (Walking), and C (Head Down)
    Crystal, 1950-1958; $95.00
    Amber, 1965-1973; $110.00
    Olive Green, 1965-1973; $110.00
    Cobalt, 1965-1973; $125.00
    Amber Mist, 1965-1973; $110.00
    Olive Green Mist, 1965-1973; $110.00
    Cobalt Mist, 1965-1973; $125.00
2633 Fish Set:
    Fish A (Vertical), Crystal, 1950-1957; $125.00
    Fish B (Horizontal), Crystal, 1950-1957; $165.00
2634 Mermaid, Crystal, 1950-1962; $195.00
2634 Floating Garden, 13" base for Mermaid, Crystal, 1950-1960; $85.00

Lute and Lotus, Silver Mist, Ebony with Gold Decoration

2635 Madonna (offered with lighted base)
    Crystal, 1950-1974; $95.00
    Silver Mist, 1956-1974; $125.00
    Lighted Base; $25.00
2626 Chinese Lute, 12"
    Silver Mist, 1956-1958; $250.00
    Decoration 522, Ebony with Gold, 1954-1957; $500.00
2626½ Chinese Lotus, 12"
    Silver Mist, 1956-1962; $250.00
    Decoration 522, Ebony with Gold, 1954-1957; $500.00
2676 Hen and Nest (see Milk Glass)
2680 Stage Coach (see Milk Glass)
2782 Fish Nappy (see Milk Glass)
2715 St. Francis (offered with lighted base)

Madonna and Child, Small Madonnas which were sold through Fostoria Outlet Stores, Madonna on Ebony Base, St. Francis

Silver Mist, 1957-1973; $400.00
Lighted Base; $25.00
2797 Sacred Heart (offered with lighted base)
Silver Mist, 1967-1973; $500.00
Lighted Base; $25.00
2798 Madonna and Child (offered with lighted base)
Silver Mist, 1967-1973; $500.00
Lighted Base; $25.00
2821/304 Stork
Crystal, 1971-1973; $37.00
Lemon, 1971-1973; $40.00
Olive Green, 1971-1973; $40.00
Silver Mist, 1971-1973; $37.00
Lemon Mist, 1971-1973; $40.00
Olive Green Mist, 1971-1973; $40.00
2821/357 Cat
Crystal, 1971-1973; $35.00
Lemon, 1971-1973; $40.00
Olive Green, 1971-1973; $40.00
Silver Mist, 1971-1973; $37.00
Lemon Mist, 1971-1973; $40.00
Olive Green Mist, 1971-1973; $40.00
2821/410 Dolphin
Crystal, 1971-1973; $25.00
Lemon, 1971-1973; $35.00
Olive Green, 1971-1973; $35.00
Silver Mist, 1971-1973; $30.00
Lemon Mist, 1971-1973; $35.00
Olive Green Mist, 1971-1973; $35.00
2821/420 Frog
Crystal, 1971-1973; $35.00
Lemon, 1971-1973; $40.00
Olive Green, 1971-1973; $40.00
Silver Mist, 1971-1973; $37.00
Lemon Mist, 1971-1973; $40.00
Olive Green Mist, 1971-1973; $40.00
2821/452 Lady Bug
Crystal, 1971-1973; $35.00
Lemon, 1971-1973; $40.00
Olive Green, 1971-1973; $40.00
Silver Mist, 1971-1973; $37.00
Lemon Mist, 1971-1973; $40.00
Olive Green Mist, 1971-1973; $40.00
2821/527 Owl
Crystal, 1971-1973; $35.00
Lemon, 1971-1973; $40.00
Olive Green, 1971-1973; $40.00
Silver Mist, 1971-1973; $37.00
Lemon Mist, 1971-1973; $40.00
Olive Green Mist, 1971-1973; $40.00
2321/627 Baby Rabbit
Crystal, 1971-1973; $22.00
Lemon, 1971-1973; $25.00
Olive Green, 1971-1973; $25.00
Silver Mist, 1971-1973; $22.00
Lemon Mist, 1971-1973; $25.00
Olive Green Mist, 1971-1973; $25.00

Chanticleer, Ebony with Gold Decoration, Milk Glass

Table Ornaments: Topaz Pelican, Silver Mist Pelican, Polar Bear, Seal, Penguin, Topaz Penguin

Duck Set, Cobalt Mist; Squirrels, Amber Mist

2821/628 Mama Rabbit
  Crystal, 1971-1973; $35.00
  Lemon, 1971-1973; $40.00
  Olive Green, 1971-1973; $40.00
  Silver Mist, 1971-1973; $37.00
  Lemon Mist, 1971-1973; $40.00
  Olive Green Mist, 1971-1973; $40.00
4165 Santa Claus, 1955 (six months), Market (see Milk Glass)

Colts, Standing and Reclining; Deer Standing, Milk Glass, Blue (Special Edition for Blue Colt Collectibles), Deer Reclining

Frog, Whale, Owl (purchased from Fostoria Outlet Store), Rabbits in Blue, Lemon, and Lemon Frost, Stork

Sea Shell Bookend, Mermaid and Bowl, Vertical and Horizontal Fish, and Seahorse (which although technically a bookend, seems to fit with figurals)

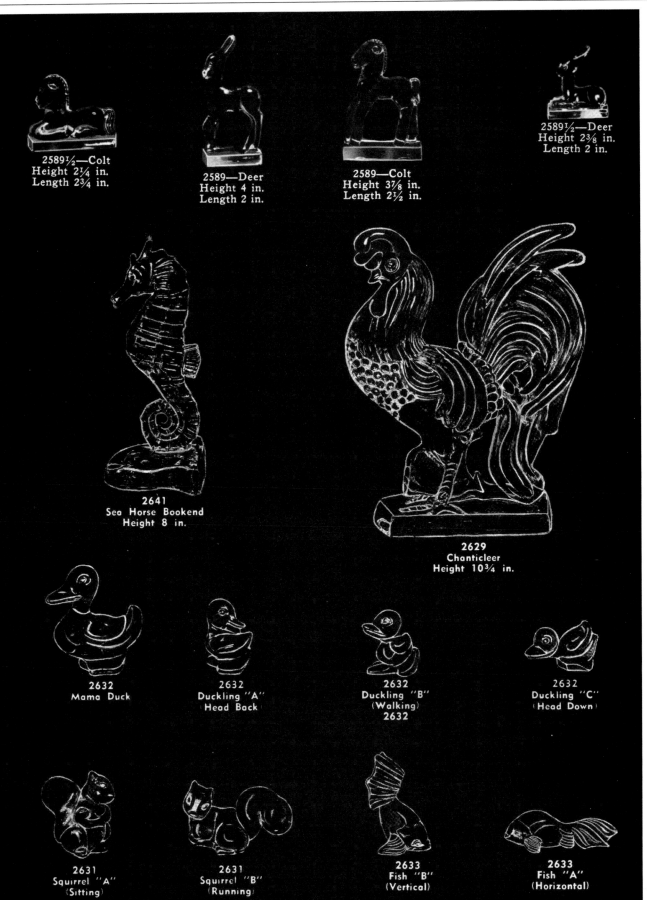

2589½—Colt
Height 2¼ in.
Length 2¾ in.

2589—Deer
Height 4 in.
Length 2 in.

2589—Colt
Height 3⅞ in.
Length 2½ in.

2589½—Deer
Height 2⅜ in.
Length 2 in.

2641
Sea Horse Bookend
Height 8 in.

2629
Chanticleer
Height 10¾ in.

2632
Mama Duck

2632
Duckling "A"
(Head Back)

2632
Duckling "B"
(Walking)
2632

2632
Duckling "C"
(Head Down)

2631
Squirrel "A"
(Sitting)

2631
Squirrel "B"
(Running)

2633
Fish "B"
(Vertical)

2633
Fish "A"
(Horizontal)

2531—Seal
Height 3⅞ in.

2531—Polar Bear
Height 4¾ in.

2531
Penguin
Height 4½ in.

2531—Pelican
Height 4 in.

2634
Mermaid & Bowl Centerpiece
Height 11½ in. Diameter 13 in.

2634
Mermaid
Height 10⅛ in.

2634 — 13 in.
Floating Garden

2635
Madonna
Decoration No. 525 Silver Mist
Height 10 in.

2635
Madonna with Base (Lighted)
Decoration No. 525 Silver Mist
Height 11¾ in.

2626
Chinese Lotus
Decoration No. 525 Silver Mist
Height 12¼ in.

2626
Chinese Lute
Decoration No. 525 Silver Mist
Height 12¼ in.

| 2635 | 2715 | 2797 | 2798 |
| 470-471-473 | 469-470-473 | 473-625 | 472-473 |

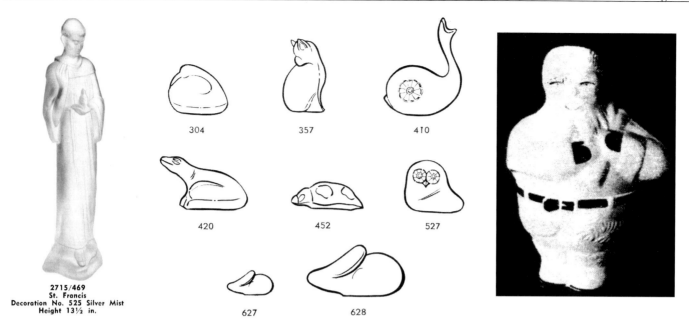

2715/469
St. Francis
Decoration No. 525 Silver Mist
Height 13½ in.

304

357

410

420

452

527

627

628

FUNCTIONAL SCULPTURES/ASH TRAYS

1980 – 1981
Frosted Crystal

Standing upright, these animal heads make interesting decorative accents. Lying flat they may be used as ash trays. Milbra's first trip to the Fostoria factory in Moundsville, West Virginia, was in June of 1980. The first of these sculptures had just been finished and was being shown with pride. The Ram has not been seen as often as the Hound and Lion. The original price was $15.00 each. (See also Smoker Items.)

FU01/116 Lion; $42.00
FU02/116 Ram; $45.00
FU03/116 Hound; $42.00

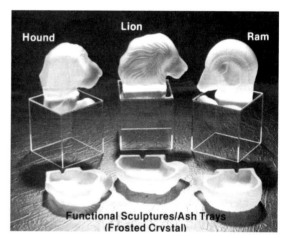

Functional Sculptures/Ash Trays
(Frosted Crystal)

GEORGE AND MARTHA WASHINGTON PLAQUES

Fostoria was working with Pickard China in 1975 – 1976 when the George and Martha plaques were designed using White Bisque profiles on a Crystal background. These originally sold for $40.00 a pair.

2913/597 George and Martha Washington Plaques, 1975-1976; $85.00 pair

George and Martha Washington Plaques, Silver Mist Cardinal Head (see p. 141)

FINGER BOWLS

DESSERT SERVICE . . . The fork, spoon. fingerbowl and doily are placed on a glass plate and set before each guest. Guest removes and places them as shown. after which dessert is served on the plate.

Before World War II finger bowls were used extensively for formal dining. They were always placed on a napkin or doily with a liner or dessert plate underneath. The bowl was half filled with water. A mint leaf or fragrant flower petals or slice of lemon enhanced the visual and aromatic pleasantness of the occasion when added to the bowl. The guest was to delicately dip sticky fingertips into the water and blot them on a napkin. Finger bowls were most often used with the dessert course. After 1943 finger bowls served a dual purpose, that of a dessert bowl or a finger bowl.

After 1930 only the 869 finger bowl was listed as having a plate. The instructions beneath the picture to the left are taken from a 1944 teaching handbook called "Let Tables Glisten." It was prepared by the Fostoria Glass Company to aid homemaking teachers as they instructed students in proper table setting technique.

When the finger bowl used a plate, the two pieces are priced as a set.

766 Finger Bowl, pre 1924-1943, 1736 6" Plate Plain or Narrow Optic. Made in all the regular colors of this period and in Regal Blue, Burgundy, and Empire Green.
Crystal; $15.00
Colors; $35 to $45.00

858 Finger Bowl, pre 1924-1928, 2283 6" Plate, Crystal or MOP; $15.00

869 Finger Bowl, RO, 1925-1943, 2283 6" Plate. Made in Crystal and all the colors of the period except Ebony.
Crystal; $15.00
Colors; $35.00 to $45.00

890 Finger Bowl (Listed with 890 stemware through 1932, then changed to 869)
Crystal; $15.00
Rose, $35.00
Green, $35.00

1769 Finger Bowl, 2283 6" Plate
Crystal, RO, 1924-1942; $15.00
Crystal, Dimple Optic, 1936-1943; $28.00
Topaz, Dimple Optic, 1932-1942; $42.00
Wisteria, Dimple Optic, 1932-1935; $64.00
Regal Blue, Burgundy, Empire Green, Ruby, 1934-1942 (no optic); $48.00

Amber Vernon 869; Topaz June 869 Finger Bowl and Plate; 4021 Manor; 869 Blue, RO; Green Rogene 766 Finger Bowl (not listed in color)

4095 Finger Bowl (made from the 4095 4½" footed nappy), 2283 6" Plate
Crystal, RO, 1925-1936; $18.00
Green, SO, 1925-1937; $22.00
Blue Foot, RO, 1925-1927; $28.00
Green Foot, SO, 1925-1938; $22.00
Amber Foot, LO, 1925-1935; $22.00
Rose Bowl, RO, 1928-1934; $28.00
    Azure Bowl, RO, 1928-1934; $28.00
    Green Bowl, RO, 1925-1935; $26.00

4021 Finger Bowl
    Crystal, 1929-1943; $22.00
    Green Foot, 1929-1940; $28.00
    Amber Foot, 1929-1940; $28.00
    Ebony Foot, 1929-1940; $28.00
    Rose Bowl, 1930-1940; $35.00
    Topaz/Gold Tint Bowl, 1930-1943; $35.00
    Wisteria Bowl, 1931-1938; $57.00

4185/495 Dessert/Finger Bowl, 1965-1970; $18.00

Ruby 1769; 4185 with Rose Cutting

6002 Finger Bowl, 1930-1933
  Green Base, $38.00
  Ebony Base, $38.00
  Rose Bowl, $38.00
  Topaz Bowl, $38.00

Wisteria 869 Finger Bowl; 2440 Lafayette dessert plate. Shown with doily as used.

1769—Finger Bowl.
2283—6 in. F. B. Plate.
Spiral Optic.

No. 858 Finger Bowl.
No. 2283-6 in. Finger Bowl Plate.

No. 766 Finger Bowl
No. 2283-6 in. Plate

869—Finger Bowl, Optic
Height 2 in.   Diameter 4½ in.
766—Finger Bowl, Plain
Same Shape as 869
2283—6 in. Plate

No. 1769 Finger Bowl
No. 2283-6 in. Plate

No. 4095 Finger Bowl

4021—Finger Bowl
Height 2¼ in.   Diameter 4⅜ in.

DESIGN PATENT NO. 80971

1769—Finger Bowl
Height 2 in.   Diameter 4⅛ in.

6002 Finger Bowl

2512 GLASS FRUIT

July 1934 – 1937

Although listed in the July Supplement in 1934, these luscious specimens were shown first in 1935. Perfect for the strong colors introduced at the same time, all six pieces were also made in Crystal, decorated with Silver and called the Silvered Line. The Orange and Peach were not made in Empire Green. As was the case with many novelty items, this line was short lived and pieces are seldom seen. Interestingly, the regular colors sold for fifty cents per dozen and the Silvered Line for seventy-five cents per dozen. The few pieces we have seen were hollow, not solid. Since we have not seen a piece with a price tag, it would be impossible to offer current values.

Regal Blue Peach, Burgundy Orange (courtesy of Carol and Larry Bartholf)

Grape
    Regal Blue, Burgundy, Empire Green,
    Silver Decoration
Orange
    Regal Blue, Burgundy
    Silver Decoration
Banana
    Regal Blue, Burgundy, Empire Green
    Silver Decoration
Apple
    Regal Blue, Burgundy, Empire Green
    Silver Decoration
Pear
    Regal Blue, Burgundy, Empire Green
    Silver Decoration
Peach
    Regal Blue, Burgundy
    Silver Decoration

2512—Grapes

2512—Orange

2512—Banana

2512—Apple

2512—Pear

2512—Peach

2378 ICE BUCKETS, SUGAR PAILS, and WHIP CREAM PAILS

Ice tubs with tab handles and an underplate had been in use for a long time in the home, in hotels, and in restaurants. In 1927 the 2378 Ice Bucket with bail handle appeared in Amber, Blue, Green, and Orchid, and could be had with a metal ice drainer and tongs. This bucket was used exclusively until 1929 when an ice bucket was added to the Fairfax pattern, and by 1932, the 2378 bucket was no longer being offered. A few etched patterns from this period had both styles. Sizes of these two ice buckets are identical; the only way to tell them apart is through the optic ridges inside the Fairfax bucket. (See Fostoria Tableware: 1924 – 1943.) Many pressed patterns had ice buckets or tubs that were used for etched, cut and decorated designs. The number is the clue to the original pattern, i.e., 2375 Fairfax.

Sugar and whip cream pails first appeared in 1928. Nowadays we would consistently say "whipped" cream, but Fostoria sometimes added the "ped" and more often did not. We were recently told that whip cream meant the unwhipped cream, and whipped cream referred to cream that had been whipped to stand in peaks. Some desserts called for the unwhipped cream, and in fine families one would surely serve whichever cream (whipped or unwhipped) the dessert required. The little sugar pail was perfect for the new, at that time, sugar cubes. After 1930, neither pail was listed. Sugar and whip cream pails were used for several cut, etched, and decorated designs, and were made with spiral optic and in all the colors of this period. Possibilities for collecting are quite extensive. Gold finished handles and tongs were used with Amber and Topaz, and on patterns with iridescent and gold decoration. Handles on all three, ice tongs and sugar tongs, and the 2378 Ice Bucket Drainer were available in Nickle Plated, Silver Plated, or Gold Finished. The whip cream pail used the 2375 Glass Ladle.

2378 Sugar Pail, NP Handle
  Crystal, 1928-1930; $34.00
  Amber, 1928-1930; $37.00
  Green, 1928-1930; $44.00
  Rose, 1928-1930; $44.00
  Azure, 1928-1930; $48.00
  Orchid, 1928; $57.00
  Topaz, 1929-1930; $44.00
2378 Sugar Pail, SO
  Crystal, 1928; $35.00
  Amber, 1928-1930; $42.00
  Green, 1928-1930; $48.00
  Rose, 1928-1930; $52.00
  Azure, 1928-1930; $55.00
  Orchid, 1928; $65.00
2378 Whip Cream Pail
  Crystal, 1928-1930; $32.00
  Amber, 1928-1930; $35.00
  Green, 1928-1930; $42.00
  Rose, 1928-1930; $42.00
  Azure, 1928-1930; $48.00
  Orchid, 1928; $55.00
  Topaz, 1929-1930; $42.00
2378 Whip Cream Pail, SO
  Crystal, 1928; $30.00
  Amber, 1928-1930; $38.00
  Green, 1928-1930; $45.00
  Rose, 1928-1930; $47.00
  Azure, 1928-1930; $48.00
  Orchid, 1928; $57.00
2378 Ice Bucket
  Crystal, 1927-1931; $38.00
  Amber, 1927-1932; $42.00
  Green, 1927-1932; $47.00

  Rose, 1928-1932; $47.00
  Azure, 1928-1932; $48.00
  Orchid, 1927-1928; $55.00
  Blue, 1927; $58.00
2378 Ice Bucket, SO
  Amber, 1928-1930; $46.00
  Green, 1928-1930; $50.00
  Rose, 1928-1930; $50.00
  Azure, 1928-1930; $52.00

Azure June Sugar Pail; Azure Versailles Whipped Cream Pail; Blue Vesper Ice Bucket; Rose Sugar Pail, unknown cutting; Oak Leaf Ice Bucket and Whip Cream Pail; Green Paradise Ice Bucket; Green Versailles Whip Cream Pail; Green SO Sugar Pail

2451 ICE DISH and LINERS

Elegant table settings often included dishes in which to serve chilled foods such as juice, seafood, and fruit. Most of these dishes included an insert for the chilled food which was then nestled into the chipped ice in the dish itself. Different sized and shaped liners (or inserts) were used to suit the food being served.

Several styles of grapefruit bowls were offered as well. Early ones were flat bowls with a liner to hold the fruit, but before the era of elegant dining waned, tall and short-stemmed grapefruits, as well as the simple flat bowl and liner were made available in many patterns. (See *Fostoria Stemware* and *Fostoria Tableware: 1924 – 1943*.)

The 2451 ice dish was independent of the pressed patterns, but was used with many of the etched and cut patterns. Six liners were offered with the ice dish, three pressed and three blown. The bottoms of the pressed liners are usually ground and polished. The blown liners were offered in colors to match the ice dish, but pressed liners were made only in crystal. The liners were standard sizes and will fit any Fostoria ice dish from any pattern. Wisteria liners were made for the Hermitage ice dishes from 1932 – 1935. The Regal Blue ice dishes used Crystal liners.

A long time Fostoria dealer and collector, Barbara Adt, recently suggested, "A new use for an old tradition… candles placed front and center along the length of a dining room table… in prized icer bowls once used for appetizers. Make an elegant centerpiece to adorn a festive table. Add flowers or a garland intertwined between two or three candles for a decorative flair." If one looks at the choice of colors available, the possibilities for creating a beautiful table with ice dishes as candleholders are greatly expanded.

Regal Blue 2451 Ice Dish, Crystal Tomato Juice Liner

2451 Ice Dish
   Crystal, 1931-1971; $15.00
   Amber, 1931-1940; $18.00
   Green, 1931-1940; $20.00
   Rose, 1931-1940; $20.00
   Azure, 1931-1940; $20.00
   Topaz/Gold Tint, 1931-1940; $20.00
   Regal Blue, 1934-1940; $32.00

2479 Liners (Pressed)
   Crystal (any size); $8.00

2451 Liners (Blown)
   Crystal (any size); $15.00
   Amber (any size); $18.00
   Green (any size); $18.00
   Azure (any size); $20.00
   Topaz/Gold Tint (any size); $18.00
   Rose (any size); $20.00
   Wisteria (any size); $35.00

2479—4 oz. Crab
Meat Liner
Crystal

2479
5 oz. Tomato
Juice Liner
Crystal

2479—4 oz. Fruit
Cocktail Liner
Crystal

2451—4 oz. Crab
Meat Liner
Ro-Az-Gr-Am-
Crys-Tz-Wis

2451—5 oz. Fruit
Cocktail Liner
Ro-Az-Gr-Am-
Crys-Tz-Wis

2451—5 oz. Tomato
Juice Liner
Ro-Az-Gr-Am-Crys-
Tz-Wis

2451—Ice Dish
Ro-Az-Gr-Am-Eb-Crys-Tz
2451—7 in. Ice Dish Plate
Ro-Az-Gr-Am-Crys-Tz

JUGS and TANKARDS

Water pitchers were usually called jugs and sometimes tankards by the Fostoria Company. From the beginning jugs had been an important part of production. Few covers have survived. In pattern listings there was often a note indicating that the cover was not etched or cut.

An innovation for jugs appeared with the automatous jugs. The 1518 automatous jug was made in 6, 8, 12, 16, 18, 24, and 32 ounce sizes. The 8 ounce and 12 ounce sizes later were changed to 2194 and used as syrups. The lid for the automatous jug was a metal spring top which fit inside the top of the glass jug. When the jug was tipped over for pouring, the contents pushed against the metal top, forcing it open. When the jug was returned to an upright position, the lid "automatically" closed. The top was easily removed for cleaning. Before the automatous jug, tops had been permanently affixed, or were made to screw on. The Fostoria automatous lid is easily identified since it fits completely inside the top of the jug while lids of other companies fit over the top. This is especially evident with the syrup (see Syrups).

Prior to 1928, most jugs came in several sizes. The only clue we have as to the meaning of the -4, for example, following the line number comes from a 1901 catalog featuring the 300 line both with numbers and equivalent ounces. No. 1 was 8 oz.; No. 2, 10½ oz.; No. 3, 15 oz.; No. 3½, 21 oz.; No. 4, 31 oz.; No. 5, 42 oz.; No. 6, 54 oz.; and No. 7; 65 oz.

It has been difficult to determine if a 316 jug really existed or if a printing error is responsible for its invention. The only time it is shown is with the Fresno pattern, and it looks identical to the 318. The price listing for the Fresno pattern includes a 318 jug but not a 316 jug making us nearly certain that 316 was intended to read 318.

Several beautiful jugs were available with dinner services including the 6011 and the 4020, but by far, the one most often used was the gracefully elegant 5000 jug. Since it was a No. 7 jug, we may surmise that it holds about 65 ounces.

For pictures of jugs not shown here, please refer to *Fostoria Stemware, Fostoria Tableware: 1924 – 1943, Fostoria Tableware: 1944 – 1986,* and *Bar and Refreshment*.

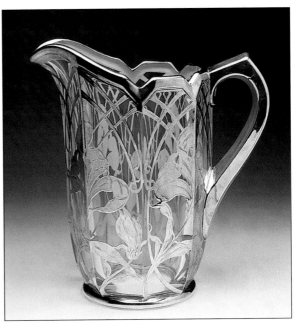

1630 Alexis ½-gallon Tall Pitcher with Silver Overlay, courtesy of Tom and Aleeta Herr

Abbreviations used:

CN = Cut Neck   RO = Regular Optic
SO = Spiral Optic   LO = Loop Optic

300 Jug, pre 1924-1928; $75.00
300½ Jug, pre 1924-1928; $80.00
303 Jug, pre 1924-1940; $65.00
316 Jug (See 318)
317-7 Jug, Plain or CN; $65.00
317½-7 Jug, Plain or CN, and Cover, pre 1920-1927; $75.00
318 Jug, Optic, pre 1920-1940; $78.00
724 Jug, pre 1920-1928; $74.00
890-7 Jug, 1929-1932
   Crystal, $125.00
   Solid Rose, $195.00
   Solid Green, $195.00
1227-7 Jug, Plain or CN, pre 1920-1924; $65.00
1236 Jug (Solid Crystal, or Solid Colors)
   Crystal, pre 1920-1928; $95.00
   Blue, 1925-1927; $200.00
   Green, 1925-1928; $175.00
   Amber, 1925-1928; $150.00
1518 Jug, Automatic removable top; 6, 8, 12, 16, 24, 32 oz., 1924; $12.00-$45.00
1761 Tankard, Claret, pre 1920-1928; $125.00
1787 Tankard, 1924; $65.00

1793 Jug, 75 oz., 1924-1928; $75.00
1852-6, 1852-8 Jug, 1922-1928; $75.00
1992 Jug, 3-pint Pressed, 1924-1928; $58.00
1992 Jug, quart, Pressed, 1924-1928; $48.00

Mayflower 4140 Jug, Oriental 317½ Jug and Cover, Woodland 300 Jug

153

2010 Jug, 63 oz., Plain or Optic, 1924-1928; $65.00
2018-7 Jug, Plain or CN, 1924-1928; $65.00
2040 Jug, 1924-1926; $45.00
2082 Jug, Plain or Spiral Optic, 37, 47, 60 oz.
    Crystal, 1924-1928; $26.00-$38.00
    Solid Green, SO, 1924-1928; $38.00-$57.00
2100 Tankard, pre 1920-1928; $65.00
2104 Jug and Tumbler, pre 1924; $125.00
2230-7 Jug and Cover, pre 1924-1928; $95.00
2270-7 Jug, Plain or Optic
    Crystal, pre 1924-1940; $70.00
    Amber, 1924-1928; $90.00
    Blue, 1924-1927; $125.00
    Green, 1924-1928; $110.00
2270-7 Jug and Cover, Plain or Optic
    Crystal, pre 1924-1928; $84.00
    Amber, 1924-1928; $95.00
    Blue, 1924-1927; $145.00
    Green, 1924-1928; $125.00
2464 Jug, Ice
    Crystal, 1933-1943; $175.00
    Rose, 1933-1934; $295.00
    Green, 1933-1934; $295.00
    Amber, 1933-1934; $250.00
    Topaz, 1933-1934; $295.00
2503 Wine Jug (see Bar and Refreshment)
2518 Jug (see Bar and Refreshment)
2666 Jug (see Contour)
4020 Jug, ½ gal
    Crystal, 1931-1940; $150.00
    Ebony Base, 1931-1939; $195.00
    Green Base, 1931-1936; $225.00
    Amber Base, 1931-1936; $195.00
    Wisteria Base, 1931-1934; $375.00
    Green Bowl, 1931-1934; $250.00
    Rose Bowl, 1931-1936; $250.00
    Topaz Bowl, 1931-1936; $235.00
    Wisteria Bowl, 1931-1937; $425.00
4095-4, -5, -7 Jug, Footed
    Crystal, RO, 1924-1928; $150.00
    Solid Green, SO, 1925-1937; $175.00
    Green Base, SO, 1925-1939; $150.00
    Amber Base, LO, 1925-1939; $150.00
    Blue Base, RO, 1925-1927; $225.00
    Green Bowl, RO, 1928-1934; $175.00
    Azure Bowl, RO, 1928-1936; $175.00
    Rose Bowl, RO, 1928-1939; $150.00
4140 Refreshment Set (see Bar and Refreshment)
4141 Refreshment Set (see Bar and Refreshment)
4142 Refreshment Set (see Bar and Refreshment)
5000-7 Jug, Footed, RO
    Crystal, 1926-1956; $135.00
    Solid Green, 1926-1930; $250.00
    Green Base, 1926-1940; $200.00
    Green Bowl, 1927-1937; $225.00
    Amber Base, 1926-1937; $175.00
    Amber Bowl, 1927-1937; $200.00

Green Seville 5084 Jug, 870 Footed Iced Tea Tumbler; Amber 5084 Jug, Seville 870 Goblet

    Solid Amber, 1926-1940; $225.00
    Blue Base, 1926-1927; $250.00
    Solid Blue, 1926-1927; $300.00
    Orchid Bowl, 1927-1928; $265.00
    Solid Orchid, 1927-1928; $275.00
    Solid Azure, 1928-1938; $275.00
    Azure Bowl, 1928-1939; $260.00
    Rose Bowl, 1928-1937; $260.00
    Topaz/Gold Tint Bowl, 1929-1939; $245.00
5084-7 Jug, Footed, RO
    Crystal, 1926-1943; $125.00
    Rose, 1928-1940; $135.00
    Green, 1926-1940; $135.00
    Amber, 1926-1936; $135.00
    Blue, 1926-1927; $225.00
6011 Jug, Footed
    Crystal, 1934-1943; $125.00
    Regal Blue Bowl, 1934-1940; $450.00
    Burgundy Bowl, 1934-1937; $500.00
    Empire Green Bowl, 1934-1940; $450.00
    Amber Base, 1934-1940; $195.00

4095 Amber Foot, LO; 4095 Blue Foot, unknown cutting; Blue Priscilla Handled Lemonade; 4095 Silver Mist, Green Foot; Blue Priscilla

Spray 2666 Jug, Regal Blue
6011 Jug and Footed Ice Tea
Tumbler, Christiana 6011 Jug

Topaz Trojan 5000 Jug, Orchid
5000 Jug, Palmetto 5000 Jug

300 Claret Jug. Height 12 in.
Capacity 58 oz.

300 No. 1 Tankard.
Capacity 8 oz.
Packed 15 doz. in bbl.

300 No. 2 Tankard.
Capacity 10½ oz.
Packed 12 doz. in bbl.

300 No. 4 Tankard.
Capacity 31 oz.
Packed 4 doz. in bbl.

300 No. 3½ Tankard.
Capacity 21 oz.
Packed 6 doz. in bbl.

300 No. 3 Tankard.
Capacity 15 oz.
Packed 9 doz. in bbl.

317 No. 7. Etched 48.
Packed 1¼ doz. in bbl.

317 No. 7 Jug, Cut Neck and Star.
Packed 1¼ doz. in bbl.

00½ No. 7. Capacity 58 oz. Packed 1½ doz. in bbl.
This Jug is made in 4, 5, 6, 7 sizes.

318. No. 6, Optic. Packed 2 doz. in bbl.
Made also in five sizes, Nos. 4, 5, 6, 7, 8.

724 No. 7 Jug, 2 Quart. Packed 1½ doz. in bbl.
Also in No. 6 size. Packed 2 doz. in bbl.

318. No. 7. Etched 48. Packed 2 doz. in bbl.
Made also in No. 6 size. " 2 " "
        "   " 5 "   " 3 " "
        "   " 4 "   " 3½ " "
        "   " 8 "   " 4 " "

No. 303-No. 7 Jug.

No. 1787-No. 3 Jug.

No. 2040/3. Jug.

No. 1852-6 Jug.

No. 4095. No. 7 Footed Jug.

No. 2194-8 oz. Syrup, N. T.

The 2194 Syrup illustrates the "automatous top" which opened automatically when liquid was poured.

1236—No. 6 Jug, Optic.

2270—Jug, Optic.
Also made in Amber, Blue and Green.

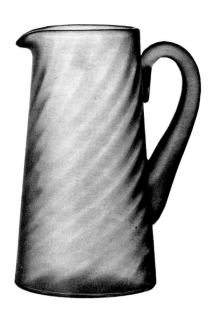

2082—No. 7 Jug.
Spiral Optic.

5100—No. 7 Jug, Optic.

5084—No. 7 Jug, Optic.

2464—Ice Jug
Capacity ½ Gal.
Ro-Gr-Am-Crys-Tz

4020—Footed Jug
Capacity ½ Gallon
Height 8¾ in.

6011—Footed Jug
Cap. 53 oz. Height 8⅞ in.

890—7 Ftd. Jug.

LAMPS

The Fostoria Glass Company was known for its beautiful hand-painted lamps and vases before 1924. The 1910 Lamp Catalog which, fortunately for hand-painted vase lovers, includes quite a few of those gems as well as some miscellaneous items, follows this section. Although the lamps in the catalog are shown with two decorations, note that many list a third decoration. The lovely Victoria lamp was made when the company was still in Fostoria, Ohio.

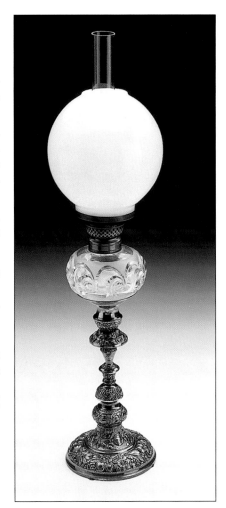

183 Victoria Oil Lamp, all original parts

No. 1 Banquet Lamp, 25", 1939-1942; $400.00 Market

No. 1½ Banquet Lamp, Low Standard, 1939-1942; $295.00

No. 2 Banquet Lamp, 18", 1939-1942; $300.00

No. 21 Princess Lamp: No. 21 Lustre Base with Font and Chimney, shade with fringe beads; Market

2325 Electric Boudoir Lamp, Large and Small sizes, Ebony, 1924-1925; $75.00-$95.00

No. 734 D.
No. 2 Burner and Chimney.

No. 734 C.
No. 2 Burner and Chimney.

No. 734 B.
No. 2 Burner and Chimney.

No. 734 A.
No. 1 Burner and Chimney.

No. 734 O.
No. 1 Burner and Chimney.

No. 734 Footed.
No. 1 Burner and Chimney.

No. 734 Flat
No. 1 Burner and Chimney.

No. 191 D.
No. 2 Burner and Chimney.

No. 191 C.
No. 2 Burner and Chimney.

No. 191 B.
No. 2 Burner and Chimney.

No. 191 A.
No. 1 burner and Chimney.

No. 191 O.
No. 1 Burner and Chimney.

No. 191 Footed.
No. 1 Burner and Chimney.

No. 191 Squat.
No. 1 Burner and Chimney

No. 734 Sewing Lamp.
Packed 1 doz. complete in 35c. bbl.

No. 2325. **Large Electric Boudoir Lamp**
Standard—Ebony Glass
Height, including shade, 15 inches. Stem hollow for wire

No. 2325. **Small Electric Boudoir Lamp**
Standard—Ebony Glass
Height, including shade, 12 inches. Stem hollow for wire

No. 1 Banquet Lamp
Height 25 inches

No. 2 Banquet Lamp
Height 18 inches

1910 LAMP AND VASE CATALOG

Season of 1910

FANCY DECORATED

LAMPS, VASES, ETC.

ALL FIRED COLORS

FOSTORIA GLASS COMPANY
M O U N D S V I L L E ,   W E S T   V I R G I N I A

PERMANENT SAMPLE ROOMS

New York City	56 West Broadway	John Nixon
Chicago, Ill.	807 Masonic Temple	H. A. Marshall
Boston, Mass.	105 Federal Street	H. T. Edwards
Philadelphia, Pa.	213 Commercial Bldg.	Jos. Tomkinson
Baltimore, Md.	304 W. Baltimore Street	W. T. Owen
Dallas, Texas	909 23 Elm Street	H. J. Blakeney
Buffalo, N. Y.	352 Main Street	A. H. Sharpe
San Francisco, Cal.	86 Third Street, Room 203	B. F. Heastand

To the Trade

We take pleasure in handing you our Catalog for 1910, of Decorated Lamps, Vases, Etc., and beg to call your attention to the pleasing variety of decorations and excellent finish of our goods. Shown in Gilt, Gold, Oxidized Copper and Brush Brass finishes. "Royal" Center Draft Burners. Rochester Chimneys.

Fostoria Glass Company
Moundsville, W. Va.

*We aim to excel in
Design and Quality*

TAMPA
Height 15 inches.   Globe 7½ inches
Dec. B.   Poppy, Green Tint

TAMPA
Height 15 inches.   Shade 7 inches
Dec. C.   Rose, Blue Tint

TAMPA—Dec. A.   Pansy, Coral Red Tint

GEM
Height 16 inches.   Globe 7½ inches
Dec. A.   Wild Rose, Pink Tint

GEM
Height 16 inches.   Globe 7½ inches
Dec. B.   Rose, Blue Tint

GEM—Dec. C.   Poppy, Brown Tint

ELMO
Height 16 inches.   Globe 7½ inches
Dec. B.   Pansies, Green Tint

ELMO
Height 16 inches.   Globe 7½ inches
Dec. C.   Rose, Red Tint

ELMO—Dec. A.   Wild Rose, Pink Tint

VERA
Height 18 inch.   Shade 7 inche
Dec. B.   Rose, Green Tint

VERA
Height 18 inches.   Globe 7½ inches
Dec. C.   Cupids, Blue Tint

VERA—Dec. A.   Pansy, Ruby Tint

161

DUKE
Height 18 inches.   Globe 8 inches
Dec. A.   Pansy, Ruby Tint

DUKE
Height 18 inches.   Shade 7 inches
Dec. B.   Wild Rose, Green Tint

DUKE—Dec. C.   Poppy, Brown Tint

HUEY
Height 19 inches.   Globe 8 inches
Dec. A.   Pansy, Pink and Yellow Tints

HUEY
Height 19 inches.   Globe 8 inches
Dec. C.   Peonies, Ruby and Yellow Tints

HUEY—Dec. B.   Wild Lily, Blue and Yellow Tints

LEVAN
Height 19½ inches.   Shade 10 inches
Dec. B.   Roses, Dark Green and Black Tints

LEVAN
Height 20½ inches.   Globe 9 inches
Dec. C.   Roses, Blue and Yellow Tinted

LEVAN—Dec. A.   Wild Rose and Scroll, Pink and Ivory Tints

DUCHESS
Height 19½ inches.   Shade 10 inches
Dec. A.   Poppy, Ruby and Yellow Tints

DUCHESS
Height 21 inches.   Globe 9 inches
Dec. B.   Wild Rose, Green Tint

DUCHESS—Dec. C.   Pansy, Brown and Green

HILDA
Height 22 inches.   Globe 9 inches
Dec. B.   Poppy, Dark Green Tint

HILDA
Height 22 inches.   Globe 9 inches
Dec. C.   Rose, Ruby, Green and Yellow Tints

HILDA—Dec. A.   Peony, Carmine and Ivory Tints

EMPIRE
Height 20½ inches.   Globe 10 inches
Dec. A.   Roses, Ruby Tinted

EMPIRE
Height 20½ inches.   Globe 10 inches
Dec. B.   Seaweed, Green Tinted

SINBAD
Height 22 inches.   Globe 9 inches
Dec. A.   Chrysanthemum, Ruby Tint

SINBAD
Height 22 inches.   Globe 9 inches
Dec. B.   Rose, Green and Yellow Tinted

SINBAD—Dec. C.   Poppy, Brown and Yellow Tinted

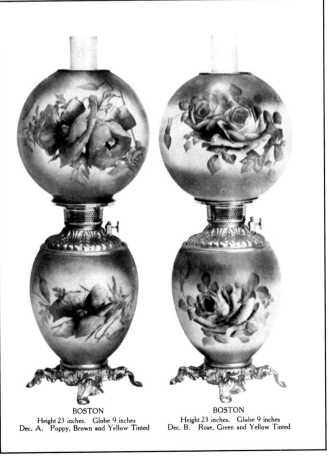

BOSTON
Height 23 inches.   Globe 9 inches
Dec. A.   Poppy, Brown and Yellow Tinted

BOSTON
Height 23 inches.   Globe 9 inches
Dec. B.   Rose, Green and Yellow Tinted

163

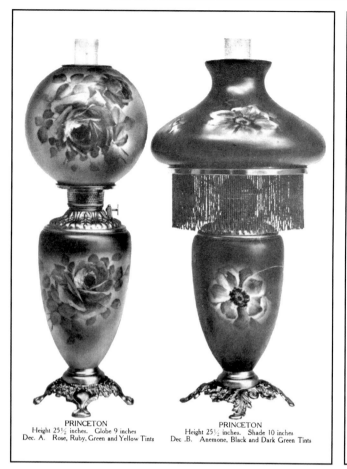

PRINCETON
Height 25½ inches. Globe 9 inches
Dec. A. Rose, Ruby, Green and Yellow Tints

PRINCETON
Height 25½ inches. Shade 10 inches
Dec. B. Anemone, Black and Dark Green Tints

HARMON
Height 23 inches. Globe 10 inches
Dec. A. Wild Rose, Ruby Tinted

HARMON
Height 23 inches. Globe 10 inches
Dec. B. Poppy, Green and Yellow Tinted

OSBORN
Height 23½ inches. Globe 10 inches
Dec. A. Rose and Cupid. Ivory Tinted

PLAZA
Height 25 inches. Globe 10 inches
Dec. A. Pansy, Ruby and Yellow Tints

OSBORN—Dec. B. Rose and Cupid, Blue and Yellow Tinted

PLAZA
Height 25 inches. Globe 10 inches
Dec. B. Wild Rose, Green and Yellow Tinted

PLAZA
Height 25 inches. Shade 10 inches
Dec. C. Poppy, Brown and Green Tints

HARVEY
Height 22½ inches. Globe 10 inches
Dec. B. Blackberry Blossom, Ivory and Carmine Tints

HARVEY
Height 22½ inches. Globe 10 inches
Dec. C. Carnation, Ruby, Green and Yellow Tints

HARVEY—Dec. A. Cupids, Pink, Blue and Yellow Tints

PEORIA
Height 25½ inches. Shade 10 inches.
Dec. A. Rose, Ruby Tinted

PEORIA
Height 25½ inches. Globe 10 inches
Dec. C. Rose and Scroll, Celadon Green Tint

PEORIA—Dec. B. Wild Rose, Pink and Green Tints

BERNARD
Height 27 inches. Globe 10 inches
Dec. A. Wild Rose, Pink Tinted

BERNARD
Height 27 inches. Globe 10 inches
Dec. B. Rose, Dark Green Tint

BERNARD—Dec. C. Chrysanthemums, Ruby and Ivory Tints

EDSON
Height 28 inches. Shade 10 inches
Dec. B. Roses, Green and Yellow Tints

EDSON
Height 28 inches. Globe 10 Inches
Dec. C. Leaf, Brown and Green Tints

EDSON—Dec. A. Orchid, Pink and Green Tints

165

GLENDALE
Height 26 inches.   Globe 10 inches
Dec. A.   Roses, Ruby Tinted

GLENDALE
Height 26 inches.   Globe 10 inches
Dec. B.   Poppy, Brown Tinted

TOLEDO
Height 21 inches.   Globe 10 inches
Dec. A.   Rose, Pink, Ivory and Green Tints

TOLEDO
Height 21 inches.   Globe 10 inches
Dec. B.   Wild Rose, Ivory and Green Tints

DENVER
Height 28½ inches.   Globe 11 inches
Dec. A.   Rose and Scroll, Ruby,
Green and Yellow Tints

DENVER
Height 28½ inches.   Globe 11 inches
Dec. B.   Chrysanthemums
Brown and Yellow Tints

PALACE
Height 26 inches.   Globe 11 inches
Dec. B. Leaf, Dark Brown, Green and Yellow Tints

PALACE
Height 26 inches.   Globe 11 inches
Dec. A.   Wild Rose, Ruby, Blue and Ivory Tints

IDEAL
Height 27½ inches.   Globe 11 inches
Dec. A.   Peony, Ruby Tint

IDEAL
Height 27½ inches.   Globe 11 inches
Dec. B.   Clematis, Dark Green Tint

WILTON
Height 27½ inches.   Globe 11 inches
Dec. A,   Ivory and Light Green Tints

WILTON
Height 27½ inches.   Globe 11 inches
Dec.   B.   Dark French Grey and Green Tints

RALEIGH
Height 29 inches.   Globe 11 inches
Dec. A.   Brown Tinted

RALEIGH
Height 29 inches.   Globe 11 inches
Dec. B.   Dark Green Tinted

PAXTON
Height 25½ inches.   Globe 12 inches
Dec. A.   Wild Roses, Ruby,
Green and Yellow Tints

PAXTON
Height 25½ inches.   Globe 12 inches
Dec. B.   Roses, Ivory
Pink and Blue Tinted

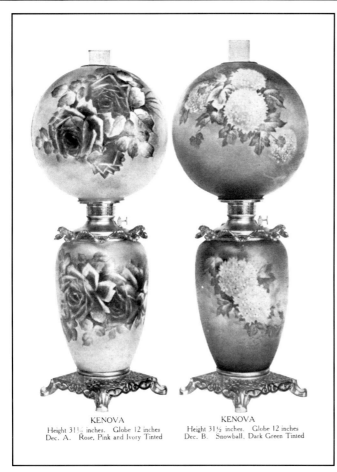

KENOVA
Height 31½ inches. Globe 12 inches
Dec. A. Rose, Pink and Ivory Tinted

KENOVA
Height 31½ inches. Globe 12 inches
Dec. B. Snowball, Dark Green Tinted

No. 1150 Vase
Height 14½ inches. Dec. No. 1
Dark Brown Tinted

No. 1150 Vase
Height 14½ inches. Dec. No. 4
Light Brown Tinted

No. 1150 Vase
Squirrel Dec.
Either Brown or Green Tints

No. 1151 Vase
Height 12½ inches. Elk Dec.
Either Brown or Green Tints

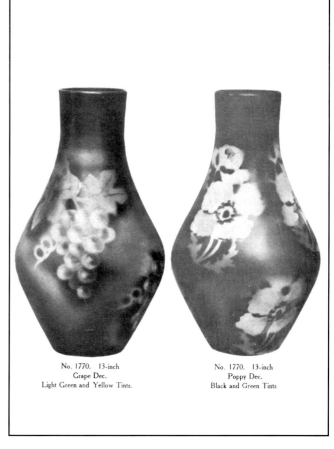

No. 1770. 13-inch
Grape Dec.
Light Green and Yellow Tints.

No. 1770. 13-inch
Poppy Dec.
Black and Green Tints

No. 1771. 13-inch. Rose Dec.
Green and Yellow Tints

No. 1771. 13-inch. Poppy Dec.
Brown and Yellow Tints

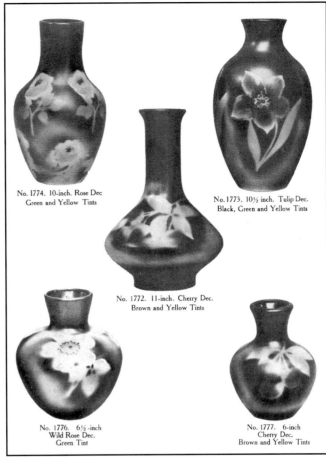

No. 1774. 10-inch. Rose Dec
Green and Yellow Tints

No. 1773. 10½ inch. Tulip Dec.
Black, Green and Yellow Tints

No. 1772. 11-inch. Cherry Dec.
Brown and Yellow Tints

No. 1776. 6½-inch
Wild Rose Dec.
Green Tint

No. 1777. 6-inch
Cherry Dec.
Brown and Yellow Tints

10-inch Globe. Dec. 401

9-inch Globe. Dec. 401

10-inch Globe. Dec. 402

9-inch Globe. Dec. 402

10-inch Globe. Dec. 403

9-inch Globe. Dec. 403

Persian Red Lamps—Solid Colors

No. 2 LAMP
With 8-inch Globe. Height 18½ inches

No. 5 LAMP
With 8½-inch Globe. Height 18½ inches

No. 1151 Vase
Height 12½ inches.   Dec. No .2
Green Tinted

No. 1151 Vase
Height 12½ inches.   Dec, No. 3
Green Tinted

No. 321.   Dec. D
Height 20 inches

No. 1775 7-inch Vase

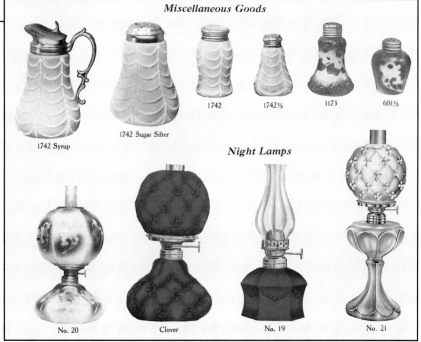

Miscellaneous Goods

1742 Syrup

1742 Sugar Sifter

1742

1742½

1173

601½

Night Lamps

No. 20

Clover

No. 19

No. 21

Not Tinted

**No. 200
Assortment**

14-inch Shade. Dec. 201

Fount. Dec. 201

10-inch Shade. Dec. 201

14-inch Shade. Dec. 202.

Fount. Dec. 202

10-inch Shade. Dec. 202

14-inch Shade. Dec. 203

Fount. Dec. 203

10-inch Shade. Dec. 203

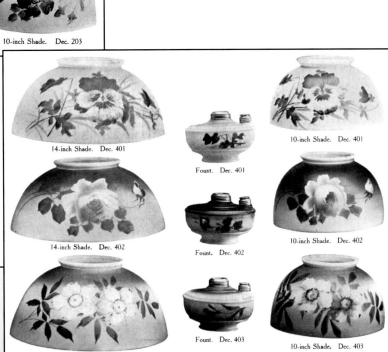

14-inch Shade. Dec. 401

Fount. Dec. 401

10-inch Shade. Dec. 401

14-inch Shade. Dec. 402

Fount. Dec. 402

10-inch Shade. Dec. 402

14-inch Shade. Dec. 403

Fount. Dec. 403

10-inch Shade. Dec. 403

Persian Red Lamps—Solid Colors

No. 1 LAMP
With 9½-inch Globe. Height 23½ inches

No. 17 LAMP
With 9½-inch Globe. Height 23½ inches

MARMALADES, MUSTARDS, and MAYONNAISE SETS

Marmalades and mustards are usually the same basic shape but the marmalade is larger. Mayonnaise sets usually consist of a bowl, plate, and ladle. The 2315 mayonnaise sets, used extensively in the 1920s and made in color, are shown in *Fostoria Tableware: 1924 – 1943*. The most widely recognized mayonnaise sets are the 2375 Fairfax, and the 2496 Baroque since they were used with many etched patterns. However, mustards and mayonnaise sets were to be found in most of the pressed patterns. We have not attempted to relist all the patterns which had a marmalade, mustard, or mayonnaise. Ladles and spoons for these pieces are difficult to find, especially the 2375 ladle which was the only one made in colors (see Spoons and Ladles).

The covers for earlier marmalades and mustards could be notched for a spoon or left unnotched. The later ones were all notched. The mustard and mayonnaise were listed with glass spoons, but the marmalade used a stainless steel spoon.

1968 Marmalade, Blown, Plain, pre 1924-1928; $32.00

4087 Marmalade and Cover, Plain or Optic, Silver plated Metal Spoon (see Appetizers, Buffet, and Relish)
Crystal, 1922-1942; $47.00
Amber, 1929-1931; $64.00
Green, 1929-1931; $67.00
Rose, 1929-1932; $67.00
Azure, 1929-1932; $67.00
Regal Blue, 1934-1940; $68.00
Burgundy, 1934-1940; $68.00
Empire Green, 1934-1935; $75.00

4089 Marmalade, Plain or Optic, pre 1924-1928; $32.00

1831 Mustard and Cover, Blown, Plain or Optic (see Appetizers, Buffet, and Relish)
Crystal, pre 1924-1938; $28.00
Regal Blue, 1934-1938; $52.00
Burgundy, 1934-1938; $52.00
Empire Green, 1934-1938; $52.00

2496 Mustard (See Baroque)

810 Mayonnaise, 3 piece, pre 1924-1928; $35.00

1831 Mustard, New Vintage Etching; 4089 Marmalade, cut; Amber 4087 Marmalade, LO; 1968 Marmalade, Poupee Etching

858 Mayonnaise, 3 piece, pre 1924-1928; $35.00

1769 Mayonnaise, 3 piece, pre 1924-1928; $35.00

2138 Mayonnaise, Plate and 2138 Spoon, Crystal, pre 1924-1928; $67.00

2315 Mayonnaise sets (See Twenty-Three Fifteen)

2375 Mayonnaise (See Fairfax)

2496 Mayonnaise (See Baroque)

No. 1968 Marmalade and Cover.
No. 1831 Mustard and Cover.
No. 1831 Mustard and Cover.
No. 4087 Marmalade and Cover.
No. 4089. Marmalade and Cover.
No. 810-3 Piece Mayonnaise Set.
NO. 2138 - 3 Piece Mayonnaise Set
No. 1769-3 Piece Mayonnaise Set.
No. 858-3 Piece Mayonnaise Set.

PLATES

Plates tend to be useful, but do not attract much attention otherwise. The Fostoria Company made plates for every conceivable use as well as offering them in numerous sizes, colors and optics. We are including plates made in color in 1924 and through the end of production that do not belong to a pattern and have not been shown previously. It is apparent that numbers 2283 and 2337 were favorites used over and over with patterns needing a plate. One discovery is the 2364 16" torte in colors. It was not offered with the Sonata pattern, but was always listed separately.

One thing to watch for when purchasing used plates is excessive scratching. Prices always assume mint condition.

The 2290 13" cupped plate was used as part of the 2284 epergne set shown with vases. An octagon-shaped plate carried over to an octagon-shaped tray. The snack plates were made to accommodate a tumbler or a cup.

2283 Plate, 5"
  Crystal, 1925-1943; $2.00
  Amber, 1925-1934; $3.00
  Green, 1925-1934; $3.00
  Blue, 1925-1927; $4.00
2283 Plate, 6"
  Crystal, 1924-1943; $2.00
  Amber, 1924-1940; $3.00
  Green, 1924-1940; $3.00
  Blue, 1925-1927; $4.00
  Canary, 1924-1926; $4.00
  Orchid, 1927-1928; $4.00
  Rose, 1928-1940; $3.00
  Azure, 1929-1932; $4.00
2283 Plate, 7"
  Crystal, 1924-1943; $3.00
  Amber, 1924-1940; $4.00
  Green, 1924-1936; $4.00
  Blue, 1925-1927; $6.00
  Canary, 1924-1926; $6.00
  Orchid, 1927-1928; $6.00
  Rose, 1928-1940; $5.00
  Azure, 1928-1932; $5.00
2283 Plate, 7", Cut 175, 177, or 178
  Crystal, $10.00
  Amber, $10.00
  Green, $12.00
  Canary, $24.00
2283 Plate, 8"
  Crystal, 1924-1943; $3.00
  Amber, 1924-1935; $4.00
  Green, 1924-1937; $4.00
  Blue, 1925-1927; $6.00
  Canary, 1924-1926; $6.00
  Orchid, 1927-1928; $6.00
  Rose, 1928-1934; $5.00
  Azure, 1928-1932; $5.00
2283 Plate, 9"
  Crystal, 1925-1928; $6.00
  Amber, 1925-1928; $9.00
  Green, 1925-1928; $10.00
  Blue, 1925-1927; $15.00
2283 Plate, 10"
  Crystal, 1925-1928; $8.00
  Amber, 1925-1928; $10.00
  Green, 1925-1928; $12.00
  Blue, 1925-1927; $18.00

2283 Plate, 11"
  Crystal, 1925-1928; $10.00
  Amber, 1925-1928; $12.00
  Green, 1925-1928; $13.00
  Blue, 1925-1927; $20.00
  Canary, 1925-1926; $20.00
2283 Plate, 12"
  Amber, 1927-1943; $12.00
  Green, 1927; $13.00
  Blue, 1927; $20.00
2283 Plate, 13" Flared
  Amber, 1925-1930; $15.00
  Green, 1925-1930; $18.00
  Blue, 1925-1927; $25.00
  Canary, 1925-1926; $30.00
  Orchid, 1927-1928; $25.00
  Rose, 1928-1930; $25.00
2283 Plate, 6" RO
  Crystal, 1928-1943; $2.00
  Amber, 1927-1939; $3.00
  Green, 1927-1939; $3.00
  Blue, 1927; $5.00
  Orchid, 1927; $5.00

Blue Brunswick 2283, Amethyst 2337, Green Spiral Optic 2283, Mother of Pearl Loop Optic 2337

Rose, 1928-1940; $4.00
Azure, 1928-1932; $4.00
Topaz, 1931-1940; $3.00
2283 Plate, 7" RO
Crystal, 1928-1943; $3.00
Amber, 1927-1932; $4.00
Green, 1927-1932; $4.00
Blue, 1927; $6.00
2283 Plate, 8" RO
Crystal, 1928-1943; $3.00
Amber, 1927-1932; $4.00
Green, 1927-1932; $4.00
Blue, 1927; $6.00
2283 Plate, 6" SO
Crystal, 1925-1934; $3.00
Amber, 1925-1934; $4.00
Green, 1925-1934; $4.00
Blue, 1925-1927; $6.00
Orchid, 1927-1928; $6.00
Rose, 1928-1934; $5.00
Azure, 1928-1934; $5.00
2283 Plate, 7" SO
Crystal, 1925-1934; $4.00
Amber, 1925-1934; $5.00
Green, 1925-1934; $6.00
Blue, 1925-1927; $8.00
Canary, 1925-1926; $8.00
Orchid, 1927-1928; $8.00
Rose, 1928-1934; $7.00
Azure, 1928-1934; $7.00
2283 Plate, 8" SO
Crystal, 1925-1934; $4.00
Amber, 1925-1934; $5.00
Green, 1925-1934; $6.00
Blue, 1925-1927; $8.00
Canary, 1925-1926; $8.00
Orchid, 1927-1928; $8.00
Rose, 1928-1934; $7.00
Azure, 1928-1934; $7.00
2283 Plate, 9" SO
Amber, 1929-1930; $6.00
Green, 1929-1930; $9.00
Rose, 1929-1930; $10.00
Azure, 1929-1930; $12.00
2283 Plate, 10" SO
Amber, 1929-1930; $15.00
Green, 1929-1930; $18.00
Rose, 1929-1930; $20.00
Azure, 1929-1930; $24.00
2283 Plate, 13" SO
Amber, 1925-1929; $16.00
Green, 1925-1929; $18.00
Blue, 1925-1927; $25.00
Canary, 1925-1926; $25.00
Orchid, 1927-1928; $25.00
Rose, 1928-1929; $22.00
Azure, 1928-1929; $24.00

No. 2283   No. 7 Salad Plate, Cut 178
Made in Crystal, Green, Amber or Canary

No. 2283   No. 7 Salad Plate, Cut 177
Made in Crystal, Green, Amber or Canary

No. 2283   No. 7 Salad Plate, Cut 175
Made in Crystal, Green, Amber or Canary

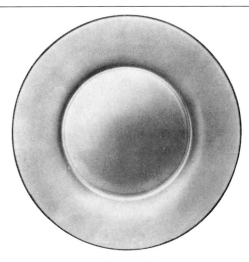

2283—8 in. Plate.
Made in 6, 7, 8, and 13 in.
Also made in orchid 6, 7, 8, and 13 in.
5 in. made in Amber and Green only.

2290 Plate, 7" Deep Salad
    Amber, 1925-1927; $5.00
    Green, 1925-1927; $7.00
    Blue, 1925-1927; $9.00
    Canary, 1925-1926; $9.00
    Ebony, 1925-1926; $7.00
2290 Plate, 8" Deep Salad
    Amber, 1924-1927; $5.00
    Green, 1924-1927; $8.00
    Blue, 1925-1927; $9.00
    Canary, 1924-1926; $9.00
    Ebony, 1925-1926; $7.00
2290 Plate, 13" Flared, RO
    Amber, 1924-1927; $15.00
    Green, 1924-1927; $18.00
    Blue, 1925-1927; $25.00
    Canary, 1924-1926; $25.00
2290 Plate, 13" Cupped, used with the 2284 3-piece
    Epergne (see Vases)
2316 Plate, 8" Soup
    Amber, 1925-1926; $5.00
    Green, 1925-1926; $8.00
    Blue, 1925-1926; $9.00
2330 Plate/Sherbet, 6", one piece, Green, 1925-1926; $24.00
2332 Plate, 7" Mayonnaise (Used with 2315 Mayonnaise,
    although most of the time the Mayonnaise was shown
    without a plate.)
    Crystal, 1925-1934; $5.00
    Amber, 1925-1934; $7.00
    Green, 1925-1934; $8.00
    Blue, 1925-1934; $10.00
    Canary, 1925-1926; $10.00
    Orchid, 1927-1928; $10.00
    Rose, 1928-1932; $9.00
    Azure, 1928-1932; $9.00
2337 Plate, 6"
    Crystal, 1934-1973; $4.00
    Regal Blue, 1934-1942; $12.00
    Burgundy, 1934-1942; $12.00

Empire Green, 1934-1942; $12.00
Ruby, 1935-1942; $14.00
2337 Plate, 7"
    Crystal, 1934-1976; $5.00
    Amber, 1926-1927; $7.00
    Green, 1926-1927; $8.00
    Blue, 1926-1927; $10.00
    Regal Blue, 1934-1942; $12.00
    Burgundy, 1934-1942; $12.00
    Empire Green, 1934-1942; 1950-1964; $12.00
    Ruby, 1935-1942; $14.00
    Amethyst, 1950-1964; $12.00
    Gold, 1962-1970; $10.00
    Lilac, 1962-1974; $12.00
    Gray Mist, 1962-1974; $8.00
    Pink, 1963-1974; $12.00
    Green Mist, 1968-1974; $8.00
    Onyx, 1971-1974; $8.00
    Blue, 1972-1974; $8.00
    Plum 1972-1974; $10.00
2337 Plate, 8"
    Crystal, 1934-1976; $6.00
    Amber, 1926-1927; $8.00
    Green, 1926-1927; $10.00
    Blue, 1926-1927; $12.00
    Regal Blue, 1934-1942; $16.00
    Burgundy, 1934-1942; $16.00
    Empire Green, 1934-1942; $16.00
    Ruby, 1935-1942; $18.00
2337 Plate, 11"
    Crystal, 1934-1943; $10.00
    Regal Blue, 1934-1942; $25.00
    Burgundy, 1934-1942; $25.00
    Empire Green, 1934-1942; $25.00
    Ruby, 1935-1942; $25.00

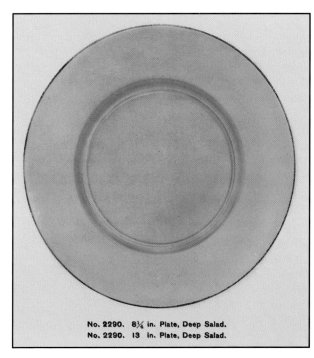

No. 2290. 8¾ in. Plate, Deep Salad.
No. 2290. 13 in. Plate, Deep Salad.

2337 Plate, 6" RO, 1935-1958; $4.00
2337 Plate, 7" RO, 1935-1958; $5.00
2337 Plate, 8" RO, 1935-1958; $6.00
2337 Plate, 9", 1938-1970; $10.00
2337 Plate, 10" Dinner, 1957-1970; $12.00
2337 Plate, 6" LO, 1942-1943; $8.00
2337 Plate, 7" LO, 1939-1974; $10.00
2337 Plate, 8" LO, 1940-1943; $12.00
2337 Plate, 7" Niagara Optic, 1953-1965; $10.00
2337 Plate, 7" Narrow Optic, 1956-1970; $10.00
2341 Plate, 8" Figured Edge
    Amber, 1925-1926; $18.00
    Green, 1925-1926; $20.00
    Blue, 1925-1926; $25.00
    Canary, 1925-1926; $25.00
2342 Plate, 6" Octagon
    Amber, 1929-1934; $6.00
    Green, 1929-1934; $7.00
    Rose, 1929-1934; $7.00
    Azure, 1929-1934; $8.00
2342 Plate, 7" Octagon
    Crystal, 1925-1937; $5.00
    Amber, 1925-1934; $7.00
    Green, 1925-1937; $8.00
    Blue, 1925-1927; $12.00
    Canary, 1925-1926; $12.00
    Orchid, 1927-1928; $12.00
    Rose, 1928-1937; $9.00
2342 Plate, 8" Octagon
    Crystal, 1925-1932; $6.00
    Amber, 1925-1932; $8.00
    Green, 1925-1932; $9.00
    Blue, 1925-1927; $12.00
    Canary, 1925-1926; $12.00
    Orchid, 1927-1928; $12.00
    Rose, 1928-1932; $10.00
    Azure, 1929-1932; $10.00
2342 Plate, 13" Octagon
    Amber, 1925-1930; $44.00
    Green, 1925-1930; $48.00
    Blue, 1925-1927; $55.00
    Canary, 1925-1926; $55.00
    Orchid, 1927-1928; $50.00
    Rose, 1928-1930; $48.00
    Azure, 1929-1930; $50.00
2348 Plate, 8"
    Amber, 1926-1929; $10.00
    Green, 1926-1929; $12.00
    Blue, 1926-1927; $15.00
    Canary, 1926; $15.00
2356 Plate, 8"
    Amber, 1926-1929; $12.00
    Green, 1926-1930; $15.00
    Blue, 1926-1927; $18.00
    Canary, 1926; $18.00
    Orchid, 1927-1928; $18.00

No. 2330. Sherbet and Plate, (One Piece.)
(Made in Green only)

2364 Plate, 14" Torte (See Sonata)
2364 Plate, 16" (Sonata)
    Crystal, 1931-1943; $45.00
    Green, 1931-1935; $74.00
    Amber, 1931-1940; $70.00
    Ebony, 1931-1936; $55.00
    Rose, 1931-1935; $75.00
    Topaz/Gold Tint, 1931-1940; $65.00
    Regal Blue, 1934-1937; $87.00
    Burgundy, 1934-1937; $85.00
    Empire Green, 1934-1935; $95.00
2492 Plate, 8½" Fish Canape (See Bar and Refreshment)
2541 Plate, Snack, 1935-1939; $12.00
2665 Plate, 7", 1952-1958; $10.00
2665 Plate, 8", 1952-1960; $10.00

No. 2341. 8 in. Plate.

No. 2342. 8 in. Plate.

No. 2316. 8 in. Soup Plate.
(Made in Crystal, Amber, Blue and Green)

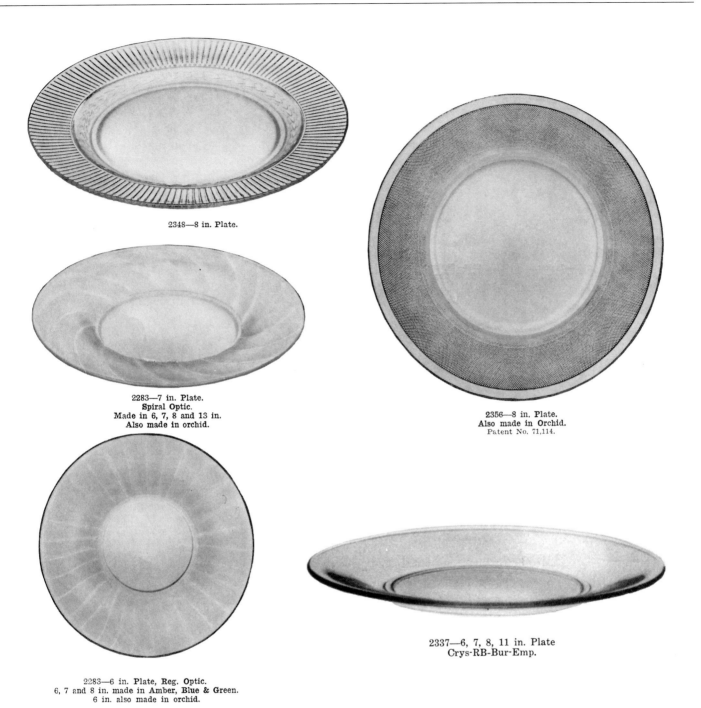

2348—8 in. Plate.

2283—7 in. Plate.
Spiral Optic.
Made in 6, 7, 8 and 13 in.
Also made in orchid.

2356—8 in. Plate.
Also made in Orchid.
Patent No. 71,114.

2283—6 in. Plate, Reg. Optic.
6, 7 and 8 in. made in Amber, Blue & Green.
6 in. also made in orchid.

2337—6, 7, 8, 11 in. Plate
Crys-RB-Bur-Emp.

2541—Snack Plate
6¾ in. Square

SALAD DRESSING and OIL BOTTLES

In the early years from 1900 to 1920 there were numerous oil and vinegar bottles used. Most pressed patterns had at least one, some had several sizes. A few of these carried over with patterns that continued production after 1920. By 1924 the 1465 and 312 were used with most cut and etched patterns. After 1928 oil bottles independent of a pressed pattern disappeared as most pressed tableware patterns offered one or more sizes of oil bottles. Not so with salad dressing bottles. The 2169 salad dressing bottle was used with the Oriental pattern and was slightly larger than the 2083, although similar in shape. The 2083 had been in use prior to 1924 and continued to be made through 1943 in crystal. It was also made in colors for a few years. The 2375 salad dressing bottle, also made in colors, was used extensively for cut and etched patterns. The 2375 Fairfax footed oil was used for patterns in color. These bottles in color especially with the etched patterns are fast becoming among the hard to find pieces.

312, Plain or CN, Optic, pre 1924-1928; $32.00
1465, 5 oz., Plain or CN, Optic, 1924-1928; $32.00
1465, 7 oz., Plain or CN, Optic, 1924-1928; $32.00
2083 Salad Dressing Bottle, Plain or Optic, "Vinegar and Oil" optional
    Crystal, 1924-1943; $58.00
    Amber, 1930-1932; $64.00
    Green, 1930-1932; $75.00
    Rose, 1930-1932; $75.00
    Azure, 1930-1932; $85.00
    Topaz, 1930-1932; $75.00
2056 (see American)
2375 (see Fairfax)
2412 (see Colony)
2449 (see Hermitage)
2510 (see Sunray)
2560 (see Coronet)
2574 (see Raleigh)
2630 (see Century)
2666 (see Contour)

No. 2169 Salad Dressing Bottle.

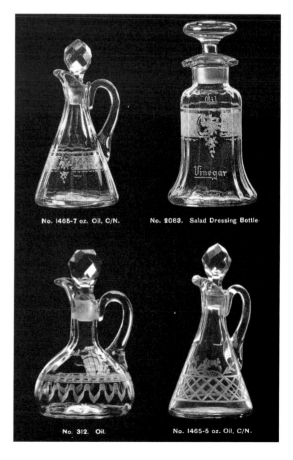

Mayflower 2560 Oil, Topaz Trojan 2375 Footed Oil, I.C. Pattern Oil, Topaz 2419 Mayfair Oil

Amber 2375 Salad Dressing Bottle, Navarre 2083 Salad Dressing Bottle, Topaz 2083 Salad Dressing Bottle

No. 1465-7 oz. Oil, C/N.   No. 2083. Salad Dressing Bottle.

No. 312. Oil.   No. 1465-5 oz. Oil, C/N.

SHAKERS and OPEN SALTS

Shakers were more popular in the 1920s and 1930s, gradually replacing the open salt on American tables. Interestingly, advertising from this period occasionally shows a shaker paired with the 4095 footed salt. Fostoria offered a variety of shaker tops over the years, and most of these are listed at the end of this section. The Fostoria glass top, or FGT as it is commonly found listed, is the most sought after and most difficult to find in mint condition. All glass tops were crystal with the exception of the 2111 shaker which had a top the same color as the shaker, and the Winburn milk glass shaker which was offered with a milk glass top. The 2449 Hermitage and 2510 Sunray glass tops were dome shaped. All other glass tops were flat. The most popular of the all glass shakers was, and continues to be, the 2375 Fairfax. No shakers were offered from 1944 to 1947. By 1949 all glass tops had been replaced with chrome.

The Priscilla and Hartford pieces shown in the photographs are from the turn of the century.

Shakers are priced as a pair. For information on shakers that belonged to particular lines, such as Sonata or Colony, the reader is asked to refer to *Fostoria Tableware: 1924 – 1943* and *Fostoria Tableware: 1944 – 1986*.

614 Shaker, FGT, Crystal, 1935-1942; $28.00
713½ Shaker, FGT
    Crystal, 1929-1930; $28.00
    Amber, 1929-1930; $35.00
    Green, 1929-1934; $38.00
800 Shaker, FGT, Crystal, 1935-1943; $28.00
880 Salt, Footed Open, Crystal, pre 1924-1929;
    $20.00
1913½ Salt, Open
    Amber, 1926-1932; $22.00
    Green, 1926-1932; $22.00
    Blue, 1926-1927; $26.00
2022 Shaker, 1918-1928; $32.00
2056 Shaker (see American)
2111 Shaker, FGT
    Crystal, 1924-1942; $28.00
    Amber, 1924-1940; $32.00
    Blue, 1924-1927; $45.00
    Green, 1924-1940; $34.00
    Canary, 1924-1926; $45.00
    Rose, 1928-1939; $35.00
    Azure, 1928-1939; $37.00
    Topaz/Gold Tint, 1930-1939; $35.00
    Orchid, 1927-1928; $35.00
2127 Shaker, FGT
    Crystal, 1924-1932; $28.00
    Amber, 1924-1932; $36.00
    Blue, 1924-1927; $45.00
    Green, 1924-1932; $38.00
    Canary, 1924-1926; $45.00
2128 Shaker, FGT
    Crystal, 1924-1932; $28.00
    Amber, 1924-1932; $36.00
    Blue, 1924-1927; $45.00
    Green, 1924-1932; $38.00
    Canary, 1924-1926; $45.00
2222 Footed Salt (Colonial), pre 1924-1928;
    $18.00
2235 Shaker, FGT, PT (used almost exclusively with etched and cut patterns in the 1920s)
    Crystal, 1922-1942; $25.00
    Regal Blue, 1935-1940; $45.00
    Burgundy, 1935-1939; $45.00
    Empire Green, 1935-1940; $45.00

676 Priscilla Shakers, Sterling Embossed Tops; 501 Hartford Shakers, Hard Nickel Tops; Individual Salt

2236 Shaker, FGT
    Amber, 1930-1938; $38.00
    Green, 1930-1937; $40.00
    Rose, 1930-1932; $45.00
    Topaz/Gold Tint, 1930-1938; $40.00
2263 Salt, Individual Open, Crystal, 1924-1927; $20.00
2364 Shaker (see Sonata)
2375 Shaker, Footed, FGT (see Fairfax)
2412 Shaker (see Colony)

1913½ Salts on 2000 Condiment Tray

2419 Shaker, FGT (see Mayfair)
2449 Shaker (see Hermitage)
2496 Shaker, FGT (see Baroque)
2510 Shaker (see Sunray)
2521 Bird Salt
    Crystal, 1936-1940; $20.00
    Regal Blue, 1934-1939; $32.00
    Burgundy, 1934-1939; $32.00
    Empire Green, 1934-1939; $32.00
    Ruby, 1934-1939; $35.00
    Milk glass (see Milk Glass)
2560 Shaker (see Coronet)
2574 Shaker (see Raleigh)
2593 Salt, Individual, Crystal, 1940-1943; $22.00
2630 Shaker (see Century)
2666 Shaker (see Contour)
2719 Shaker (see Jamestown)
4020 Shaker, SPT
    Crystal, 1931-1932; $77.00
    Amber Base, 1931-1932; $98.00
    Green Base, 1931-1932; $125.00
    Rose Bowl, 1931-1932; $125.00
    Topaz Bowl, 1931-1932; $125.00
    Ebony Base, 1931-1932; $110.00
    Wisteria Base, 1931-1932; $145.00
4095 Salt, Individual Footed
    Crystal, RO, 1925-1927; $20.00
    Crystal, SO, 1925; $22.00
    Amber, RO, 1926-1927; $25.00
    Amber Foot, LO, 1925-1927; $25.00
    Green, RO, SO, 1925-1927; $28.00

Henry Ford Museum Copper Blue Salt; Milk Glass Bird Salt; 4095 Almond, Green Foot; 4095 Salt, Green Foot

    Green Foot, SO, 1925-1927; $28.00
    Blue, RO, 1926-1927; $30.00
    Blue Foot, RO, 1925-1927; $30.00
    Rose Bowl, RO, 1928-1930; $28.00
    Azure Bowl, RO, 1928-1930; $30.00
    Topaz Bowl, 1929-1930; $28.00
5100 Shaker, Optic, SPT, FGT
    Crystal, 1924-1932; $64.00
    Amber Foot, 1924-1926; $95.00
    Solid Amber, 1924-1932; $95.00
    Blue Foot, 1924-1926; $125.00
    Solid Blue, 1924-1927; $125.00
    Green Foot, 1924-1926; $110.00
    Solid Green, 1924-1932; $110.00

Blue 2127 Shaker, Crystal and Green 2111 Shakers, 2235 Crystal with Cattail Cutting, 5100 Green Shaker with Fostoria Glass Top (FGT), 2128 Amber

2364 Sonata Shaker with Romance Etching, FGT; 2630 Century Shaker with Heather Etching, Chrome Top; 2022 Woodland Etching; 2560 Coronet Shaker with Mayflower Etching; 2364 Chintz Shaker, Chrome Top

2375 Green Fairfax Shaker, FGT; Gold Tint Regular Baroque Shaker, FGT; 4020 Manor Shaker, SPT; 2419 Mayfair Shaker with Manor Etching, FGT; Azure Fairfax, Sterling Silver Top; Gold Tint Baroque Individual, FGT

2675 Peach Randolph Shaker, Chrome Top; 1704 Winburn Milk Glass Shakers with Milk Glass Tops; 1871 Shaker, Chrome Top F

713½—Shaker, F. G. T.
Height 3 in.

2111—Shaker, F. G. T.
Height 2⅛ in.

800—Shaker, F. G. T.
Height 2½ in.

2235—Shaker, F. G. T.
Height 2½ in.

614
Shaker, F. G. T.
Height 3 in.

SHAKER TOPS

These tops were still being offered in 1924:
GTop: Glass disc in metal band
PTop: Pearl disc in non-corrosive band
XXX Top: Nickel Silver with extra heavy plate
SPT: Silver Plated Top
NC: Non-Corrosive Top
FGT: Fostoria Glass Top
HNT: Hard Nickel Top

After 1928, shaker tops were glass or silver plated. By 1949 these tops were replaced by chrome. The 2449 Hermitage and 2510 Sunray glass tops were dome shaped. All others were flat.
Chrome Tops:
A, Regular for Jamestown, American
C, Individual for Colony, Century, American
B, Regular for Century
E, Contour
F, Lead Crystal

2111—Shaker.
F. G. Top.
Also made in Orchid.

2127—Shaker.
F. G. Top.

2222—Ftd. Salt.

2236   Shaker, G. T.
Ro-Gr-Am-Tz
Priced on page 40

4020   Footed Shaker
Solid Crystal
Gr-Am-Eb-Wis Base
with Crys Bowl
Crys Base with
Ro-Tz Bowl
Priced on page 40

4095—Salt, optic.
Solid colors or colored foot.

5100—Shaker, Optic.
F. G. Top.
Also made in orchid.

1913½—Ind. Salt.
2000—Condiment Tray.

1934 House and Garden

No.2235 Shaker, Pearl Top.

No.2263 Ind. Salt,
Eng. 26.

No.880 Ftd. Salt, Eng. 26.

2593—Individual Salt
Height ¾ in.   1½ in. Square

SILVER MIST
Decoration 525

As one follows Silver Mist through the price lists, it is evident that Fostoria was not always sure where it belonged. First listed with decorations in 1934, for the rest of the 1930s it is usually found listed with plate etchings. Silver Mist was not given a number until 1950 when, on the Madonna, it is listed as Decoration 525. As such, it represents a contradiction for the Fostoria Glass Company, and is one of the few patterns that was identified by name and not by number first.

As a pattern, Silver Mist took pieces from many other lines. The majority of pieces were made in Silver Mist from 1934 through 1940. Figurals and bookends were added in 1935 and 1940 respectively. This first period of Silver Mist ended in 1943 and did not return until 1950. This listing includes pieces from the 1934 – 1943 period with the pieces introduced in 1950 being included with such patterns as Garden Center, Henry Ford Museum, and Lotus Giftware (see *Fostoria Tableware: 1944 – 1986*). Oftentimes during that later period, the Silver Mist was used on color (see also Figurals). Prices would be about 10% above the same item in Crystal.

2419 Ash Tray, 1935-1938
2457 Ash Tray, 1934-1940
2520 Ash Tray, 1934-1943
2534 Ash Tray, 1935-1942
2538 Ash Tray/Place Card Holder, 1935-1943
2538 Berry Set, 9 pieces, 1935-1943, 11" Nappy, eight 4½" Nappies
2521 Bird, 1935-1938
2494 Bitters Bottle, 1934-1938
2517 Bon Bon, 1935-1938
2536 Bowl, 9" Handled, 1935-1940
2484 Bowl, 10" Handled, 1934-1938
4024 Bowl, 10" Footed, 1934-1936
4024 Candlestick, 6", Silver Mist base, 1934-1935
2472 Candlestick, Duo, 1934-1938
2496 Candlestick, Duo, 1935-1938
2496 Candlestick, Trindle, 1935-1938
2484 Candlestick, 2-light, 1934-1938
2484 Candlestick, 2-light with Drips, 1934-1938 (see Candlesticks for photograph)
2484½ Candle Drips, 3½", 1934-1938
2535 Candlestick, 5½", 1935-1940
4099 Candy Jar and Cover, 1935-1938
2511 Cheese and Cracker, 1934
2391 Cigarette Box, Large, and Cover, 1934-1940
5092 Cigarette, 1934-1938
2518 Cocktail, 3 oz. Footed, 1935-1940
4115½ Cocktail, 4 oz. Footed, 1935-1938
2518 Cocktail Shaker, Gold Top, 1934-1938
2518½ Cocktail Shaker, Gold Top, 1935-1940
2525 Cocktail Shaker, Gold Top, 1935-1940
2525½ Cocktail Shaker, Gold Top, 1935-1940
2519 Cologne and Stopper; 1935-1939
2589 Colt, Standing, 1940-1943
2589 Colt, Reclining, 1940-1943
4024 Comport, 5" Silver Mist base, 1935-1938
4024 Cordial, 1934-1938
2494 Cordial Set, 10 pieces, 1934-1935, Cordial Tray, 2494 Cordial Bottle, eight 4024 Cordials
2494 Cordial Set, 7 pieces, 1934-1938, Cordial Bottle, six 4024 Cordials
2494 Decanter and Stopper, 1934-1938
2502 Decanter and Stopper, 1934-1935
2518 Decanter and Stopper, 1935-1940

2502 Decanter Set, 7 pieces, 1934-1935, Decanter and six 2502 Whiskeys
2589 Deer, Standing, 1940-1943
2589 Deer Reclining, 1940-1943
2585 Eagle Bookend, 1940-1943
2585 Eagle Bookend with Stars Carving, 1940-1943
2580 Elephant Bookend, 1939-1943
2492 Fish Canape, 1934-1938 (see Bar and Refreshment)
2564 Horse Bookend, 1939-1943
2518 Jug, 1935-1940
2517 Lemon, 1935-1938
2440 Mayonnaise, 2-part (see Lafayette)
2513 Mayonnaise, Plate, Crystal Ladle, 1935-1940
2513 Mint, 4" Handled, 1935-1940
2538 Nappy, 4½", 1935-1943
2538 Nappy, 6", 1935-1943
2538 Nappy, 11", 1935-1943
2531 Pelican, 1935-1940
2531 Penguin, 1935-1940
2440 Plate, 13" Torte (see Lafayette)
2531 Polar Bear, 1935-1940
2513 Preserve, 5" Handled, 1935-1940

2496 Baroque Trindle Candlestick, 2419 Mayfair 4-part Relish, Seafood Cocktail, 2440 Lafayette 2-part Relish, 2496 Baroque 3-part Candy Box and Cover

183

2519 Puff and Cover, 1935-1939
2440 Relish, 2-part Handled (see Lafayette)
2440 Relish, 3-part Handled (see Lafayette)
2419 Relish, 4-part (see Mayfair)
2419 Relish, 5-part (see Mayfair)
2513 Relish, 2-part, 1935-1940
2513 Relish, 3-part, 1935-1940
2538 Salad Set, 9 pieces, 1935-1943, 11" Nappy, eight 6" Nappies
2440 Sauce Dish, 6½" Oval (see Lafayette)
2497 Seafood Cocktail, 1934-1943
2531 Seal, 1935-1940
4024 Sherry, 1934-1938
2497½ Sugar and Cream, 1935-1940
2517 Sweetmeat, 1935-1938
2429 Tray, Cordial, 1934-1935
2440 Tray, 8½" Oval (see Lafayette)
2518 Tumbler, 10 oz., 1935-1940
2404 Vase, 6", 1934-1938
2428 Vase, 9", 1934-1938
2428 Vase, 13", 1934-1943
2489 Vase, 5½", 1934-1938

2522 Vase, 8", 1935-1938
2523 Vase, 6½", 1935-1938
4103 Vase, 4", 1934-1938
4110 Vase, 7½", 1934-1935
4116 Vase, 4" Bubble Ball, 1935-1938
4116 Vase, 5" Bubble Ball, 1935-1938
4116 Vase, 6" Bubble Ball, 1935-1938
4116 Vase, 7" Bubble Ball, 1935-1938
4116 Vase, 8" Bubble Ball, 1935-1940
4116 Vase, 9" Bubble Ball, 1935-1940
4129 Vase, 2½" Bubble Ball, 1935-1940
5088 Vase, 8" Bud, 1934-1938
5091 Vase, 6½" Bud, 1935
887 Whiskey, 1¾ oz, optic, 1934-1938
2502 Whiskey, 1934-1935
2518 Whiskey, 2 oz., 1935-1940
2494 Whiskey Set, 7 pieces, 1934-1938, Decanter and six 887 Whiskeys, 1¾ oz., optic
2518 Wine, 5 oz., 1935-1940
2503 Wine Jug, 1934-1935
2494 Wine Set, 7 pieces, 1934-1938, Wine Decanter and six 4024 Sherries

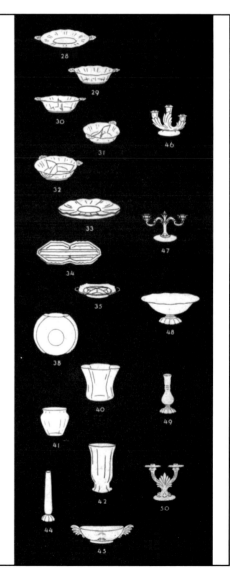

SILVER MIST

CRYSTAL GLASS
WITH A
SOFT, SMOOTH MAT FINISH

28.	2440	8½-in. Oval Tray		40.	2489	5½-in. Vase
29.	2440	6½-in. Oval Sauce Dish		41.	4103	4-in. Vase
30.	2440	6½-in. 2-Part Mayonnaise		42.	4110	7½-in. Vase
31.	2440	2-Part Hld. Relish		43.	4116	4-in. Bubble Ball
32.	2440	3-Part Hld. Relish		43.	4116	5-in. Bubble Ball
33.	2440	13-in. Torte Plate		43.	4116	6-in. Bubble Ball
34.	2419	5-Part Relish		44.	5088	8-in. Bud Vase
35.	2419	4-Part Relish		45.	2484	10-in. Handled Bowl
36.	2497	Seafood Cocktail		46.	2496	Trindle Candlestick
37.	4099	Candy Jar and Cover		47.	2472	Duo Candlestick
38.	2404	6-in. Vase		48.	4024	10½-in. Footed Bowl
39.	2428	9-in. Vase		49.	4024	6-in. Candlestick
39.	2428	13-in. Vase		50.	2484	2-Light Candle and Drips

The 2374 nut bowl was later offered as a comport, and the almonds and open salts were sometimes used interchangeably, i.e. the Bird Salt could be used as an almond. These tiny dishes seem made for children, but were an integral part of any fine dinner service.

315 Thin Bowl, 1938-1943, 4½", 5", 6", 7", 8"; $5.00-$15.00
766 Almond, Small, pre 1924-1928; $15.00
766 Bon Bon, 4½" Plain or Optic, 1924-1928; $14.00
858 Sweetmeat, 4½" Plain or Optic, Pre 1924-1927; $15.00
863 Almond, Small, 1924-1928; $15.00
880 Bon Bon, 4½" Plain or Optic, 1924-1927; $18.00
2374 Bowl, 6" Nut (see Comports, Nappies, and Jellies)
    Crystal, 1928-1932; $24.00
    Amber, 1928-1932; $25.00
    Green, 1928-1932; $25.00
    Rose, 1928-1932; $28.00
    Azure, 1928-1932; $28.00
2374 Bowl, Individual Nut
    Crystal, 1928-1943; $16.00
    Amber, 1928-1940; $18.00
    Green, 1928-1940; $20.00
    Rose, 1928-1940; $22.00
    Azure, 1928-1942; $24.00
    Topaz/Gold Tint, 1929-1940; $22.00
    Regal Blue, 1934-1936; $26.00
    Burgundy, 1934-1937; $26.00
    Empire Green, 1934-1937; $26.00
2394 Bowl, 6"
    Crystal, 1929-1936; $16.00
    Amber, 1929-1936; $18.00
    Green, 1929-1936; $18.00
    Rose, 1929-1934; $20.00
    Azure, 1929-1934; $22.00
    Topaz, 1929-1934; $18.00
2394 Bowl, 4½" Mint
    Crystal, 1929-1936; $14.00
    Amber, 1929-1938; $15.00
    Green, 1929-1932; $16.00
    Rose, 1929-1934; $16.00
    Azure, 1929-1938; $20.00
    Topaz, 1929-1934; $16.00
2402 Bowl, 6" Mint
    Crystal, 1929-1930; $12.00
    Amber, 1929-1938; $14.00
    Green, 1929-1932; $16.00
    Rose, 1929-1938; $16.00
    Azure, 1929-1936; $18.00
    Topaz, 1929-1936; $16.00
    Ebony 1929-1938; $16.00
2513 Bowl, Individual Almond (see Milk Glass)
    Crystal, 1934-1943; $11.00
    Regal Blue, 1934-1942; $22.00
    Burgundy, 1934-1942; $22.00
    Empire Green, 1934-1942; $22.00

1630 Alexis Almond; 4095 Almond, Blue Foot; 766 Almond with 212 Etching; 2513 Almonds in Crystal and Milk Glass

2517 Sweetmeat (see Appetizers, Buffet, and Relish)
    Crystal, 1934-1943; $16.00
    Regal Blue, 1934-1942; $20.00
    Burgundy, 1934-1939; $20.00
    Empire Green, 1934-1940; $20.00
    Ruby, 1934-1939; $20.00
2517 Bon Bon (see Appetizers, Buffet, and Relish)
    Crystal, 1934-1943; $16.00
    Regal Blue, 1934-1942; $20.00
    Burgundy, 1934-1940; $20.00
    Empire Green, 1934-1939; $20.00
    Ruby, 1934-1939; $20.00
2517 Lemon (see Appetizers, Buffet, and Relish)
    Crystal, 1934-1943; $16.00
    Regal Blue, 1934-1942; $20.00
    Burgundy, 1934-1940; $20.00
    Empire Green, 1934-1939; $20.00
    Ruby, 1934-1939; $20.00
2521 Bird Salt or Almond (see Shakers and Open Salts)
2546 Quadrangle Bowl (see Bowls, Centerpieces, and

4020 Almonds in Ebony, Green, Wisteria, Topaz, and Crystal; 2374 Individual Nut in Topaz; Wisteria 2440 Almond; and Green 2374 Individual Nut

Console Bowls)
4020 Individual Almond, 1931-1934
  Crystal; $18.00
  Amber; $20.00
  Green; $20.00
  Ebony; $22.00
  Rose; $24.00
  Topaz; $22.00
  Wisteria; $32.00
4095 Almond
  Crystal, RO, 1925-1935; $14.00
  Amber, RO, 1931; $16.00
  Amber Foot, LO, 1925-1937; $16.00
  Green, SO, 1931; $18.00
  Green Bowl, RO, 1928-1931; $18.00
  Green Foot, SO, 1925-1936; $18.00
  Blue Foot, RO, 1925-1927; $22.00
  Rose Bowl, RO, 1928-1931; $22.00
  Azure Bowl, RO, 1928-1931; $24.00
4152 Bowl, Snack

2394 Amber 4½" Mint, Green 6" Bowl

Crystal, 1952-1963; $12.00
Cinnamon, 1952-1954; $15.00
Spruce, 1952-1963; $15.00
Chartreuse, 1952-1963; $15.00
Ebony, 1954-1958; $15.00

4020—Individual Nut
Ro-Gr-Am-Eb-Crys-Tz-Wis

No. 4095·Footed Almond.

2394 6-in. Bowl
2394 Mint
Ro-Az-Gr-Am-Crys-Tz

2374 Individual Nut
Ro-Az-Gr-Am-Crys-Tz

2402 Mint
Ro-Az-Gr-Am-Eb-Tz

2374—6 in. Nut Bowl.
Ro-Az-Gr-Am-Crys.
Priced Page 17.

2517—5¼ in. Handled
Sweetmeat

2513
Individual Almond

2517—5¼ in. Handled
Bon Bon

2517—6 in. Handled Lemon

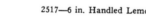

315—Thin Bowl
See Price List For Sizes

No. 766 Bon Bon.

No. 858. Sweetmeat.

No. 880. Bon Bon.

SMOKING ACCESSORIES

One can almost trace the evolution of the smoking habit by the number and variety of smoking accessories. In 1918 three ash trays were listed besides the one from the American pattern. In 1925 four ash trays in graduated sizes made to nest are shown. There was a gradual increase in number available from this time on. In 1924 only the 2106 Vogue match box and cigarette box are shown. A group of cigarette holder/ash tray combinations, an innovative idea, appeared in 1925. The color and crystal combination was probably a carry over from the stemware being made at that time.

By 1939 the listings had increased from half a dozen items to more than a page in the price list. The peak period for smoking items had to be 1939 – 1944. After the war fewer ash trays and cigarette holders were offered. From 1970 on, most smoker items were listed with giftware and lead crystal. Many pressed patterns had smoking accessories and these are listed with the pattern.

Cigarette boxes may be found etched or cut or, less frequently, decorated. We found it interesting that in 1950 three ash trays, 2608, 2609, and 2610 were made with slots for book matches. No new designs were offered after 1961 with the exception of the Functional Sculptures/Ash Trays (see Figurals).

When the 2427 cigarette box was made in 1929 – 1932, it had horizontal ridges on the base; when reintroduced in 1939 it was plain and made in crystal only. Our most baffling challenge came with the discovery of the 2618 cigarette box and cover with Oriental etching. Oriental was discontinued in 1928, but there is no listing of a 2618 cigarette box until 1942.

1372 (see Coin)
2056 (see American)
2106 Cigarette Box and Cover, Small
    Amber, 1924-1927; $20.00
    Blue, 1924-1927; $32.00
    Green, 1924-1927; $22.00
    Canary, 1924-1926; $37.00
2106 Cigarette Box and Cover, Large
    Amber, 1924-1927; $57.00
    Blue, 1924-1927; $68.00
    Green, 1924-1927; $57.00
    Canary, 1924-1926; $75.00
2106 Match Box and Cover
    Amber, 1924-1926; $52.00
    Blue, 1924-1926; $60.00
    Green, 1924-1926; $52.00
    Canary, 1924-1926; $65.00
2306 Smoker Set, 4 piece
    Crystal, 1929-1943; $20.00
    Amber, 1926-1940; $40.00
    Blue, 1926-1927; $45.00
    Green, 1926-1940; $40.00
    Ebony, 1925-1929; $40.00
    Rose, 1929-1939; $40.00
    Azure, 1929-1940; $40.00
2306 Ash Trays, 2¾", 3⅛", 3½", 4" (Priced each)
    Crystal, 1929-1943; $5.00
    Amber, 1926-1943; $8.00
    Blue, 1926-1927; $12.00
    Green, 1926-1940; $8.00
    Ebony, 1925-1929; $10.00
    Rose, 1929-1939; $10.00
    Azure, 1929-1940; $10.00
2349 Cigarette Holder/ Round Ash Tray
    Amber, 1925-1927; $38.00
    Blue, 1925-1927; $42.00
    Green, 1925-1927; $38.00
    Canary, 1925-1926; $47.00
    Ebony, 1925-1927; $38.00

2351 Cigarette Holder/Ash Tray, Amber and Amber Foot; Small Green 2391 Cigarette and Cover; 2349 Cigarette Holder in Green and Blue

2351 Cigarette Holder/Ash Tray
Crystal, 1925-1927; $34.00

5092 Blown Cigarette Holder/Ash Tray in Crystal, Empire Green Bowl, Green Foot, Regal Blue Bowl, Blue Foot, Ruby Bowl, Blue

Amber, 1925-1927; $40.00
Blue, 1925-1927; $45.00
Green, 1925-1927; $42.00
Canary, 1925; $65.00
Ebony, 1926-1927; $40.00
2351 Cigarette Holder/Oval Ash Tray,
    Colored Foot
    Amber, 1925-1926; $44.00
    Blue, 1925-1927; $47.00
    Green, 1925-1926; $45.00
    Canary, 1925; $65.00
2354 Cigarette
    Crystal, 1925-1927; $34.00
    Amber, 1925-1927; $40.00
    Blue, 1925-1927; $45.00
    Green, 1925-1927; $42.00
    Ebony, 1926-1927; $40.00
2354 Cigarette, Colored Foot
    Amber, 1925-1927; $44.00
    Blue, 1925-1927; $47.00
    Green, 1925-1927; $45.00
2391 Cigarette and Cover, Small
    Crystal, 1928-1943; $34.00
    Amber, 1928-1932; $38.00
    Green, 1929-1934; $38.00
    Ebony, 1928-1938; $35.00
    Orchid, 1928; $48.00
    Rose, 1928-1934; $38.00
    Azure, 1928; $48.00
2391 Cigarette and Cover, Large
    Crystal, 1928-1943; $42.00
    Amber, 1928-1934; $48.00
    Green, 1928-1939; $48.00
    Ebony, 1928-1939; $44.00
    Orchid, 1928; $65.00
    Rose, 1928-1934; $48.00
    Azure, 1928; $67.00
    Regal Blue, 1934-1939; $65.00
    Burgundy, 1934-1935; $75.00
    Empire Green, 1934-1939; $65.00
    Ruby, 1935-1940; $65.00
2391 Cigarette and Cover
    Cut A, B, C in Azure, Green, and Rose
    Small, 1928; $54.00
    Large, 1928; $65.00
2420 Ash Tray Set, 3 pieces, Small, Medium, and
    Large
    Ebony, 1930-1932; $58.00
2424 Ash Trays (see Kent)
2427 Cigarette Box, divided and Cover
    Crystal, 1929-1932, ridged; $52.00
    Amber, 1929-1932; $65.00
    Green, 1929-1932; $65.00
    Ebony, 1929-1932; $65.00
    Rose, 1929-1932; $65.00
    Azure, 1929-1932; $70.00
    Topaz, 1929-1932; $70.00

2419 Mayfair Ash Tray with Rosette Carving, Empire Green, Burgundy; 2618 Cigarette Box and Cover, Paradise Etching; 2375 Fairfax Ash Try in Azure, Rose, and Green; Azure Versailles 2350 Pioneer Small Ash Tray

Crystal, 1939-1943, plain; $48.00
2427 Ash Tray, Oblong, Crystal 1939-1958; $10.00
2457 Ash Tray
    Crystal 1933-1939; $15.00
    Amber, 1933-1939; $18.00
    Regal Blue, 1933-1939; $32.00
    Burgundy, 1933-1939; $32.00
    Empire Green, 1933-1935; $32.00
2496 Smoker Set (see Baroque)
2510 (see Sunray)
2515 Ash Tray, 1935-1940; $10.00
2516 Ash Tray, 1939-1958; $12.00
2520 Ash Tray, 1935-1943; $10.00
2530 Ash Tray
    Crystal, 1935-1937; $12.00
    Ebony, 1935-1939; $15.00
2534 Ash Tray
    Crystal, 1935-1942; $10.00
    Regal Blue, 1935-1940; $32.00

Topaz 2427 ridged, divided Cigarette Box, no cover; 2496 Baroque Ash Tray; Topaz Spool Cigarette and Cover, Round Ash Tray, 3-piece Ash Tray Set in Azure, Crystal, and Topaz, Crystal Oblong Cigarette Box and Cover

Burgundy, 1935-1942; $32.00
Empire Green, 1935-1939; $32.00
2538 Ash Tray/Place Card Holder
Crystal, 1937-1962; $15.00
Silver Mist, 1937-1942; $15.00
Ebony, 1954-1962; $18.00
Azure, 1937-1939; $26.00
2550 Spool (see Spool)
2566 Fish Ash Tray, 1938-1943; $44.00
2596 Cigarette Box and Cover, 1940-1943; $57.00
2596 Ash Tray, 4" Square, 1940-1943; $16.00
2592 (see Myriad)
2608 Ash Tray, 4½" Round, 1942-1958; $10.00
2609 Ash Tray, 4" Oblong, 1942-1961; $5.00
2610 Ash Tray, 3½" Shell, 1942-1957; $10.00
2618 Cigarette Box and Cover
Crystal, 1942-1974; $40.00
Ebony, 1954-1962; $45.00
2618 Ash Tray, 4" Square, 1942-1961; $10.00
2618 Ash Tray, 4½" Oblong, 1942-1970; $10.00
2622 Ash Tray, 4½", 1950-1961; $8.00
2623 Ash Tray, 5", 1950-1958; $10.00
2625 Ash Tray, 5", 1950-1954; $12.00
2625 Ash Tray, 6½", 1950-1961; $15.00
2625 Ash Tray Set, 2 piece, 1950-1954; $25.00
2628 Cigarette Box and Cover, 1949-1957; $55.00
2628 Ash Tray, 4¼", 1949-1954; $10.00
2667 Cigarette Holder
Crystal, 1953-1961; $15.00
Ebony, 1953-1962; $18.00
2667 Ash Tray, 5"
Crystal, 1953-1974; $6.00
Ebony 1954-1962; $8.00
2667 Ash Tray, 7"
Crystal 1953-1974; $10.00
Ebony, 1954-1962; $14.00
2667 Ash Tray, 9"
Crystal, 1953-1974; $12.00
Ebony, 1954-1962; $18.00
2667 Ash Tray Set, 3 piece, 1953-1974; $30.00
2667 Smoking Set, 3 piece, 1953-1961; $32.00
2667 Smoking Set, 4 piece, 1953-1958; $40.00
2691 Individual Cigarette, 1956-1957; $20.00
2691 Individual Ash Tray, 1956-1957; $14.00
2731 Cigarette Box and Cover, 1960-1976; $48.00
2731 Ash Tray, 4" Oblong, 1960-1976; $5.00
2731 Ash Tray, 5" Round, 1960-1976; $6.00
2731 Ash Tray, 7½" Round
Crystal, 1960-1976; $12.00
Amber, 1960-1967; $15.00
Green, 1960-1967; $15.00
Blue, 1960-1967; $18.00
2746 Ash Tray, 6" Footed
Ruby Mist, 1961-1965; $42.00
Green Texture, 1961-1965; $54.00
2747 Ash Tray, 4½"
Crystal, 1961-1967; $8.00
Amber, 1961-1967; $10.00

2391 Large Cigarette and Cover, Rosette Carving; 1372 Coin Cigarette Urns in Amber amd Green (note difference in tops); Cigarette Box and Cover; 2675 Randolph Milk Glass Ash Tray; Coin Ash Tray (lid to cigarette); 2731 Ash Tray, 2638 Contour One Lip Ash Tray

Green, 1961-1967; $10.00
2747 Ash Tray, 6"
Crystal, 1961-1967; $10.00
Amber, 1961-1967; $14.00
Green, 1961-1967; $14.00
2747 Ash Tray Set, 2 piece
Crystal, 1961-1967; $18.00
Amber, 1961-1967; $24.00
Green, 1961-1967; $24.00
2748 Mortar Ash Tray
Amber Mist, 1961-1965; $28.00
Pink Mist, 1961-1965; $38.00
2752 (see Facets)
2753 Ash Tray, 5½"
Crystal, 1961-1968; $8.00
Brown, 1961-1965; $10.00
Gold, 1961-1965; $10.00
2753 Ash Tray, 7½"
Crystal, 1961-1968; $10.00
Brown, 1961-1965; $12.00
Gold, 1961-1965; $15.00

2592 Myriad Cigarette Box and Cover; 2538 Place Card Holder/Ash Tray in Azure and Crystal; 2566 Fish Ash Tray; 2412 Colony Cigarette Box and Cover; 2592 Myriad Crystal Oblong Ash Tray, Individual Ash Tray, Ebony with Gold Decoration

2753 Ash Tray, 10½"
  Crystal, 1961-1968; $14.00
  Brown, 1961-1965; $15.00
  Gold, $1961-1965; $15.00
2753 Ash Tray Set, 3 piece
  Crystal 1961-1968; $32.00
  Brown, 1961-1965; $35.00
  Gold, 1961-1965; $37.00
4148 Cigarette Holder, 1940-1943; $35.00
4148 Ash Tray, 1940-1943; $10.00
5092 Cigarette Holder/Ash Tray, Blown
  Crystal, 1925-1938; $58.00
  Amber, 1925-1930; $65.00
  Blue, 1925-1927; $78.00
  Green, 1925-1930; $67.00
  Rose, 1929-1930; $67.00
  Azure, 1929-1930; $68.00
5092 Cigarette Holder/Ash Tray, Colored Foot
  Amber, 1925-1927; 1939-1940; $60.00
  Blue, 1925-1927; $75.00
  Green, 1925-1927; 1939-1940; $65.00
5092 Cigarette Holder/Ash Tray, Colored Bowl

2667 Ebony Cigarette Holder, 2746 6" Footed Ash Tray in Ruby Mist and Green Textured, 2748 Pink Mist Mortar Ash Tray, 2623 Ash Tray, 2667 7" Ash Tray, 2628 two-handled Ash Tray

  Ruby, 1935; $125.00
  Regal Blue, 1934-1935; $125.00
  Burgundy, 1934-1938; $95.00
  Empire Green, 1934-1938; $95.00
FU01 Functional Sculptures/Ash Trays (see Figurals)

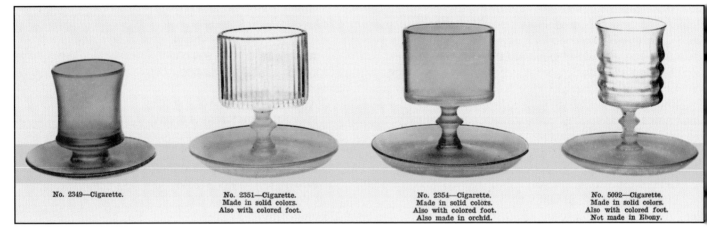

No. 2349—Cigarette.

No. 2351—Cigarette.
Made in solid colors.
Also with colored foot.

No. 2354—Cigarette.
Made in solid colors.
Also with colored foot.
Also made in orchid.

No. 5092—Cigarette.
Made in solid colors.
Also with colored foot.
Not made in Ebony.

2538—Place Card Holder
Also used for Nut Dish
or Ash Tray
Height 2¾ in.

Place Card Holder
in Use

2550½—3 Pce. Ash Tray Set
Height Nested 1⅞ in.
Set consisting of:
1/12 Doz. 2550½ Lge. Ash Tray
1/12 Doz. 2550½ Med. Ash Tray
1/12 Doz. 2550½ Ind. Ash Tray

2412—4½ in. Square Ash Tray

2496—5-Piece Smoker Set
Consisting of:
1/12 Doz. 2496—Cigarette Box and Cover
1/3 Doz. 2496—Oblong Ash Tray

2566—Fish Ash Tray
Diameter 5¼ in.

No. 2106—Large Cigarette and Cover.
Not made in Ebony.

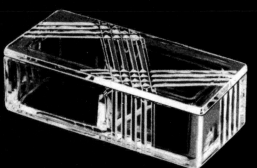

2306—3 Piece Smoker Set
Cutting No. 811
Set Consisting of:
2306—3   in. Ash Tray
2306—3½ in. Ash Tray
2306—4   in. Ash Tray

4148—2¼ in.
Cigarette Holder, Blown
Laurel Design
Cutting No. 776
Top Diameter 2 in.

4148—2½ in.
Individual Ash Tray
Laurel Design
Cutting No. 776

2427—Oblong Cigarette Box and Cover
Cutting No. 810
Length 7 in.   Height 2¼ in.
Width 3⅛ in.
Each side holds 35 Cigarettes

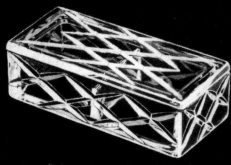

2427—Oblong Cigarette Box and Cover
Cutting No. 809
Length 7 in.   Height 2¼ in.
Width 3⅛ in.
Each side holds 35 Cigarettes

2427—Oblong Ash Tray
Cutting No. 809
Length 3½ in.   Width 2¾ in.

2550½—Oblong Cigarette Box and Cover
Cutting No. 808
Height 2⅛ in.   Length 4¾ in.
Width 3⅜ in.

2550—Round Ash Tray
Cutting No. 808
Diameter 3¼ in.

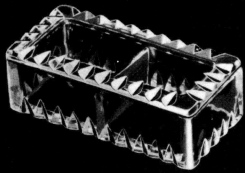

2427—Oblong Cigarette Box and Cover
Cutting No. 808
Length 7 in.   Height 2¼ in.
Width 3⅛ in.
Each side holds 35 Cigarettes

2427—Oblong Ash Tray
Cutting No. 808
Length 3½ in.   Width 2¾ in.

2516—Ash Tray
Cutting No. 808
Height 2⅛ in.   Diameter 5 in.

2419—Ash Tray
4 in. Square

2391—Large Cigarette and Cover
Length 4¾ in.—Width 3½ in.
2391—Small Cigarette and Cover
Length 3½ in.—Width 2¾ in.

2306—4 Piece Smoker Set

2520——Ash Tray
Length 4½ in.

5092—Cigarette Holder
Height 4½ in.
Capacity 20 Cigarettes

2350—Small Ash Tray
Diameter 3¾ in.
2350—Large Ash Tray
Diameter 5 in.

2530—Ash Tray
Diameter 5¼ in.

2457—Ash Tray
Length 5⅛ in.
Width 2½ in.

2056—Oval Ash Tray
Length 5½ in.

2056—Cigarette Box
and Cover
Length 4¾ in.
Width 3½ in.

2515—Ash Tray
Diameter 3 in.

2534—Ash Tray
Length 5 in.   Width 3½ in.

2449—5 Piece Ash Tray Set
Height 3 in.

2449—Ash Tray
Diameter 2¾ in.

2510
Square Ash Tray
3 in. Square

2510½
Individual Ash Tray
Diameter 2⅜ in.

2510—5 Piece Smoker Set
Consisting of
1/12 Doz. 2510 Cigarette and Cover
1/3 Doz. 2510 Square Ash Tray
2510½—Smoker Set
same as above except with
2510½ Ind. Ash Trays

2510
Cigarette and Cover
Height 3⅞ in.

2608—Round Ash Tray
Diameter 4¼ in.
Slot for book matches

2609—Oblong Ash Tray
Length 4 in.   Width 2 in.
Slot for book matches

2610—Shell Ash Tray
Length 3½ in.   Width 3¼ in.
Slot for book matches

2618—4½ in. Oblong Ash Tray

2618—Cigarette Box & Cover
Length 5½ in.   Width 4¼ in.
Height 1½ in.
Cigarette Capacity 40

2618—4 in. Square Ash Tray

2592—Oblong Cigarette Box and Cover
Length 6 in.   Width 3½ in.
Height with cover 3¼ in.
Cigarette Capacity 48

2592—Oblong Ash Tray
Length 3¾ in. Width 2¾ in.

2592—Individual Ash Tray
Length 3 in.   Width 2¼ in.

2306—4 Piece Smoker Set
Consisting of:
1/12 Doz. 2¾ in. Ash Tray
1/12 Doz. 3 in. Ash Tray
1/12 Doz. 3½ in. Ash Tray
1/12 Doz. 4 in. Ash Tray

2596—4 in. Square Ash Tray

2596—Cigarette Box and Cover
Length 4 in.   Width 3½ in.
Cigarette Capacity 30

4148—2¼ in.
Cigarette Holder, Blown
Top Diameter 2 in.
Cigarette Capacity 14

4148—2½ in.
Individual Ash Tray, Blown

193

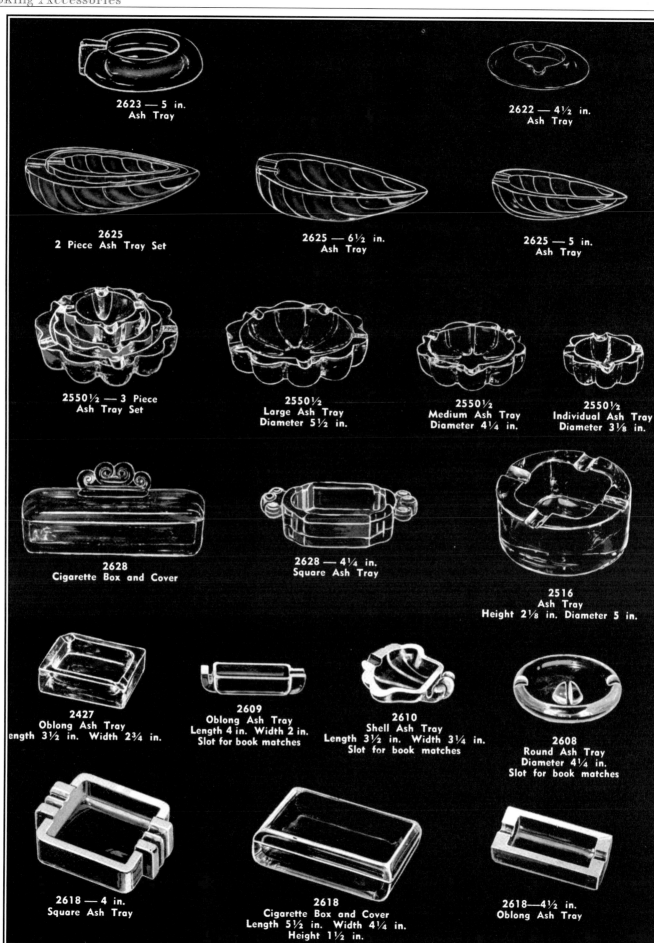

2623 — 5 in.
Ash Tray

2622 — 4½ in.
Ash Tray

2625
2 Piece Ash Tray Set

2625 — 6½ in.
Ash Tray

2625 — 5 in.
Ash Tray

2550½ — 3 Piece
Ash Tray Set

2550½
Large Ash Tray
Diameter 5½ in.

2550½
Medium Ash Tray
Diameter 4¼ in.

2550½
Individual Ash Tray
Diameter 3⅛ in.

2628
Cigarette Box and Cover

2628 — 4¼ in.
Square Ash Tray

2516
Ash Tray
Height 2⅛ in. Diameter 5 in.

2427
Oblong Ash Tray
Length 3½ in. Width 2¾ in.

2609
Oblong Ash Tray
Length 4 in. Width 2 in.
Slot for book matches

2610
Shell Ash Tray
Length 3½ in. Width 3¼ in.
Slot for book matches

2608
Round Ash Tray
Diameter 4¼ in.
Slot for book matches

2618 — 4 in.
Square Ash Tray

2618
Cigarette Box and Cover
Length 5½ in. Width 4¼ in.
Height 1½ in.

2618—4½ in.
Oblong Ash Tray

2667—5 in.
Ash Tray

2667—7 in.
Ash Tray

2667—9 in.
Ash Tray

2667-3 Piece
Ash Tray Set
Consisting of:
1/12 Doz. 2667—5 in. Ash Tray
1/12 Doz. 2667—7 in. Ash Tray
1/12 Doz. 2667—9 in. Ash Tray

2667
Cigarette Holder
Height 2¾ in.

2667—3 Piece
Smoking Set
Consisting of:
1/12 Doz. 2667—5 in. Ash Tray
1/12 Doz. 2667—7 in. Ash Tray
1/12 Doz. 2667 Cigarette Holder

2667—4 Piece
Smoking Set
Consisting of:
1/12 Doz. 2667—5 in. Ash Tray
1/12 Doz. 2667—7 in. Ash Tray
1/12 Doz. 2667—9 in. Ash Tray
1/12 Doz. 2667—Cigarette Holder

2731/374
Cigarette Box and Cover
Height 1¾ in.
Length 5¾ in. Width 4½ in.

2731/114—7½ in.
Round Ash Tray

2731/115
Oblong Ash Tray
Length 4 in.

2427 Cigarette Box and Cover
Ro-Az-Gr-Am-Eb-Crys-Tz
Priced on page 40

2420 3-Piece Ash Tray Set
Ebony only
Priced on page 40

2618
Cigarette Box and Cover
Length 5 ½ in.   Width 4 ¼ in.

2427—Oblong Ash Tray
Length 3½ in.
Width 2¾ in.

2427—Oblong Cigarette Box and Cover
Length 7 in.   Height 2¼ in.
Width 3⅛ in.
Each Side Holds 35 Cigarettes

2516—Ash Tray
Height 2⅛ in.
Diameter 5 in.

No. 2306. Smoker Set.
(Four Ash Trays Nested)
(**Made in Crystal and Ebony**)

2747/107

2747/111

2747/119

2748/113

2752/120

2752/124

2746/118

2752/374

2753/108

2753/111

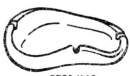

2753/119

2753/124

Miscellaneous Etched Smoking Accessories

1927

2354 Cigarette, Etched Dog
  Crystal, $87.00
  Amber, $110.00
  Blue, $125.00
  Green, $115.00
  Ebony, $115.00
2354 Cigarette, Etched Horse
  Crystal, $94.00
  Amber, $110.00
  Blue, $125.00
  Green, $115.00
  Ebony, $115.00

2354 Cigarette, Etched Cupid
  Crystal, $125.00
  Amber, $145.00
  Blue, $175.00
  Green, $165.00
  Ebony, $157.00
2354 Cigarette, Etched Deer
  Crystal, $110.00
  Amber, $125.00
  Blue, $150.00
  Green, $135.00
  Ebony, $135.00

2354—Cigarette.
Etched Dog.

2354—Cigarette.
Etched Horse.

2354—Cigarette.
Etched Cupid.

2354—Cigarette.
Etched Deer.

Miscellaneous Rock Crystal Cuttings

1940 – 1943

Cut 808:
2427 Oblong Ash Tray; $12.00
2427 Oblong Cigarette and Cover; $56.00
2516 Ash Tray; $18.00
2550 Ash Tray; $10.00
2550½ Cigarette and Cover; $52.00

Cut 809:
2427 Oblong Ash Tray; $12.00
2427 Oblong Cigarette and Cover; $56.00
Cut 810:
2427 Oblong Cigarette and cover; $56.00
Cut 811:
2306 Smoker Set, 3 piece; $22.00

2391—Small Cigarette.
Cut A.

2391—Large Cigarette.
Cut C.

SPOONS and LADLES

Four spoons were listed in 1924 as sanitary glass spoons. The 3½" mustard spoon is shorter than the later one and the shape is undetermined. A horseradish spoon is shown in the jar in 1901 but may not be the same as the sanitary one. Without a picture, the high ball and ice tea spoons are not able to be identified. The 2138 ladle is ground flat on the bottom to fit the bottom of the mayonnaise bowl. It was used until 1928 in the 2138 mayonnaise which is shown with several patterns (see Rogene, *Fostoria Tableware: 1924 – 1943*).

Since Fostoria never made a glass punch bowl ladle, one wonders if the Most Perfect Dipper was intended for this use. A metal wire holds the glass bowl and screws into the wooden handle. It was shown in 1901 and was still being made in 1924. A plastic punch ladle was offered in 1953 through 1982. The glass punch ladle shown in the photograph has the Wakefield cutting. Milbra purchased it from William (Bill) Suter who was a cutter at the Fostoria factory for many years, and who cut the design on this ladle. It was never a production item, and the blank ladle may not have been made at Fostoria.

In 1928 the 2375 Fairfax ladle became the only mayonnaise ladle used in all patterns until it was replaced with a stainless steel spoon in 1965. This ladle was also used in the 2378 whip cream pail. The glass ladle first offered with the 2375 Mayonnaise in crystal and colors is generally thicker than the 2138, and the tip of the handle has a chopped-off look. Sometimes the 2375 ladle is more slender and curved, and other times it is fatter and straighter, but always the handle ends dramatically with a flat tip. After the colored ladles were discontinued, a crystal one was used until 1965.

The mustard and mustard spoon were first offered in the Hermitage pattern, and the spoon was made in crystal only. Glass ladles and spoons are becoming more rare with each passing year, but add value and authenticity to any piece which used them.

Sanitary, 1924:
   Mustard, 3½"; $20.00
   Horseradish, 4"; $22.00
   High ball, 6"; $16.00
   Ice Tea, 8"; $18.00
Most Perfect Dipper, pre 1924; Market
2056 Crushed Fruit Spoon, 9" (see American)
979 Plastic Ladle, 1953-1982; $15.00
2138 Ladle, used with 2138 Mayonnaise Set, pre 1924-1928; $24.00

2375 Mayonnaise Ladle (see Fairfax)
   Crystal, 1928-1965; $20.00
   Amber, 1928-1935; $34.00
   Green, 1928-1938; $35.00
   Rose, 1928-1935; $42.00
   Azure, 1928-1934; $50.00
   Topaz/Gold Tint, 1929-1938; $42.00
   Orchid, 1928; $55.00
2449 Mustard Spoon (see Hermitage)
987 Salad Fork and Spoon (Wood),1935-1972 (see Bowls, Centerpieces, and Console Bowls); $25.00

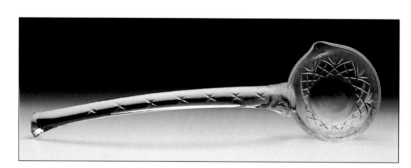

Glass Punch Ladle, Wakefield cut by William (Bill) Suter

2138 Ladle and Mustard Spoon

*2375 Ladles in
all colors made*

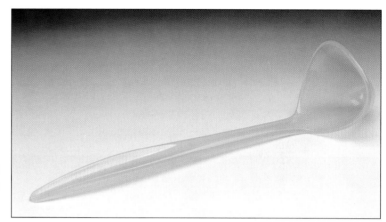

*Plastic Punch
Ladle*

Most Perfect Dipper Made.

As the handle is flexible, and the wire held into the wood by a pin, which makes it
impossible to detach handle from dipper.

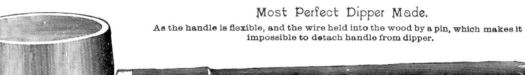

Crystal Dipper.
Packed ½ gro. in bbl

456 Horseradish and Spoon.
No Handle.

456 Horseradish.
Handled and Spoon.

199

233 Ruth, about 1891

Syrups were a stock item for many years. Early patterns often provided a regular 8 ounce or 12 ounce size as well as a larger molasses and a 6 ounce individual size. Around 1920 a "spring loaded" metal lid that fit inside the rim of the syrup was used. It was labeled "automatous" by Fostoria because it opened automatically when tipped for liquid to pour out. Used on both the 2194 syrups and the 1518 six ounce, eight ounce, and twelve ounce jugs, it was advertised as being insect proof. The 1518 and 2194 syrups were identical except the rim on the 1518 was not smooth. We found one listing in 1925 of the 2017 seven ounce molasses, but it was not pictured. Other than syrups offered with patterns, the 2586 Sani-Cut Syrup, first offered in 1940, was the final syrup made. It was used for Chintz, Navarre, Buttercup, Meadow Rose, Mayflower, and Willowmere etchings, and for Laurel and Pilgrim cuttings. Since it was produced for such a short time it is considered rare whether plain or etched or cut. The molasses cans shown are from the 1901 catalog.

1518 Syrup, 8 oz., 12 oz., pre 1924-1928; $48.00
2194 Syrup, 8 oz., 12 oz., pre 1924-1928; $48.00

2017 Molasses, 7 oz., plain or optic, pre 1924-1925; $48.00
2586 Sani Cut Syrup, 9 oz., 1940-1943; $125.00

2056 American, Glass Top; Topaz 2419 Mayfair

No. 2194-8 oz. Syrup.

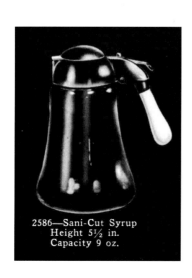

2586—Sani-Cut Syrup
Height 5½ in.
Capacity 9 oz.

2194 Lotus Etching; Arrow Cutting

600 Heavy Britannia Syrup Top.
Capacity 6 oz.
Packed 6 doz. in bbl.

417 Syrup.
Silver Plated Top and Handle.
Capacity 4½ oz.
Packed 12 doz. in bbl.

444 Syrup, Small.
Silver Plated Top and Handle.
Capacity 6 oz.
Packed 12 doz. in bbl.

726 Can.
Silver Plated Top and Handle.
Capacity 5½ oz.
Packed 12 doz. in bbl.

675 Syrup, Brit. Top.
Capacity 8 oz.
Packed 8 doz. in bbl.

951 Syrup, Tin Top, No. 1 Sand Blast.
Capacity 18 oz.   Packed 6 doz. in bbl.

597 Tin Top.
Capacity 16 oz.
Packed 7 doz. in bbl.

598 Tin Top.
Capacity 15 oz.
Packed 7 doz. in bbl.

601 Spun Nickel Top.
Capacity 14 oz.
Packed 6 doz. in bbl.

603 Spun Nickel Top.
Capacity 15 oz.
Packed 6 doz. in bbl.

789 Syrup, 8½ oz.
Packed 8 doz. in bbl.

956 Syrup, Capacity 12 oz.
Packed 6 doz. in bbl.

1000 Syrup, Capacity 10½ oz.
Packed 7 doz. in bbl.

961 Syrup, Glass Lip.
Capacity 14 oz. Packed 6 doz. in bbl.

921 Syrup, Glass Lip, 16 oz.
6 doz. to bbl.

Before 1920, Fostoria made either pressed or mold blown vases almost exclusively. The hand-painted opal ware vases were popular from before 1900 to around 1918. Some of those are shown in the 1910 Lamp and Vase Catalog. At that time several blown shapes were shown with various etchings and cuttings — some named, some numbered and some simply labeled "deep etched" or "cut." Some of these shapes were used for patterns which continued to be made in crystal through the 1920s. Early vases were often referred to as bouquet holders. Four pages from a 1901 catalog are included in this section simply to make the information on vases as complete as possible, although many of the early offerings are listed but not shown. The 300 vases in 12", 18", and 24" sizes were used for deep etched designs, and 1845 vases in 6", 8", 10", and 12" were listed in both Crystal and Topaz from July 1933 and January 1934, but no picture was offered in catalogs at that time probably because the vase was a reintroduction from the teens. Fostoria made two styles of wall vases, both very short lived and seldom seen today.

With the advent of color in 1924, many new designs were created, some in several sizes and variations such as optics (regular, narrow, spiral, loop) and straight, flared, or cupped edges. On a few, the rim of the flared vase was rolled over to create a rolled edge, or crimped to make a fluted top. Thus, from one basic mold, several different styles of vases could be made. A vase collection from the period of 1920 through 1943 could contain several hundred vases if all sizes and colors were included. We have tried to show every vase Fostoria made after 1924, but unfortunately were unable to find pictures in a few cases.

Few vases were made after World War II that did not belong to a specific pattern until 1952 when some of the earlier shapes were reintroduced and made in 1950s colors. The quality of vase production continued as did the obvious hand crafting. Two vases in the Heirloom pressed pattern, for example, are definitely from the same mold, but may have different shapes and heights dependent on the whim of the skilled workers who produced each.

In 1977, Fostoria succeeded in creating art glass with its Designer Collection. These vases were individually hand crafted and most pieces were signed Fostoria and dated 1977 or 1978 (see Designer Collection). Group International brought colors and shapes from the Morgantown Glass Company to the Fostoria inventory. Even in 1986, the last year of the Fostoria Glass Company in Moundsville, West Virginia, bud vases were included in an imported lead crystal line (see Blown Stemware and Giftware).

45-3 Flower Set, 1921-1923; $200.00
300 Vase, 12" Etched, $175.00
622 Vase, 6½", 1924; $22.00
760 Vase, 12"
    Crystal, 1934-1937; $38.00
    Regal Blue Bowl, 1935-1937; $57.00
    Burgundy Bowl, 1935-1939; $57.00
    Ruby Bowl, 1935-1938; $57.00
    Empire Green Bowl, 1935-1939; $57.00
761 Vase, 10" Footed, 1921-1923; $195.00
762 Vase, 8" Footed, 1921-1923; $65.00
763 Vase, 9" Footed, 1921-1923; $125.00
764 Vase, 8" Footed, 1921-1923; $95.00
765 Vase, 10" Bud, 1924-1928; $38.00
864 Vase, 7½", 1924; $75.00
1001 Vase, 7", 9", 11" circa 1901; $75.00 – $95.00

183 Victoria Rose Bowl, 735 Vase, Body Acid finished, leaving the figure in bright relief, circa 1900

1002A Vase, 18 to 21" Swung, 1928; $45.00
1002B, 12 to 14" Swung, 1928; $40.00
1002C, 9 to 10" Swung, 1928; $25.00
1106 Vase, 4" Violet
    Crystal, 1924; $18.00
    Green, 1924; $22.00
1106 Vase, 5" Violet
    Crystal, 1924; $20.00
    Amber, 1925-1926; $22.00
    Green, 1924-1926; $24.00
1106 Vase, 6½" Orchid, $22.00
1106 Vase, 8", Orchid, $35.00
1106 Vase, 15" "E" Shape
    Crystal, 1924; $65.00
    Amber, 1925; $77.00
    Green, 1924-1926; $85.00
1120 Vase, 12" RO, LO
    Crystal, 1924-1928; $36.00
    Amber, 1925-1927; $45.00
    Green, 1924-1927; $55.00
1120 Vase, 15" RO, LO
    Crystal, 1924-1928; $65.00
    Amber, 1925-1927; $75.00
    Green, 1924-1927; $85.00
1120 Vase, 18", RO, LO
    Crystal, 1924-1928; $75.00
    Amber, 1925-1926; $85.00
    Green, 1924-1926; $95.00
1120 Vase, 24", LO, 1928; $125.00
1120 Vase, 36", LO, 1928; $150.00
1120 Vase, 50", 2 pieces, pre 1924; $150.00
1479 Vase, 6" RO
    Crystal, 1924-1932; $32.00
    Amber, 1925-1932; $38.00
    Green, 1925-1932; $46.00
1479 Vase, 7" RO
    Crystal, 1924-1929; $35.00
    Amber, 1925-1929; $42.00
    Green, 1925-1929; $48.00
1479 Vase, 9" RO, 1924-1928; $48.00
1491 Vase, 6", Ebony, 1925-1926; $47.00
1491 Vase, 8½"
    Ebony, 1925-1926; $55.00
1630 Alexis Vase, 1909-1924; $54.00
1663 Vase, 9" Pressed, 1928; $40.00
1663 Vase, 16" Pressed, 1928; $65.00
1681 Vase, Wall
    Crystal, 1925-1927; $65.00
    Amber, 1925-1927; $70.00
    Green, 1925-1927; $75.00
    Blue, 1925-1927; $85.00
    Ebony, 1925-1927; $65.00
1699A Vase, 13" Pressed, 1928; $50.00
1699B Vase, 11" Pressed, 1928; $40.00
1699C Vase, 9" Pressed, 1928; $35.00
1761 Vase, 10½", 1924; $60.00
1796 Vase, 9", 1921-1923, Engraving 5; $75.00

300 Vase, Deep Etch; 761 Vase with Greek Figure; 1120 18" Vase with Loop Optic

1797½ Vase, 7", Cut 116, 1921-1923; $54.00
1798 Vase, 9" Footed, 1924; $75.00

Green 1681 Wall Vase, Blue 4095½ Vase

1799½ Vase, 7¼" Deep Etched Poppy; $65.00

1827/801 Vase (see Centennial II)

1840 Vase, 10½" RO, 1928; $58.00

1840 Vase, 15" RO, 1928; $65.00

1873 Vase, 8", 1924; $45.00

1895 Vase, 8" RO
    Crystal,1933; $35.00
    Topaz, 1934; $48.00

1895 Vase, 10" RO
    Crystal, 1933; $38.00
    Topaz, 1934; $55.00

1895 Vase, 12" RO
    Crystal, 1933; $44.00
    Topaz, 1934; $65.00

1895½ Vase, 10" Heavy, 1938-1943; $37.00

1939 Vase, Center Set, 1922-1923; $250.00

2056 (see American)

2072 Vase, 8", 1923-1924; $57.00

2081 Vase, 12" or Tall Aquarium, Plain or Optic, 1928-1934; $47.00

2081 Vase, 15" or Tall Aquarium, Plain or Optic, 1928-1934; $55.00

2081 Vase, 18" or Tall Aquarium, Plain or Optic, 1928; $68.00

2137 Vase, Brush, pre 1924-1925, Cut or Decorated (see Boudoir Accessories and Jewelry); $95.00

2209 Vase, 9", 1932; $35.00

2210 Vase, 1924; $25.00

2212 Vase, 1924; $25.00

2218 Vase, Sweet Pea, pre 1924-1924; $45.00

2222 Vase, 8", 1938-1940; $48.00

2222 Vase, 10", 1938-1940; $55.00

2265 Vase, 12", 1924; $75.00

2284 Vase, 12"
    Amber, 1924-1926; $125.00
    Green, 1925-1926; $125.00

2284 Epergne Set: 2284 Vase, 2284 12" Bowl, 2290 13" Plate
    Amber, 1924-1926; $295.00
    Green, 1924-1926; $295.00

2288 Vase, Tut
    Crystal, 1924-1940; $28.00
    Amber, 1925-1931; $60.00
    Green, 1925-1935; $58.00
    Blue, 1925-1927; $75.00
    Canary, 1925-1926; $125.00
    Ebony, 1925-1940; $30.00

2292 Vase, 8" Flared
    Crystal, 1925-1930; $47.00
    Amber, 1925-1930; $55.00
    Green, 1925-1930; $60.00
    Blue, 1925-1927; $75.00
    Orchid, 1927; $75.00
    Azure, 1929-1930; $75.00
    Rose, 1928-1930; $70.00

2292 Vase, 8" Cupped
    Crystal, 1925-1930; $47.00

501 Hartford Vase, 1630 Alexis Vase, 2600 Acanthus Vase

    Green, 1925-1930; $55.00
    Azure, 1928; $125.00
    Rose, 1928-1930; $70.00

2292 Vase, 8" SO
    Amber, 1927-1930; $62.00
    Green, 1927-1930; $65.00
    Blue, 1927; $80.00
    Orchid, 1927; $80.00

2297 Vase, 8" Square Top
    Crystal, 1924-1927; $65.00
    Amber, 1924; $85.00
    Green, 1924; $95.00
    Canary, 1924; $125.00

2297 Vase, 8" Rolled Edge
    Crystal, 1924-1927; $45.00
    Amber, 1924-1927; $65.00
    Green, 1924-1927; $70.00
    Blue, 1924-1927; $85.00
    Canary, 1925-1926; $100.00

2300 Vase, 12"
    Amber, 1925-1926; $65.00
    Green, 1925-1926; $74.00

2454 Ebony Vase, 2288 Green Tut Vase, 2360 Ebony Vase, 2288 Canary Tut Vase, 2454 Ruby Vase (courtesy of Larry Baker and Don Barber)

Blue, 1925-1926; $95.00
Canary, 1925-1926; $125.00
Ebony, 1925-1926; $65.00
2312 Vase, 10" Bud, Ebony, 1925-1926; $60.00
2312 Vase, 12" Bud, Ebony, 1925-1926; $65.00
2312 Vase, 14" Bud, Ebony, 1925-1926; $70.00
2326 Vase, 7"
    Crystal, 1925-1926; $42.00
    Amber, 1925-1926; $54.00
    Green, 1925-1926; $65.00
    Blue, 1925-1926; $75.00
    Canary, 1925; $75.00
2360 Vase, 8" RO
    Amber, 1926-1927; $77.00
    Green, 1926-1927; $85.00
    Blue, 1926-1927; $98.00
    Orchid, 1927; $98.00
2360 Vase, 10", RO
    Amber, 1926-1927; $80.00
    Green, 1926-1927; $94.00
    Blue, 1926-1927; $125.00
    Ebony (Plain), 1930-1940; $75.00
    Orchid, 1927; $125.00
2369 Vase, 5" RO
    Crystal, 1927; 1939-1940; $30.00
    Amber, 1927-1929; $40.00
    Green, 1927-1929; $40.00
    Blue, 1927; $55.00
    Orchid, 1927; $50.00
2369 Vase, 7" Footed, RO
    Crystal, 1930; 1939-1943; $35.00
    Amber, 1930-1932; $45.00
    Green, 1927-1932; $45.00
    Orchid, 1927; $65.00
    Azure, 1928-1932; $55.00
    Rose, 1928-1932; $55.00
2369 Vase, 9"
    Crystal, 1928-1930; $48.00
    Amber, 1928-1930; $56.00
    Green, 1928-1930; $58.00
    Azure, 1928-1930; $65.00
    Rose, 1928-1930; $65.00
2369 Vase, 11" RO
    Crystal, 1927-1929; $60.00
    Amber, 1927-1929; $65.00
    Green, 1927-1929; $68.00
    Blue, 1927; $85.00
    Orchid, 1927-1928; $75.00
    Azure, 1930; $75.00
2373 Vase, Small Window (offered with or without cover, price with cover)
    Crystal, 1928-1932; $75.00
    Amber, 1929-1932; $82.00
    Green, 1928-1932; $85.00
    Orchid, 1928; $95.00
    Azure, 1928-1932; $95.00
    Rose, 1928-1932; $90.00
    Ebony, 1928-1932; $80.00

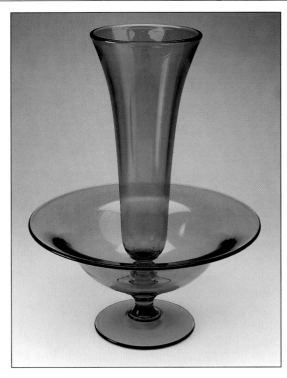

Amber 2284 Epergne Set, Vase and Bowl

2373 Vase, Large Window (offered with or without cover, priced with cover)
    Crystal, 1928-1932; $85.00
    Amber, 1929-1932; $90.00
    Green, 1928-1932; $95.00
    Orchid, 1928; $100.00
    Azure, 1928-1932; $100.00
    Rose, 1928-1932; $95.00
    Ebony, 1928-1932; $90.00

2421 Green 10½" Vase (courtesy of Larry Baker and Don Barber)

2385 Vase, 8½" Fan
 Crystal, 1928-1931; $50.00
 Green, 1928-1932; $60.00
 Orchid, 1928; $75.00
 Azure, 1928-1932; $75.00
 Rose, 1928-1932; $70.00
 Ebony, 1928-1932; $65.00
2385 Vase, 8½" Fan, Cut A, B, C in Azure, Green, and Rose, 1928 (see Smoker Items); $75.00
2387 Vase, 8"
 Crystal, 1928-1932; $52.00
 Green, 1928-1932; $57.00
 Orchid, 1928; $65.00
 Azure, 1928-1930; $65.00
 Rose, 1928-1932; $60.00
 Ebony, 1930-1932; $55.00
2387½ Vase, 8" Heavy, 1938-1940; $50.00
2396 Vase, 7" RO
 Crystal, 1927-1929; $55.00
 Amber, 1927-1929; $60.00
 Green, 1927-1929; $65.00
 Blue, 1927; $75.00
 Orchid, 1927; $70.00
2396 Vase, 9" RO
 Crystal, 1927-1929; $60.00
 Green, 1927-1929; $70.00
 Blue, 1927; $80.00
 Orchid, 1927; $75.00
 Rose, 1929; $75.00
2397 Vase, 4" Footed RO
 Green, 1928-1930; $54.00
 Azure, 1928-1930; $60.00
 Rose, 1928-1930; $55.00
2397 Vase, 6" Footed RO
 Green, 1928-1930; $60.00
 Azure, 1928-1930; $65.00
 Rose, 1928-1930; $65.00
2397 Vase, 8" Footed RO
 Green, 1928-1930; $75.00
 Azure, 1928-1930; $85.00
 Rose, 1928-1930; $80.00
2404 Vase, 6" RO
 Crystal, 1934-1943; $30.00
 Amber, 1929-1933; $40.00
 Green, 1929-1934; $42.00
 Azure, 1939-1938; $45.00
 Rose, 1930-1938; $45.00
 Ebony, 1929-1938; $40.00
 Topaz, 1929-1935; $40.00
 Regal Blue, 1934-1935; $75.00
 Empire Green, 1934-1935; $75.00
2408 Vase, 8" RO
 Amber, 1929-1932; $55.00
 Green, 1929-1932; $64.00
 Azure, 1929-1932; $75.00
 Rose, 1929-1932; $65.00
 Topaz, 1929-1932; $65.00

Navarre 2470 Vase, Manor 4107 Vase, Midnight Rose 4110 Vase

2409 Vase, 7½" RO
 Amber, 1929-1932; $55.00
 Azure, 1929-1932; $75.00
 Rose, 1929-1932; $65.00
 Ebony, 1930-1932; $55.00
 Topaz, 1929-1932; $60.00
2417 Vase, RO, SO
 Crystal, 1929-1933; $50.00
 Amber, 1929-1933; $55.00
 Green, 1929-1933; $60.00
 Azure, 1929-1930; $75.00
 Rose, 1929-1933; $65.00
 Topaz, 1929-1932; $60.00

Green and Crystal Manor 4108 5" Vases, Topaz 4108 6" Vase with Butterfly Decoration

2421 Vase, 10½" Footed RO
    Amber, 1929-1930; $68.00
    Green, 1929-1930; $75.00
    Azure, 1929-1930; $90.00
    Rose, 1929-1930; $85.00
    Ebony, 1930-1932; $68.00
2425 Vase, 8"
    Crystal, 1930-1933; $60.00
    Amber, 1930-1933; $65.00
    Green, 1930-1933; $70.00
    Azure, 1930-1933; $75.00
    Rose, 1930-1933; $70.00
    Ebony, 1930-1933; $65.00
    Topaz, 1930-1933; $65.00
2428 Vase, 6" NO
    Amber, 1930-1935; $38.00
    Green, 1930-1935; $45.00
    Rose, 1930-1940; $45.00
    Ebony, 1930-1940; 1953-1958; $50.00
    Topaz, 1931-1933; $50.00
    Wisteria, 1931-1938; $65.00
2428 Vase, 7½"
    Crystal, 1933-1938; $45.00
    Amber, 1930-1938; $50.00
    Green, 1930-1935; $55.00
    Azure, 1930-1934; $65.00
    Rose, 1930-1936; $60.00
    Ebony, 1930-1938; $50.00
    Topaz, 1930-1938; $50.00
2428 Vase, 9" NO
    Crystal, 1931-1939; $57.00
    Amber, 1930-1940; $65.00
    Green, 1930-1934; $75.00
    Rose, 1930-1940; $70.00
    Ebony, 1930-1940; 1953-1958; $65.00
    Topaz/Gold Tint, 1931-1939; $75.00
    Wisteria, 1931-1934; $165.00
2428 Vase, 10"
    Crystal, 1932-1936; $60.00
    Amber, 1930-1932; $70.00
    Green, 1930-1936; $75.00
    Azure, 1930-1934; $85.00
    Rose, 1930-1934; $85.00
    Ebony, 1930-1935; $75.00
    Topaz, 1930-1936; $75.00
2428 Vase, 13"
    Crystal, 1932-1943; $64.00
    Amber, 1930-1935; $75.00
    Green, 1930-1934; $95.00
    Rose, 1930-1934; $150.00
    Ebony, 1930-1940; 1953-1958; $75.00
    Topaz, 1931-1935; $125.00
    Wisteria, 1931-1933; $225.00
2430 (see Diadem)
2431 Vase, 7½" Wall
    Amber, 1930-1932; $70.00
    Green, 1930-1932; $75.00

Glacier GL06/757 6" Bud Vase, 2412 Colony Vase with Lotus decoration; Ruby 1827/801 Rambler Vase

    Azure, 1930-1932; $80.00
    Rose, 1930-1932; $75.00
    Ebony, 1930-1932; $65.00
2440 Vase, 7" (see Lafayette)
2449 Vase, 6" (see Hermitage)
2454 Vase, 8"
    Crystal, 1930-1939; $48.00
    Amber, 1932-1935; $58.00
    Green, 1932-1939; $55.00
    Rose, 1932-1939; $55.00
    Ebony, 1932-1938; $55.00
    Topaz/Gold Tint, 1932-1940; $54.00
    Ruby, 1936; $95.00
2467 Vase, 7½"
    Crystal, 1934-1946; $48.00
    Green, 1934-1937; $58.00
    Ebony, 1934-1938; 1953-1958; $45.00
    Topaz/Gold Tint, 1934-1938; $55.00

Topaz New Garland 2430 Vase, Topaz June 2417 Vase

2470 Vase, 8"
  Crystal, 1935-1943; $54.00
  Regal Blue, 1935-1938; $75.00
  Empire Green, 1935-1938; $75.00
  Burgundy, 1935-1939; $70.00
  Ruby, 1935-1940; $75.00
2470 Vase, 10"
  Crystal, 1933-1958; $60.00
  Green, 1933-1936; $95.00
  Azure, 1937-1938; $97.00
  Topaz/Gold Tint, 1933-1938; $75.00
  Wisteria, 1933-1942; $125.00
  Empire Green, 1934-1942; $90.00
  Burgundy, 1934-1942; $90.00
  Ruby, 1935-1942; $115.00
  Cinnamon, 1952-1956; $70.00
  Spruce, 1952-1958; $65.00
2470 Vase, 11½"
  Crystal, 1934-1943; $65.00
  Regal Blue, 1934-1939; $125.00
  Empire Green, 1934-1939; $110.00
  Burgundy, 1934-1939; $110.00
2484 Vase, 7" (see Baroque)
2485 Vase, 5" Crescent
  Crystal, 1933-1934; $100.00
  Green, 1933-1934; $125.00
  Topaz, 1933-1934; $125.00
  Ebony, 1933-1934; $125.00
2486 Vase, 7" Square
  Crystal, 1933-1934; $125.00
  Green, 1933-1934; $150.00
  Topaz, 1933-1934; $150.00
  Ebony, 1933-1934; $150.00
2485 Vase, 7" Crescent
  Crystal, 1933-1934; $125.00
  Green, 1933-1934; $150.00
  Topaz, 1933-1934; $150.00
2486 Vase, 9" Square
  Crystal, 1933-1934; $150.00
  Green, 1933-1934; $175.00
  Topaz, 1933-1934; $175.00
2489 Vase, 5½"
  Crystal, 1933-1936; $35.00
  Green, 1933-1937; $44.00
  Topaz, 1933-1935; $40.00
  Wisteria, 1933-1935; $68.00
2489 Vase, 6½"
  Crystal, 1933-1938; $40.00
  Green, 1933-1938; $48.00
  Topaz/Gold Tint, 1933-1938; $48.00
  Wisteria, 1933-1938; $70.00
2503 Vase, 7" Crimped
  Regal Blue, 1934-1942; $67.00
  Empire Green, 1934-1942; $67.00
  Burgundy, 1934-1938; $75.00
  Ruby, 1935-1936; $95.00

Azure 2397 6" Vase, Rose 4101 Vase; Amber 4103 6" Vase, Orchid 4103 4" Vase

2503 Vase, 8" Crystal Handles
  Regal Blue, 1934-1936; $125.00
  Empire Green, 1934-1936; $125.00
  Burgundy, 1934; $145.00
2510 (see Sunray)
2518 Vase, 10"
  Regal Blue, 1935-1938; $95.00
  Empire Green, 1935-1938; $95.00
  Burgundy, 1935-1938; $95.00
  Ruby, 1935-1940; $95.00
2522 Vase, 8" (Similar to 4100), Silver Mist, 1935-1939; $47.00
2523 Vase, 6½" (Similar to 4105), Silver Mist, 1935-1939; $32.00
2545 Vase, 10" (see Flame)
2550 (see Spool)
2560 (see Coronet)
2567 Vase, 6" Footed, Heavy, 1938-1943; $42.00
2567 Vase, 7½" Footed Heavy
  Crystal, 1938-1958; $45.00
  Ebony Base, 1953-1958; $75.00

2545 Azure 10" Vase

2567 Vase, 8½" Footed, Heavy, 1938-1943; $50.00
2568 Vase, 9" Footed, Heavy, 1938-1943; $54.00
2569 Vase, 9" Footed, Heavy, 1938-1943; $58.00
2570 Vase, 6¾" Flared, 1939-1943; $46.00
2570 Vase, 7" Regular, 1939-1943; $46.00
2577 Vase, 15", 1942-1943; $65.00
2579 Vase, 6" Cornucopia, 1940-1943; $45.00
2577 Vase, 5½" Wide, 1940; $35.00
2577 Vase, 6", 1940; $40.00
2577 Vase, 8½", 1940-1943; $45.00
2591 Vase, 8½", 1952-1963; $48.00
2591 Vase, 11½", 1952-1960; $65.00
2591 Vase, 15" Heavy, 1940-1943; $75.00
2592 (see Myriad)
2600 Vase, Acanthus, 1940-1957; $87.00
2611 Vase, 14", 1942-1943; $85.00
2612 Vase, 13", 1942-1943; $65.00
2614 Vase, 10", 1942-1943; $75.00
2619½ Vase, 6" Ground Bottom, 1942-1943; $34.00
2619½ Vase, 7½" Ground Bottom, 1942-1943; $40.00
2619½ Vase, 9½" Ground Bottom, 1942-1943; $48.00
2654 Vase, 9½" Footed, 1952-1961; $54.00
2656 Vase, 10" Footed
    Crystal, 1952-1963; $50.00
    Spruce, 1952-1964; $54.00
2657 Vase, 10½" Footed
    Crystal, 1952-1960; $55.00
    Cinnamon, 1952-1964; $60.00
2658 Vase, 10½" Footed
    Crystal, 1952-1954; $55.00
    Spruce, 1952-1960; $60.00
2659 Vase, 10" Footed
    Crystal, 1952-1954; $65.00
    Cinnamon, 1952-1954; $75.00
2659 Vase, 8" Footed
    Crystal, 1952-1954; $57.00
    Cinnamon, 1952-1954; $67.00
2660 Vase, 8" Flip
    Crystal, 1952-1958; $37.00
    Cinnamon, 1952-1963; $40.00
    Spruce, 1952-1963; $40.00
2692 (see Garden Center Items)
2702 Brass and Glass Candleholder/Vase, 6¾", 8", 9½",
    1956-1962 (see also p. 74, 84); $22.00 – $28.00
2723 Epergne, 10" Bowl, three 8" Trumpet Vases
    Crystal, 1959; $125.00
    Amber, 1959; $150.00
    Amethyst, 1959; $175.00
2724 Vase (see Garden Center Items)
4020 Vase, 7½" Bud, SO
    Crystal, 1931-1940; $27.00
    Amber Base, 1931-1940; $32.00
    Green, Base, 1931-1940; $35.00
    Rose Bowl, 1931-1936; $38.00
    Ebony Base, 1931-1939; $34.00
    Topaz Bowl, 1931-1936; $38.00
4055D Vase, 7½", 1921-1928, Cut B; $45.00

*5088 Bud Vase, Topaz Bowl; 4020 Bud Vases, Crystal,
Spiral Optic; Amber Base, Spiral Optic; Ebony Base*

4056 Vase, 5", 1921-1923; $24.00
4056 Vase, 5½", 1921-1923; $24.00
4056 Vase, 6½", 1921-1923; $30.00
4056 Vase, 7½", 1921-1923; $35.00
4069 Vase, 9"
    Crystal, 1924; $47.00
    Amber, 1925-1927; $52.00
    Blue, 1925-1927; $65.00
    Green, 1925-1927; $57.00
4095 Vase, 7" SO
    Amber, 1927; $48.00
    Green, 1927; $54.00
    Blue, 1927; $67.00
    Orchid, 1927; $54.00
4095 Vase, 8" Small Flared, LO
    Crystal, 1924-1927; $47.00
    Amber, 1925-1927; $52.00

*Regal Blue 5092 Vase, 2404 Vase, 4129 2½" Bubble Ball, Empire
Green 5090 Vase, Regal Blue 4116 5" Bubble Ball, 5091 Vase*

Green, 1925-1927; $57.00
Blue, 1925-1927; $68.00
4095 Vase, 8" Small Flared SO
Amber, 1927; $52.00
Green, 1927; $57.00
Blue, 1927; $68.00
Orchid, 1927; $65.00
4095 Vase, 8" Small, Rolled Top, Plain or LO
Crystal, 1924; $50.00
Amber, 1925-1927; $54.00
Blue, 1925-1927; $68.00
4095 Vase, 9" Medium Flared, Plain or LO
Crystal, 1924-1925; $55.00
Amber, 1925-1927; $60.00
Green, 1925-1927; $65.00
Blue, 1925-1927; $74.00
4095 Vase, 9" LO
Amber, 1925-1927; $60.00
Green, 1925-1927; $65.00
Blue, 1925-1927; $74.00
4095 Vase, 10" Large Flared
Crystal, 1924-1927; $58.00
Amber, 1925-1927; $62.00
Green, 1925-1927; $67.00
Blue, 1925-1927; $75.00
4095 Vase, 9" Rolled Edge
Crystal, 1924-1927; $58.00
Amber, 1925; $60.00
Green, 1925; $65.00
Blue, 1925; $75.00
4095 Vase, 10" Rolled Edge
Crystal, 1924-1927; $60.00
Amber, 1925-1926; $65.00
Green, 1925-1926; $68.00
Blue, 1925-1926; $78.00
Canary, listed in catalog but not price list
4095½ Vase, 8" Plain, RO, SO, LO
Crystal, 1925-1927; $47.00
Amber, 1925-1927; $52.00
Amber Foot, LO, 1925-1927; $55.00
Green, 1925-1927; $57.00
Green Foot, SO, 1925-1927; $57.00
Blue, 1925-1927; $68.00
Blue Foot, RO, 1925-1927; $74.00
4100 Vase, 6" RO, LO
Crystal, 1927-1929; $28.00
Amber, 1927-1929; $35.00
Green, 1927-1929; $40.00
Blue, 1927; $48.00
Orchid, 1927; $45.00
4100 Vase, 8" RO, LO
Crystal, 1926-1934, RO only; $30.00
Amber, 1926-1934; $37.00
Green, 1926-1934; $38.00
Blue, 1926-1927; $52.00
Orchid, 1927; $47.00
Rose, 1929-1934; $45.00

2470 Vases in Ruby and Empire Green, 2428 Wisteria 13" Vase, 2409 Green 7½" Vase, 2470 Vase in Spruce

Azure, 1929-1934; $48.00
4100 Vase, 10", RO, LO
Crystal, 1927-1930; $35.00
Amber, 1927-1930; $40.00
Green, 1927-1930; $45.00
Blue, 1927; $56.00
Orchid, 1927; $50.00
Rose, 1929-1930; $52.00
4100 Vase, 12", RO
Crystal, 1927; $40.00
Amber, 1927-1932; $42.00
Green, 1927-1932; $45.00
Blue, 1927; $60.00
Orchid, 1927; $55.00
Rose, 1929-1932; $55.00
4100 Vase, 12", LO
Crystal, 1927-1928; $40.00

2373 Rose Window Box, unknown cutting; Green 4105 Vase, LO; 2385 Green Oak Leaf Fan Vase; Rose 4100 Vase with Triangle Decoration; Ebony 2409 Vase with Fern Decoration (courtesy of Kevin Coughlin and Irma Griffin)

Amber, 1927-1929; $42.00
Green, 1927-1929; $45.00
Blue, 1927; $60.00
4101 Vase, 5½"
    Amber, 1931-1934; $35.00
    Green, 1931-1934; $38.00
    Rose, 1931-1934; $38.00
    Topaz, 1931-1934; $38.00
4103 Vase, 3" RO
    Crystal, 1938-1943; $18.00
    Amber, 1927-1940; $22.00
    Green, 1927-1940; $24.00
    Blue, 1927; $30.00
    Orchid, 1927; $28.00
    Rose, 1928-1933; $28.00
    Azure, 1928-1936; $28.00
    Regal Blue, 1934-1937; $37.00
    Empire Green, 1934-1938; $37.00
    Burgundy, 1934-1937; $37.00
4103 Vase, 4" RO
    Crystal, 1929-1939; $23.00
    Amber, 1927-1940; $25.00
    Green, 1927-1940; $27.00
    Blue, 1927; $35.00
    Orchid, 1927; $30.00
    Rose, 1928-1940; $30.00
    Regal Blue, 1934-1939; $42.00
    Empire Green, 1934-1939; $42.00
    Burgundy, 1934-1939; $42.00
    Ruby, 1935-1942; $42.00
4103 Vase, 5" RO
    Crystal, 1929-1940; $25.00
    Amber, 1927-1943; $27.00
    Green, 1927-1936; $32.00
    Blue, 1927; $38.00
    Orchid, 1927; $36.00
    Rose, 1928-1933; $36.00
4103 Vase, 6" RO
    Crystal, 1929-1933; $28.00
    Amber, 1927-1933; $34.00
    Green, 1927-1933; $38.00
    Blue, 1927; $45.00
    Rose, 1929-1933; $40.00
4103½ Vase, 5" Ribbed Heavy, Crystal, 1938-1940; $28.00
4105 Vase, 6" RO
    Crystal, 1928-1931; $28.00
    Green, 1928-1931; $38.00
    Orchid, 1928; $42.00
    Rose, 1928-1931; $40.00
    Azure, 1928-1931; $45.00
4105 Vase, 6" LO
    Green, 1928-1930; $38.00
    Rose, 1928-1930; $40.00
    Azure, 1928-1930; $45.00
4105 Vase, 8" RO
    Crystal, 1928-1932; $34.00

Spruce 2658 Vase (from the collection of Terry and Carl Naas; photograph by Glenn Eppleston)(See p. 4.)

Green, 1928-1932; $40.00
Orchid, 1928; $45.00
Ebony 1930-1932; $40.00
Rose, 1928-1932; $42.00
Azure, 1928-1932; $48.00
Topaz, 1929-1932; $42.00
4105 Vase, 8" LO
    Green, 1928-1930; $40.00
    Rose, 1928-1930; $42.00
    Azure, 1928-1930; $50.00
4105 Vase, 10" RO, LO
    Green, 1928-1930; $45.00
    Rose, 1928-1930; $48.00
    Azure, 1928-1930; $55.00

Cinnamon 4121 Vase, Arcady 4121 Vase, Amber 2369 Vase

4106 Vase, 7"
  Crystal, 1931-1938; $30.00
  Amber, 1931-1934; $36.00
  Green, 1931-1934; $38.00
  Ebony 1931-1934; $36.00
  Rose, 1931-1933; $40.00
  Topaz, 1931-1934; $36.00
4107 Vase, 9"
  Crystal, 1931-1938; $40.00
  Amber, 1931-1932; $50.00
  Green, 1931-1935; $54.00
  Rose, 1931-1934; $54.00
  Topaz, 1931-1934; $54.00
  Wisteria, 1931-1938; $95.00
4107 Vase, 12"
  Crystal, 1931-1939; $47.00
  Amber, 1931-1934; $55.00
  Green, 1931-1934; $58.00
  Ebony, 1931-1934; $55.00
  Rose, 1931-1934; $60.00
  Topaz, 1931-1934; $58.00
4107 Vase, 15"
  Crystal, 1932-1942; $47.00
  Amber, 1931-1932; $65.00
  Green, 1931-1935; $65.00
  Rose, 1931-1934; $70.00
  Topaz/Gold Tint, 1931-1938; $60.00
4108 Vase, 5"
  Crystal, 1931-1934; $28.00
  Amber, 1931-1934; $32.00
  Green, 1931-1934; $34.00
  Rose, 1931-1934; $34.00
  Topaz, 1931-1934; $34.00
  Wisteria, 1931-1934; $75.00
4108 Vase, 6"
  Crystal, 1931-1934; $30.00
  Amber, 1931-1934; $35.00
  Green, 1931-1934; $38.00
  Ebony, 1932-1934; $35.00
  Rose, 1931-1934; $38.00
  Topaz, 1931-1934; $38.00
4108 Vase, 7"
  Crystal, 1931-1933; $35.00
  Amber, 1931-1933; $40.00
  Green, 1931-1933; $45.00
  Rose, 1931-1933; $45.00
  Topaz, 1931-1933; $45.00
4110 Vase, 7½"
  Crystal, 1933-1938; $42.00
  Green, 1933-1938; $47.00
  Topaz, 1933-1935; $48.00
  Wisteria, 1933-1934; $95.00
  Regal Blue, 1934-1938; $67.00
  Empire Green, 1934-1938; $67.00
  Burgundy, 1934-1938; $67.00
4111 Vase, 6½"
  Crystal, 1933-1938; $35.00

2702 Brass and Glass Combination Vases, Tall Vase with Fostoria sticker, never listed

  Green, 1933-1938; $40.00
  Ebony, 1933-1938; $38.00
  Topaz, 1933-1935; $40.00
  Wisteria, 1933-1938; $75.00
4112 Vase, 8½"
  Crystal, 1933-1939; $45.00
  Green, 1933-1938; $54.00
  Topaz/Gold Tint, 1933-1938; $54.00
  Wisteria, 1933-1934; $135.00
  Regal Blue, 1934-1938; $95.00
  Empire Green, 1934-1938; $95.00
  Burgundy, 1934-1938; $95.00
4116 Vase, 4" Bubble Ball
  Crystal, 1934-1943; $16.00
  Ebony, 1955-1958; $18.00
  Azure, 1937-1939; $20.00
  Regal Blue, 1934-1942; $20.00
  Empire Green, 1934-1942; $20.00
  Burgundy, 1934-1942; $20.00
  Ruby, 1935-1942; $20.00
  Cinnamon, 1952-1964; $18.00
  Spruce, 1952-1961; $18.00
4116 Vase, 5" Bubble Ball
  Crystal, 1934-1938; $18.00
  Azure, 1937-1939; $32.00
  Regal Blue, 1934-1942; $22.00
  Empire Green, 1934-1940; $22.00
  Burgundy, 1934-1942; $22.00
4116 Vase, 6" Bubble Ball
  Crystal, 1934-1943; $20.00
  Azure, 1937-1939; $37.00
  Regal Blue, 1934-1942; $30.00
  Empire Green, 1934-1939; $30.00
  Burgundy, 1935-1940; $30.00
  Ruby, 1935-1942; $30.00

No. 2300. 12 in. Vase.

Cinnamon, 1952-1958; $25.00
Spruce, 1952-1958; $25.00
4116 Vase, 7" Bubble Ball
Crystal, 1935-1943; $22.00
Azure, 1937-1940; $38.00
Regal Blue, 1935-1940; $36.00
Empire Green, 1935-1942; $34.00
Burgundy, 1935-1940; $36.00
Ruby, 1935-1940; $36.00
4116 Vase, 8" Bubble Ball
Crystal, 1935-1943; $25.00
Regal Blue, 1935-1939; $40.00
Empire Green, 1935-1940; $40.00
Burgundy, 1935-1939; $40.00
Ruby, 1936-1938; $45.00
4116 Vase, 9" Bubble Ball
Crystal, 1935-1943; $27.00
Azure, 1937-1938; $45.00
Regal Blue, 1935-1937; $47.00
Empire Green, 1935-1937; $47.00
Burgundy, 1935-1938; $45.00
Ruby, 1935-1937; $45.00
4116½ Vase, 5" Heavy Rib, 1938-1943; $20.00
4121 Vase, 5" RO, Crystal, 1936-1950; 1952-1958; $28.00
4121 Vase, 5" Plain
Regal Blue, 1936-1939; $47.00
Empire Green, 1936-1942; $45.00
Burgundy, 1936-1942; $45.00
Cinnamon, 1952-1963; $35.00
Spruce, 1952-1963; $35.00
Chartreuse, 1952-1963; $35.00
4123 Vase, Pansy
Crystal, 1935-1955; $18.00
Azure, 1937-1942; $27.00
Regal Blue, 1935-1942; $27.00
Empire Green, 1935-1942; $27.00
Burgundy, 1935-1942; $27.00
Ruby, 1935-1942; $27.00
Cinnamon, 1952-1956; $20.00
Spruce, 1952-1960; $18.00
Chartreuse, 1952-1954; $20.00
4124 Vase, 4½" RO
Crystal, 1936-1943; $20.00
Azure, 1937-1939; $30.00
4124 Vase, 4½" Plain
Regal Blue, 1936-1939; $34.00
Empire Green, 1936-1939; 34.00
Burgundy, 1936-1940; $34.00
4125 Vase, 7" RO, 1936-1938; $30.00
4125 Vase, 7" Plain
Regal Blue, 1936-1938; $58.00
Empire Green, 1936-1938; $58.00
Burgundy, 1936-1938; $58.00
4126 Vase, 11" LO, 1936-1939; $57.00
4126 Vase, 11" Plain, Colored Bowl
Regal Blue, 1936-1938; $125.00
Empire Green, 1936-1937; $125.00
Burgundy, 1936-1940; $95.00

1928 Good Housekeeping

4126½ Vase, 11" Footed, Heavy, 1940-1943; $50.00
4128 Vase, 5" RO
Crystal, 1936-1943; $28.00
Azure, 1937-1939; $38.00
Regal Blue, 1936-1940; $40.00

No. 2284. Epergne Set, Amber.

Empire Green, 1936-1939; $40.00
Burgundy, 1936-1942; $38.00
4129 Vase, 2½" Bubble Ball
Crystal, 1935-1943; $14.00
Azure, 1937-1940; $18.00
Regal Blue, 1935-1940; $42.00
Empire Green, 1935-1940; $42.00
Burgundy, 1935-1940; $42.00
Ruby, 1935-1943; $40.00
4130 Vase, Violet
Crystal, 1935-1954; $20.00
Azure, 1927-1942; $27.00
Regal Blue, 1935-1942; $28.00
Empire Green, 1935-1942; $28.00
Burgundy, 1935-1942; $28.00
Ruby, 1935-1942; $28.00
Cinnamon, 1953-1955; $20.00
Spruce, 1952-1956; $20.00
Chartreuse, 1952-1956; $20.00
4128½ Vase, 5" Heavy, 1938-1943; $28.00
4132½ Vase, 8" Heavy, 1938-1943; $50.00
4133 Vase, 4" LO
Crystal, 1937-1938; $37.00
Azure, 1937-1938; $55.00
Gold Tint, 1937-1938; $55.00
4134 Vase, 6" LO
Crystal, 1937-1938; $42.00
Azure, 1937; $60.00
Gold Tint, 1937; $60.00
4136 Vase, 6" Bud
Crystal, 1938-1940; $34.00
Azure, 1937-1938; $48.00
Regal Blue, 1937; $52.00
Empire Green, 1939-1940; $50.00
Burgundy, 1939-1940; $50.00
4137 Vase, 3¾"
Crystal, 1939-1943; $20.00

Azure, 1939-1940; $27.00
Regal Blue, 1937-1942; $30.00
Empire Green, 1939-1942; $30.00
Burgundy, 1939-1942; $30.00
4138 Vase, 3½" Plain
Crystal, 1938-1943; $20.00
Azure, 1938-1940; $27.00
Regal Blue, 1938-1942; $30.00
Empire Green, 1938-1942; $30.00
Burgundy, 1938-1942; $30.00
4143 Vase, 6" Footed, 1940-1953; $34.00
4143 Vase, 7½" Footed, 1940-1943; $38.00
4143½ Vase, 6" Heavy Footed, 1940-1943; $34.00
4143½ Vase, 7½" Heavy Footed, 1940-1943; $38.00
4144 Vase, 3"
Crystal, 1940-1943; $18.00
Regal Blue, 1940-1942; $25.00
Empire Green, 1940-1942; $25.00
Burgundy, 1940-1942; $25.00
4145 Vase, 3"
Crystal, 1941-1943; $18.00
Regal Blue, 1941-1942; $25.00
Empire Green, 1941-1942; $25.00
Burgundy, 1941-1942; $25.00
4152 (see Garden Center Items)
4166 Vase, 6" Bud
Silver Mist, 1960; $20.00
Silver Mist Spruce, 1960; $20.00
5079 Vase, 9" Bud, 1924; $28.00
5085 Vase, 8" Bud
Crystal, Pre 1924-1925; $35.00
Amber, 1925-1926; $48.00
Green, 1925-1926; $54.00
Blue, 1925-1926; $65.00
5085 Vase, 8" Bud SO
Amber, 1927-1934; $52.00
Green, 1927-1934; $58.00

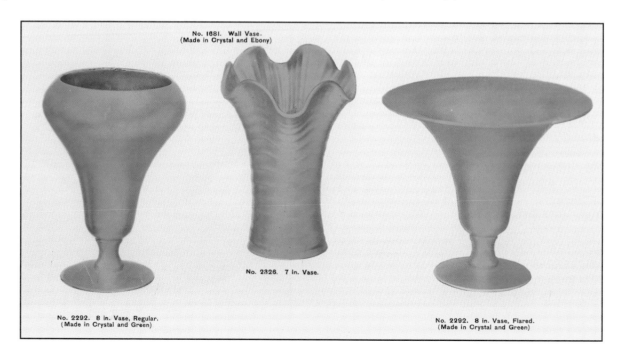

No. 1681. Wall Vase.
(Made in Crystal and Ebony)

No. 2326. 7 in. Vase.

No. 2292. 8 in. Vase, Regular.
(Made in Crystal and Green)

No. 2292. 8 in. Vase, Flared.
(Made in Crystal and Green)

Blue, 1927; $75.00
Orchid, 1927; $70.00
Rose, 1928-1934; $58.00
Azure, 1928-1932; $65.00
5086 Vase, 9" Bud
Crystal, pre 1924-1932; $50.00
Amber, 1925-1926; $60.00
Green, 1925-1926; $65.00
Blue, 1925-1926; $78.00
5086 Vase, 9" Bud SO
Amber, 1927-1934; $60.00
Green, 1927-1934; $65.00
Blue, 1927; $85.00
Orchid, 1927; $85.00
Rose, 1928-1934; $65.00
5087 Vase, 8" Bud
Crystal, pre 1924-1925; $42.00
Amber, 1925-1926; $52.00
Blue, 1925-1926; $65.00
5087 Vase, 8" Bud, SO
Crystal, 1927-1928; $30.00
Amber, 1927-1934; $52.00
Green, 1927-1934; $58.00
Blue, 1927; $75.00
Orchid, 1927; $70.00
Rose, 1928-1934; $58.00
5088 Vase, 5" Bud
Crystal, 1936-1939; $28.00
Ebony, 1936-1939; $32.00
Green Base, 1936-1939; $36.00
Wisteria Base, 1936; $45.00
Ebony Base, 1936-1939; $34.00
Topaz Bowl, 1926-1927; $36.00
Regal Blue Bowl, 1936-1939; $40.00
Empire Green Bowl, 1936-1939; $40.00
5088 Vase, 8" Bud
Crystal, 1935-1940; $34.00
Ebony, 1934-1939; $34.00
Green Base, 1934-1939; $40.00
Ebony Base, 1934-1939; $40.00
Topaz/Gold Tint Bowl, 1934-1937; $40.00
Wisteria Base, 1934-1938; $57.00
Regal Blue Bowl, 1934-1939; $58.00
Empire Green Bowl, 1934-1939; $58.00
Burgundy Bowl, 1934-1935; $60.00
5088 Vase, 8" Bud RO
Crystal, 1931-1943; $34.00
Ebony, 1931-1939; $34.00
Amber Base, 1931-1939; $52.00
Green Base, 1931-1939; $58.00
Ebony Base, 1931-1939; $52.00
Wisteria Base, 1931-1934; $64.00
Regal Blue Bowl, 1934-1940; $58.00
Empire Green Bowl, 1934-1938; $58.00
Burgundy Bowl 1934-1939; $60.00
5090 Vase, 8" Bud
Crystal, 1935-1939; $32.00

Regal Blue, 1935-1939; $57.00
Empire Green, 1935-1939; $57.00
Burgundy , 1935-1939; $57.00
Ruby, 1935-1938; $60.00
5091 Vase, 6½" Bud
Crystal, 1935-1942; $26.00
Regal Blue, 1935-1939; $45.00
Empire Green, 1935-1939; $45.00
Burgundy, 1935-1939; $45.00
Ruby, 1935-1936; $50.00
5092 Vase, 8" Bud
Crystal, 1935-1939; $34.00
Regal Blue Bowl, 1935-1939; $58.00
Empire Green Bowl, 1935-1939; $58.00
Burgundy Bowl, 1935-1939; $58.00
Ruby Bowl, 1935-1936; $60.00
5100 Vase, 10" Footed RO
Crystal, Plain, 1939-1943; $50.00
Amber, 1927-1932; $72.00
Green, 1927-1932; $85.00
Orchid, 1927; $95.00
5300 Vase, 7" Footed Bud, 1940-1943; $47.00
5301 Vase, 8" Footed Bud, 1940-1943; $56.00
6021 Vase, 6" Footed Bud
Crystal, 1938-1943; 1950-1958; $28.00
Azure, 1938-1939; $47.00
Regal Blue, 1938-1939; $54.00
Burgundy, 1938-1939; $54.00
Empire Green, 1938-1939; $54.00
Cinnamon, 1952-1958; $35.00
6021 Vase, 9" Bud, 1938-1943; $38.00

No. 4095. Large Vase.   No. 4095. Large Vase, Rolled Edge.

466 5-in. Vase.
Packed 12 doz. in bbl.
Made also in 7 inch.
Packed 7 doz. in bbl.

184 9-inch Vase.
Packed 8 doz. in bbl.

184 14-inch Vase.
Packed 1 doz. in bbl.

272 14-inch Vase.
Packed 2 doz. in bbl.

272 11½-inch Vase.
Packed 3 doz. in bbl.

272 8-inch Vase.
Packed 10 doz. in bbl.

272 5½-inch Vase.
Packed 15 doz. in bbl.

184 11-inch Vase.
Packed 2½ doz. in bbl.

195 5-inch Vase.
Packed 12 doz in bbl.

600 6½-inch Rose Bowl.
Packed 2 doz. in bbl.

195 9-inch Vase.
Packed 4 doz. in bbl.

600 11-inch Vase.
Packed 4 doz. in bbl.

600 9-inch Vase.
Packed 5 doz. in bbl.

600 7-inch Vase.
Packed 8 doz. in bbl.

402 7-inch.
Packed 10 doz. in bbl.

402 8-inch.
Packed 8 doz. in bbl.

402 10-inch.
Packed 5 doz. in bbl.

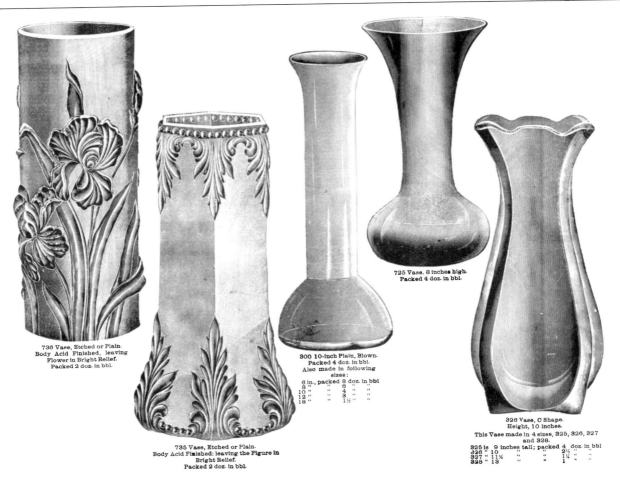

736 Vase, Etched or Plain.
Body Acid Finished, leaving
Flower in Bright Relief.
Packed 2 doz. in bbl.

735 Vase, Etched or Plain.
Body Acid Finished: leaving the Figure in
Bright Relief.
Packed 2 doz. in bbl.

300 10-inch Plain, Blown.
Packed 4 doz. in bbl.
Also made in following
sizes:

6 in., packed 8 doz. in bbl
8 "   "   6 "   "   "
10 "   "   4 "   "   "
12 "   "   3 "   "   "
18 "   "   1½ "   "   "

725 Vase, 8 inches high.
Packed 4 doz. in bbl.

326 Vase, C Shape.
Height, 10 inches.
This Vase made in 4 sizes, 325, 326, 327
and 328.
325 is 9 inches tall; packed 4 doz. in bbl
326 " 10   "   "   2½ "   "   "
327 " 11½   "   "   1¼ "   "   "
328 " 13   "   "   1 "   "   "

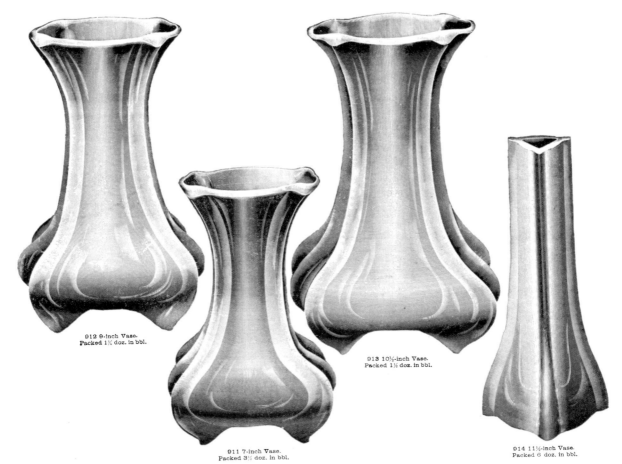

912 9-inch Vase.
Packed 1¼ doz. in bbl.

911 7-inch Vase.
Packed 3½ doz. in bbl.

913 10½-inch Vase.
Packed 1½ doz. in bbl.

914 11½-inch Vase.
Packed 6 doz. in bbl.

No. 1106 Orchid Vase
Small, Height 6½ in.
Large, Height 8 in.

No. 1966 8 in. Blown Flower Bowl
With 6 in. Wire Screen. Silver Plated.
Price, $1.10 each.

No. 1848 Flower Bowl
(With Silver Plated Mesh)
Deep Etched Art Nauvoe.
Price, $1.00 each.

No. 1848 6 in. Pressed Flower Bowl
With Wire Screen. Silver Plated.
Price, 75 cents each.

No. 1624 1-2 8 in.
Deep Etched Landscape
with Floral Border.
Price, $1.00 each.

No. 1694 8 in.
Deep Etched Marine Scene,
with Art Nauvoe Panel.
Price, $1.00 each.

No. 1796 9 in.
Cut and Engraved No. 5.
Price, $1.50 each.

No. 1797 1-2 7 in.
Cutting 116.
Price, 60 cents each.

No. 1797 1-2 7 in.
Deep Etched Persian Design.
Price, 75 cents each.

No. 4069 9-inch Vase,
Cut 138
Top Diameter 3 inches

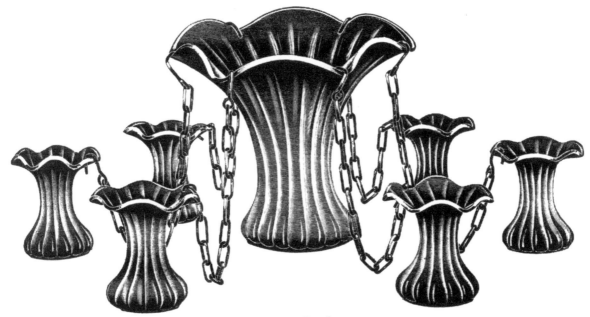

No. 1939 Center Set
Large 7 3-4 inches high.
Small 4 1-2 inches high.

No. 761 10 in.
Deep Etched Greek Figure.
Price, $1.50 each.

No. 1761 10½-inch Vase,
Cut 138
Top Diameter 3¼ inches

No. 48-3 Flower Set
(With Silver Plated Mesh.)
Cut 116 Mission Cutting.
Plate Cut Mat Star.
Price, $3.25 each Set.

No. 1491
6 in. **Vase**, Ebony.

No. 1491
8½ in. **Vase**, Ebony.

No. 2312
10 in. **Vase**, Ebony.

No. 1681. Wall Vase.
(Made in Crystal and Ebony)

*(Note the slight differ-
ence in the wall vases.)*

1120—15 in. Vase, Loop Optic.
Made in 12 and 15 in.
Not made in Blue or Orchid.

4095—8 in. Vase, **Spiral Optic.**
Made in 8, 9 and 10 in.
Not made in Orchid.

2292—8 in. Vase, Spiral Optic.
Made plain or Spiral Optic.
Made in ebony and crystal—Plain only.

1681—8 in. Wall Vase.
Made in ebony; Not made in orchid.

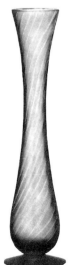

5086—9 in. Vase.
Spiral Optic.

5087—8 in. Vase.
Spiral Optic.

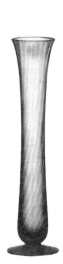

5085—8 in. Vase.
Spiral Optic.

4095½—8 in. Vase.
Spiral Optic.
Not made in orchid.

4095—7 in. Vase.
Spiral Optic.

1479—6 in. Vase.
Not made in blue or orchid.

4100—6 in. Vase.
Regular Optic.
Made in 6, 8, 10 and 12 in.
Made in Regular or Loop Optic.

5100—10 in. Vase, Optic.
Not made in Blue or Crystal.

4100—8 in. Vase, Loop Optic.
Made in 6, 8, 10 and 12 in.
Made in Regular and Loop Optic.

2485—7 in. Crescent Vase—Gr-Crys-Tz
2486—9 in. Square Vase—Gr-Crys-Tz
2485—5 in. Crescent Vase—Gr-Eb-Crys-Tz
2486—7 in. Square Vase—Gr-Eb-Crys-Tz

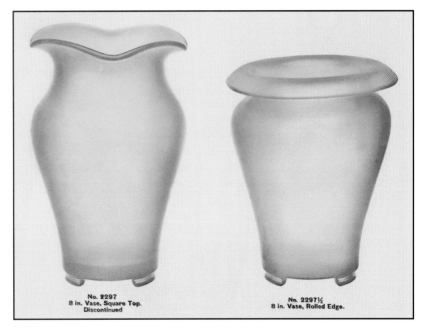

No. 2297
8 in. Vase, Square Top.
Discontinued

No. 2297½
8 in. Vase, Rolled Edge.

4106—7 in. Vase
Ro-Gr-Am-Eb-Crys-Tz

4110—7½ in. Vase
Gr-Crys-Tz-Wis

4112—8½ in. Vase
Gr-Crys-Tz-Wis

4111—6½ in. Vase
Gr-Eb-Crys-Tz-Wis

760
12 in. Vase

2360—10 in. Vase, Hld.

2428—6 in. Vase, Narrow
Diameter 2⅜ in.
2428—9 in. Vase, Narrow
Diameter 3½ in.
2428—13 in. Vase, Narrow
Diameter 5 in.
2428—7½ in. Vase, Wide
Diameter 5⅞ in.
2428—10 in. Vase, Wide
Diameter 5⅞ in.

2449—6 in. Vase

2440—7 in. Vase

2454—8 in. Vase

2404—6 in. Vase

2288—8½ in. Tut Vase, Hld

2467—7½ in. Vase

2470—8 in. Vase
2470—10 in. Vase
2470—11½ in. Vase

4103—3 in. Vase,
4103—4 in. Vase,
4103—5 in. Vase,

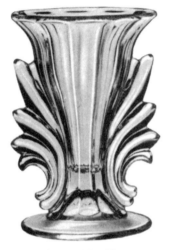

2484—7-in. Vase

2489—6½ in. Vase

2503—7 in. Crimped Vase

4107— 9 in. Vase
4107—12 in. Vase
4107—15 in. Vase

2489—5½ in. Vase

2518—10 in. Vase

4126—11 in. Vase

4125—7 in. Vase

4128—5 in. Vase

2510—Sweet Pea Vase
Height 5¼ in.   Width 6 in.

2510—3½ in. Rose Bowl
2510—5 in. Rose Bowl

2510—9 in. Square Footed Vase

2510—7-in. Vase

2510—6 in. Vase, Crimped

2550—6 in. Vase, Straight

2550—6 in. Vase, Flared

2496—3½ in. Rose Bowl

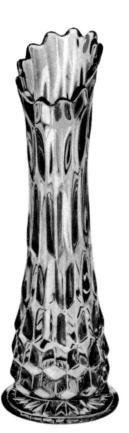

2056—Vase
Swung 9 in. to 12 in.

2496—8 in. Vase

4123—Pansy Vase
Height 3¼ in.

5091
6½ in. Bud Vase

4130—Violet Vase
Height 3⅝ in.

4121—5 in. Vase

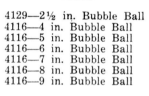

4129—2½ in. Bubble Ball
4116—4 in. Bubble Ball
4116—5 in. Bubble Ball
4116—6 in. Bubble Ball
4116—7 in. Bubble Ball
4116—8 in. Bubble Ball
4116—9 in. Bubble Ball

4124—4½ in. Vase

5092
8 in. Bud Vase

4020—7½ in. Bud Vase

5090
8 in. Bud Vase

5088—5 in. Bud Vase
5088—8 in. Bud Vase

2550½—5½ in. Vase, Straight

2550½—5 in. Vase, Flared

4133—4 in. Vase, Loop Optic

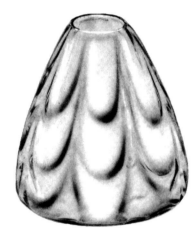

4134—6 in. Vase, Loop Optic

2056½—9½ in. Vase, Flared

2545—10 in. Vase

2222— 8 in. Vase
2222—10 in. Vase

2369—5 in. Vase, Optic
2369—7 in. Vase, Optic
2369—9 in. Vase, Optic

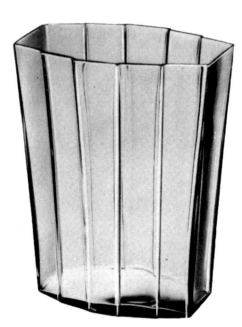

2387—8 in. Vase

2425—8 in. Vase

2408—8 in. Vase

4136
6 in. Bud Vase,
Plain

4138
3½ in. Vase,
Plain

4137
3¾ in. Vase
Plain

6021
6 in. Ftd. Bud Vase,
Plain

2430—3¾ in. Vase

5100—10 in. Vase, Plain

2430—8 in. Vase

2567—7½ in. Footed Vase, Heavy

2568—9 in. Footed Vase, Heavy

2569—9 in. Footed Vase. Heavy

4132½—8 in. Vase, Heavy

1895½—10 in. Vase, Heavy

2387½—8 in. Vase, Heavy

2659 — 10 in. Footed Vase
2659 — 8 in. Footed Vase

2654 — 9½ in.
Footed Vase

2503—8 in. Handled Vase

4116½—5 in. Ball, Ribbed, Heavy

4128½—5 in. Vase, Heavy

4103½—5 in. Vase, Ribbed, Heavy

2056½—10 in. Vase, Flared

6021—9 in. Footed Bud Vase
Plain

2412—12 in. Vase
2412—14 in. Vase

2656 — 10 in.
Footed Vase

2658 — 10½ in.
Footed Vase

2657 — 10½ in.
Footed Vase

231

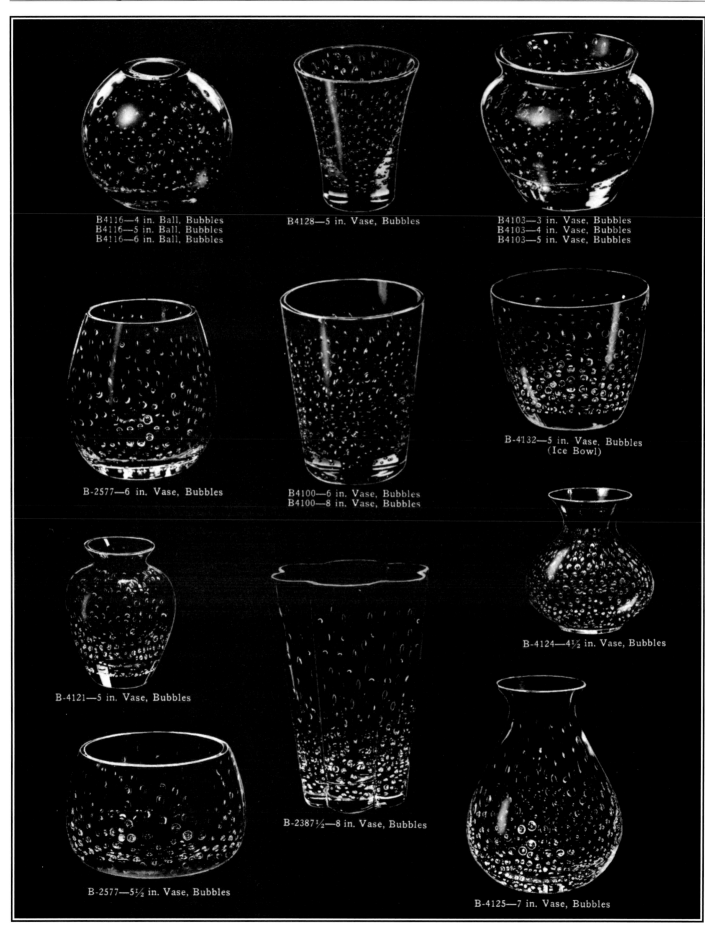

B4116—4 in. Ball, Bubbles
B4116—5 in. Ball, Bubbles
B4116—6 in. Ball, Bubbles

B4128—5 in. Vase, Bubbles

B4103—3 in. Vase, Bubbles
B4103—4 in. Vase, Bubbles
B4103—5 in. Vase, Bubbles

B-2577—6 in. Vase, Bubbles

B4100—6 in. Vase, Bubbles
B4100—8 in. Vase, Bubbles

B-4132—5 in. Vase, Bubbles
(Ice Bowl)

B-4121—5 in. Vase, Bubbles

B-4124—4½ in. Vase, Bubbles

B-2577—5½ in. Vase, Bubbles

B-2387½—8 in. Vase, Bubbles

B-4125—7 in. Vase, Bubbles

H-4116—Ball, Hammered
See Price List for Sizes

H-2577—5½ in. Wide Vase, Hammered

H-4124—4½ in. Vase, Hammered

H-4100—Vase, Hammered
See Price List for Sizes

H-4121—5 in. Vase, Hammered

H-4125—7 in. Vase, Hammered

H-2577—6 in. Vase Hammered

4144—3 in. Vase

4145—3 in. Vase

2577—5½ in. Wide Vase

4143—6 in. Footed Vase
4143½—6 in. Footed Vase, Heavy

4126½—11 in. Footed Vase, Heavy

2577—6 in. Vase

4143—7½ in. Footed Vase
4143½—7½ in. Footed Vase, Heavy

2600—7 in. Acanthus Vase

2579—6 in. Cornucopia

2577—8½ in. Vase, Heavy

5300—7 in. Footed Bud Vase

2591—15 in. Vase, Heavy

5301—8 in. Footed Bud Vase

2614—10 in. Vase

2619½—6 in. Vase
Ground Bottom

2619½—7½ in. Vase
Ground Bottom

2619½—9½ in. Vase
Ground Bottom

2577—15 in. Vase

2612—13 in. Vase

2611—14 in. Vase

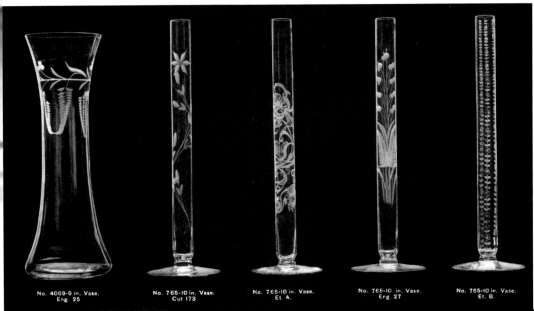

No. 4069-9 in. Vase.
Eng. 25

No. 765-10 in. Vase.
Cut 173

No. 765-10 in. Vase.
Et. A.

No. 765-10 in. Vase.
Eng. 27

No. 765-10 in. Vase.
Et. B.

No. 5085-8 in. Bud Vase.
Cut 31

No. 5086-9 in. Bud Vase.
Cut 32

No. 765-10 in. Bud Vase
Cut 30

No. 5087-8 in. Bud Vase.
Cut 83

No. 762-8 in Vase
Cut 181

No. 4055-D. Vase, Cut 182

No. 2072-8 in. Vase, Cut 182

No. 4095½-8 in. Vase, Cut 182

No. 4069-9 in. Vase, Cut 181

237

2385—8½ in. Fan Vase.
Cut B.

2385—8½ in. Fan Vase, Ftd.
Ro-Az-Gr-Eb-Crys.

2723/364
Epergne Consisting of:
1 2723/208—10″ Bowl

3 2723/312—8″ Trumpet Vase

2409 7½-in. Vase
Ro-Az-Gr-Am-Eb-Tz

4101 5½-in. Vase
Ro-Gr-Am-Tz

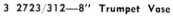
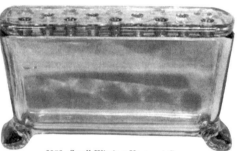

2373 Small Window Vase and Cover
2373 Large Window Vase and Cover
Ro-Az-Gr-Am-Eb-Crys

2397—4 in. Vase, Ftd. Reg. Opt.
Ro-Az-Gr.

2431—7½ in. Wall Vase.
Ro-Az-Gr-Am-Eb.

4108 5-in. Vase
Ro-Gr-Am-Crys-Tz-Wis
4108 6-in. Vase
Ro-Gr-Am-Eb-Crys-Tz
4108 7-in. Vase
Ro-Gr-Am-Crys-Tz

CORONATION CRYSTAL VASES FROM FOSTORIA

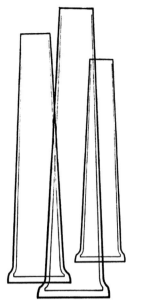

The beauty of crystal, in Coronation Crystal vases from Fostoria. Simple yet elegant, these handblown vases will complement your favorite floral arrangement. From Fostoria, the crystal for America.

CORONATION CRYSTAL VASES FROM FOSTORIA

Intricate, handcut floral designs contrast with the delicate shapes of these crystal vases, creating the mood for your favorite occasion. Enjoy! From Fostoria, the crystal for America.

2660 — 8 in.
Flip Vase

The Coronation Vases were offered through promotional material and were not included in price lists or catalogs. They were offered for sale through jewelry stores in the 1980s and carried a Fostoria paper label.

No. 1895   12-inch Vase
Etched 223

No. 1895   10-inch Vase
Etched 223

No. 1895   8-inch Vase
Etched 223

No. 1895   6-inch Vase
Etched 223

No. 300   18-inch Vase
Deep Etched

No. 300   24-inch Vase
Deep Etched

ABOUT THE AUTHORS

Milbra Long and Emily Seate complete their history of the Fostoria Glass Company from 1924 – 1986 with this volume. A retired teacher, Milbra has been a researcher for years, offering articles to many publications including *Glass Collectors Digest* and *The Daze*. She volunteered her services as chair of the research committee for the Fostoria Glass Society of America, served on the board of directors, and often wrote articles for *Facets of Fostoria*, the organization's newsletter before undertaking the Crystal for America project.

Milbra's love of glass is evident in each book of the series. Since 1994, when *Fostoria Stemware* was published, Milbra and Emily have scoured the countryside for glass to photograph, wanting to present the Fostoria Glass Company with both pictures and catalog illustrations. As they have often said, "The catalog gives the piece authenticity, but the photograph makes it real." In the process of gathering glass and information, they have made some remarkable discoveries about the company, and fondly call each discovery "a Fostoria moment."

Emily has been a writer of fiction and poetry for most of her life, with her "great American novel" still in process. She is a philosopher, preferring long hours spent in thought to just about anything, except shopping for Fostoria glassware and the possibility of fresh discovery that brings.

Together, they are mother and daughter, partners, and life-long friends.

Fostoria
THE CRYSTAL FOR AMERICA

The Crystal for America series is the most complete reference available for the Fostoria Glass Company from 1924 to 1986. *Fostoria Stemware* concentrates on Fostoria stemware etchings, cuttings, decorations, and pattern names. Production dates, colors made, other available pieces, a color identification section, and detailed line drawings make up this thorough encyclopedia. *Fostoria Tableware, 1924 – 1943,* contains over 125 full-color photographs and more than 100 original company catalog pages, with the focus on Fostoria's "golden age." Thirty-one pages devoted solely to the American pattern and an entire section on decorations, many of which have not previously been shown or identified, make this book a page-turner. The third volume in the four-book series, *Fostoria Tableware, 1944 – 1986,* covers pressed patterns, cuttings, etchings, and decorations, and includes the popular Coin, Colony, and Century patterns, the Henry Ford Museum Collection, and a host of other patterns, collections, and giftware produced by the Fostoria Glass Company in its last 42 years. Milk glass and Ebony glass have their own complete sections, as do the pieces introduced in the American and Navarre patterns during these years. Original company materials and 80 color photographs are featured throughout. Finally, *Fostoria, Useful and Ornamental,* completes the series, featuring the compotes, candlesticks, candy jars and boxes, bowls, bar and refreshment pieces, coasters, salad dressing and oil bottles, smoking accessories, syrups, jugs, marmalades, nappies, and vases that were often used with patterns, either as part of the line or as accent pieces. This final volume in the Crystal for America series includes a reproduction of the 1910 Lamp and Vase Catalog, and complete sections on Silver Mist and Carvings are included. With more than 160 color photographs, hundreds of vintage catalog illustrations, and complete listings, this final volume is the grand finale to the most complete reference available for the Fostoria Glass Company.

Stemware • ISBN: 0-89145-586-8
#3883 • 8½ x 11 • 272 Pgs. • HB • 1998 values • **$24.95**
Tableware 1924 – 1943 • ISBN: 1-57432-109-9
#5261 • 8½ x 11• 336 pages • HB • 1999 values • **$24.95**

Tableware 1944 – 1986 • ISBN: 1-57432-143-9
#5361 • 8½ x 11 • 312 Pgs • HB • 2000 values • **$24.95**
Useful & Ornamental • ISBN: 1-57432-166-8
#5604 • 8½ x 11 • 256 Pgs. • HB • 2000 values • **$29.95**

Schroeder's ANTIQUES Price Guide

. . . is the #1 bestselling antiques & collectibles value guide on the market today, and here's why . . .

Identification & Values of Over 50,000 Antiques & Collectibles

8½ x 11, 608 Pages, $12.95